MODERNIZATION OF THE AMERICAN STOCK EXCHANGE 1971–1989

MODERNIZATION OF THE AMERICAN STOCK EXCHANGE 1971–1989

by Stuart Bruchey

Libra Professor of History
University of Maine

Garland Publishing
New York & London
1991

Library of Congress Cataloging-in-Publication Data

Bruchey, Stuart Weems.
    The modernization of the American Stock Exchange 1971–1989 /
by Stuart Bruchey.
        p.   cm.
    ISBN 0-8153-0722-5
    1. American Stock Exchange. 2. Stock-exchange—United States.
I. Title.
    HG4575.2.B78   1991
    322.64'273—dc20   91–35983
                                            CIP

Design by Alison Lew.

Manufactured in the United States of America.

CONTENTS

PREFACE

The fifteenth chairman of the American Stock Exchange, James Jones, took office on November 10, 1989, shortly after the manuscript of this book was completed. It therefore seemed appropriate to add this brief preface to bring the text up to date.

Mr. Jones sees the Exchange as an institution with a long history of ingenuity and drive, and his charge as remolding this energy into a form that will break new ground in the 1990s. He envisions two principal goals for the Exchange. The first is to merit the confidence of the public investor by continuing to enhance the security and integrity of its market. The second is to make a substantial contribution to the growth that its listed companies will achieve in the coming decade.

Mr. Jones is extremely well qualified to carry out this mandate. He served in the United States Congress from 1972 to 1986, representing the First District of his native Oklahoma. While in the Congress, he was elected chairman of the House Budget Committee and served on the powerful House Ways and Means Committee for 12 years. He was recognized as a leader in the areas of budget, tax, international trade, and health care, and also through his chairmanship of the Social Security Subcommittee.

Mr. Jones was the co-author of the Jones-Steiger 1978 Tax Cut (which reduced the capital gains tax from 49% to 28% and provided for increased depreciation of assets), the 1985 Social Security Act, and other significant legislation. He also chaired the United States–Japan Trade Task Force and is the author of two "Jones Reports" on U.S.–Japan trade relations. He continues to serve on the Advisory Committee on Social Security.

Born in Muskogee, Oklahoma, in 1939, Mr. Jones received undergraduate degrees in journalism and government from the University of Oklahoma and a law degree from Georgetown University. (He is admitted to the bar in both Oklahoma and the District of Columbia.) After serving in the Army as a captain in the Counter-Intelligence Corps, he entered the public arena, first as a special assistant to President Lyndon Johnson and then, at the age of 27, as the youngest Chief of Staff in White House history.

Mr. Jones has been a member of the Board of Governors of the American Stock Exchange since January 1987 and has served on a number of corporate boards, including the Equitable Life Assurance Society of the United States, Facet Enterprises, of Tulsa, and Western National Bank. He has also been a director of numerous companies and public organizations, and a partner in the Washington law firm of Dickstein, Shapiro & Morin. A former member of the Tri-Lateral Commission, Jones is now a member of the Council on Foreign Relations.

The new CEO has pointed out that the economic portrait of the 1990s will be painted on a global canvas. Barely six weeks after he assumed the chairmanship at the American Stock Exchange, a series of modest events in its market brought the trend toward globalization into sharp focus. First, on December 28, 1989, the Exchange's final listing of the year was a foreign company—Electrochemical Industries (Frutarom) Ltd., of Israel. Six days later, it listed its first company of the new year. Again, it was a foreign company—Elan Corporation of Ireland.

Then, only a week later, the Exchange welcomed a historic new product—put warrants issued by the Kingdom of Denmark, underwritten by America's Goldman Sachs, and based on the Nikkei Stock Average of leading Japanese companies. Here was globalization in full clarity and, at the center of it, the American Stock Exchange.

Under Mr. Jones's chairmanship, the American Stock Exchange strategy will shape a strategy solidly based on advanced technology. He believes this will create unprecedented opportunities for listed companies and for the Exchange. The pursuit of new technology will be driven by a simple credo—to wed the efficiency of technology with the sound judgment, integrity, and individual responsibility of the auction market system.

"All this," according to Mr. Jones, "might seem far removed from the ancestors of the American Stock Exchange trading on the open streets in the rain and snow. But the feisty curbstone brokers, so often a step ahead of their time, funneled capital into many of the most exciting and important business ventures in our country's history. This is not so distant from the challenges facing our Exchange today. Again, the American Stock Exchange must show leadership and make an economic difference—this time, in the more sensitive, complex global arena of the 1990s."

David Finn

INTRODUCTION

I have written this book as a tribute to the American Stock Exchange. As a historian primarily interested in American economic development I felt myself drawn irresistibly to the history of an Exchange that has specialized over the years in attracting to its lists the small and mid-range companies whose risk-taking entrepreneurship is responsible for much of the technological innovation that spurs America's economic growth. Fortunately, Robert Sobel's *The Curbstone Brokers* (1970) and *Amex, A History of the American Stock Exchange, 1921–1971* (1972) detail the history of the Exchange from its beginnings to 1971. My task has been to pick up the story at that point and bring it down to 1989. With only eight months at my disposal it will be appreciated how dependent I have been on the aid of many people.

In the absence of the splendid set of Minutes of the Monthly Meetings of the Board of Governors kept for many years by Delia Emmons, my job would have been virtually impossible. I wish to thank her warmly and also to extend my appreciation to J. Bruce Ferguson of the Amex legal department not only for introducing me to the Minutes but also for providing other documents on several occasions. Lee Murray kindly made available to me a useful set of intraoffice memos and organizational charts. Sue Trowbridge came to my rescue a number of times with books I needed, and Mary Jo Bastone was also helpful in this regard. Other Amex people who freely provided information or explanations of technical terms include Lee Cutrone, Robert Shabazian, Robert Smith, and Bernie Maas. Robert Shlasko is deserving of special mention for his warmly supportive comradeship and encouragement. Had he written this account it would possess a degree of literary merit to which I cannot aspire.

Interviews with Exchange executives, past and present, provided indispensable information not captured in Board Minutes. I am especially indebted to chairman Arthur Levitt for enlightenment on key developments, not only at the Amex but also in the larger financial and political worlds to which it belongs.

Gordon Stewart also contributed much to my understanding of those worlds. I could not have labored under the gentle guidance of a more understanding person than Stewart. Marcia Mayer's help in selecting the quantitative data that appear in the Statistical Appendix was indispensable, as was her warm and cheerful support of this project from the beginning. Bernie Maas's interest in the history and his valuable reminiscences were a source of delight. So too were those of floor broker "Mike" Pascuma. John Sheehan's detailed recollections of earlier years were immensely enriching; I am also indebted to Thomas Mariam and to Keith Silverman for colorful detail on the worlds of radio and television for which they are, respectively, responsible at the Amex. Thanks are also owing a former president of the Exchange, Robert J. Birnbaum, for his willingness to find time in a busy schedule to read a draft of the manuscript. Among Amex employees who helped in numerous ways, I should like to thank Linda Jawitz, Judy Muttamara, Doreen Davis, Roland Savage, Eileen Riepe, Lisa Kravitz, Susan Mandell, Michelle Versella, "Andy" Affa, Yvrose Kolbjornsen, Carmellina Manzella, Brian Wilson, "Bud" Schutte, Lauron Lewis, Tara Trombone, Winston Hutchinson, Tina Kaferstein, Jeanne Agnello, Jim Strain, Dorothy Klock, Susan Griffin, Louis DiPasquale, Mary Cromer, and Eddie Moriando. A special debt of gratitude is owed to Ira Krawitz of the Exchange and also to Leo Balk and Heidi Christein of Garland Publishing for their considerable aid in getting the manuscript into print.

A former chairman, Paul Kolton, has my warm gratitude for the scrupulous care with which he read the manuscript, and for his suggestions for its improvement. The endless patience and good cheer with which Frances Shannon expertly typed and retyped the pages of the manuscript have earned for her a special place in my affections among those to whom I am indebted. The deepest debts of all are owing to David Finn, the distinguished photographer of sculpture who is also chairman of Ruder, Finn, and to Gordon Stewart. The former suggested that this enterprise be undertaken; the latter enabled me to see it through.

CHAPTER 1

HIGHLIGHTS FROM EARLIER YEARS

"The explorers of the Modern Era," the speaker said, "are the entrepreneurs, men with vision, with a courage to take risks and faith enough to brave the unknown." "The entrepreneurs and their small enterprises," he added, "are responsible for almost all the economic growth in the United States." The speaker was Ronald Reagan; the occasion, the President's visit to the Soviet Union in May 1988; the audience, students at Moscow State University. The President would not have had to say the same things in his own country. For students of America's economic development have long known about the dynamic role of small to middle-range business. They know that gains in productivity—in output of goods and services per unit of capital and labor—are the source of economic growth, and that technological innovation makes those gains possible. They also know that it is small business entrepreneurs who are in the forefront of the process of innovation. The one thing they might not know is that the American Stock Exchange has been and remains preeminently the home of such firms. The story of "Amex" then, helps to illuminate the larger story of America's economic growth.

The American Stock Exchange today is itself a major source of technological innovation in the provision of financial and other services to companies and to investors. Moreover, it plays a leading role in what has been well called the increasing globalization of securities markets. The main purpose of this book is to describe these innovations and to tell how the Amex came to play that role. It is the story of the modernization of the American Stock Exchange, a history of memorable accomplishments by men and women in the closing decades of the twentieth century.

But the Amex itself has a far longer history, and it is appropriate that we begin by recounting some of the highlights of those earlier years. Fortunately, two fine studies of the Exchange by Robert Sobel permit us to do so.[1] The present account depends heavily upon the pioneer researches of Professor Sobel, and represents an effort to place the story within the larger framework of the corporate response to the nation's capital needs for growth.

AMERICA, B.C. (BEFORE CORPORATIONS)

America had no stock exchanges at all during her years as a colonial dependency of Great Britain, that is, the years between the first settlement at Jamestown in 1607 and the achievement of independence in 1783. The simple fact is that there were no stocks to exchange. There were other kinds of paper, for example, tobacco notes, evidences of ownership of tobacco of a given quality that had been inspected, graded, and then deposited in a public warehouse, as the law required, to await export. Like promissory notes and even bills of exchange, tobacco notes passed from hand to hand among merchants, thus serving as money. But there is no evidence for the existence of stocks or bonds.

To be sure, the colonists formed a large number of unincorporated joint stock companies to promote a great variety of business purposes, especially in mining, fishing, and whaling, and in land speculation. Members of these companies, legally partnerships or tenancies in common, subscribed to the capital of the enterprise by investing in shares, a number of which were valued at £50 or £100. But the shares were not represented by certificates of ownership. If the original investor transferred his share to another person, the transaction was probably facilitated by making the appropriate entries in the company's books.

Most of the business done in the relatively undeveloped agro-mercantile economy of colonial America was the work of men organized in partnerships. Partnerships predominated in foreign trade, providing the capital sums required to purchase vessels and their cargoes, and spreading the risk of loss. Ownership of shares in vessels, shares as small as one-sixty-fourth, together with multiple-firm underwriting of shipments, promoted similar ends. Merchants bought and sold in local markets both for cash and on credit, and imported cargoes of dry goods, hardware, and other commodities from London on short-term credit extended by leading British mercantile houses. The chartering of the first commercial bank awaited the era of the Revolution—the year 1781.

In short, Colonial America was not a corporate world. Of course, the great trading and colonizing companies that brought English settlers to Virginia and Massachusetts in the seventeenth century were in part profit-seeking corporations that divided their capital into transferable shares. But these were English corporations, and the transfers took place in London. Corporations in America very largely took the form of towns, boroughs, and cities as populations grew. In addition to these public corporations, it is possible to distinguish a number of corporations organized for religious, charitable, educational, or business purposes. The latter were privately supported and controlled.

But business corporations were few in number and relatively unimportant. Scholars have found two in the seventeenth century, another half-dozen in the eighteenth. Making up the latter were two groups of wharf proprietors (in New Haven and Boston), three small water companies in Rhode Island, and a mutual fire insurance society in Philadelphia. The local and public service character of these corporations is self-evident.

It is sometimes said that the reason so few business corporations were organized during the nearly two centuries of our colonial dependency was the relatively undeveloped state of the economy. It is true that as late as 1790 nine out of ten people were farmers and that many of them grew crops mainly for their own consumption rather than for sale. It is true that domestic markets, while growing with population increase and especially with urbanization, were small. As late as 1775, Philadelphia, the largest city in the nation, numbered only 40,000 people. New York, the second largest city, had 25,000; Boston, 16,000; Charleston, 12,000; and Newport, 11,000.

Finally, it is also true that no large supplies of capital or labor were seeking employment, and that had they done so those who commanded them would have encountered little opposition to incorporation on the part of the British authorities.

The argument seems persuasive, but it fails to explain a highly significant development. In only 11 years, between 1789 and 1800, the newly independent American states granted charters to more than 300 business corporations! It is too much to believe that this startling growth can be attributed to a suddenly greater degree of economic maturity. Rather, the significant change lies in the legal process by which charters were obtained.

Most colonial charters were granted by royal governors in the name of the Crown, although usually with the consent of the provincial councils. The sovereign, that is to say, the executive, was recognized as the source of legal authority, with Parliamentary approval required after 1688 only in the case of a grant of exclusive or monopoly privilege. In both royal and proprietary colonies, the legal rights of the assembly to incorporate were subject to the negative of either the governor or of higher British authority.

The Revolution brought an important change in this situation. Because of the fiction that the war had been fought to free the colonists from the exactions of the Crown, a revulsion against executive authority became manifest in the early state constitutions and in our first national constitution, the Articles of Confederation (1781), as well. The power to incorporate, in a word, shifted from the executive to the legislative arm, and thus became more sensitively responsive to community pressures upon government to aid in the provision of community services. The result is plain: the overwhelming majority of those more than 300 corporations, just as in the case of the half-dozen or so colonial corporations, were essentially quasi-public in nature.

Two-thirds of them were established to provide inland navigation, turnpikes, and toll bridges. Thirty-two were empowered to underwrite insurance policies, a need deriving from expansion of the geographic area and volume of foreign commerce, especially after the outbreak of European war in 1793 opened the commercial world to American neutral vessels, increasing their risk of loss. At the same time, the increased volume of trade gave rise to a need for the short-term credit facilities of commercial banks, with the result that no less than 34 were incorporated between 1781 and 1801 (27 of them between 1790 and 1801). Commercial expansion, by increasing the size of urban populations, also increased their needs for other services, so that 32 corporations for the supply of water and 4 for the erection of docks were created in the 6-year interval between 1795 and 1801. The greater need of urban communities for protection against fire losses was reflected in the organization of nearly a dozen mutual companies between 1786 and 1800. Most insurance companies, however, were permitted to underwrite both fire and marine risks.

This surprisingly early growth of corporations contrasts markedly with British and continental European experience. This is to be explained in part by a contemporary belief that the corporate form should not be resorted to unless the public interest was involved. But there is also another part of the explanation: given a remarkable consensus among leaders of public opinion that America's freedom and independence must be rooted in economic growth, it was next to impossible at this early stage to distinguish sharply between public and private. It was the duty of government to encourage development, to make it the private interest of savers to invest in the country's future.

Invest they did. And offhand one would think that the securities made available by the great corporate burst at the turn of the century must have led to active trading in a widening market. However, this did not happen. To be sure, the launching of a new corporation sometimes led soon thereafter to speculative dealings in its stocks. The securities of a few banks and insurance companies, and an occasional bridge company, were transferred often enough to warrant newspaper quotations. Nevertheless, the stocks of these quasi-public corporations seldom found their way into speculative hands, and only a local, imperfect market for them developed.

It was speculation in the securities of the federal government that led to the development of the first organized securities market in the United States. Speculation began a half-dozen or so years before the Founding Fathers abandoned the Articles of Confederation and drew up a new constitution in 1789. Because the federal government had been denied the power to tax by the Articles, the likelihood of its being able to pay off the debt incurred in the conduct of the Revolutionary War at first seemed slight. In consequence, the value of the "war bonds of the Revolution" sank to a low of ten cents on the dollar. With brightening prospects that a new government would assume the debt of the old and be given the power to raise the necessary revenues to pay interest and gradually retire the principal, speculative purchases increased in volume.

Securities changed hands in Philadelphia, Boston, and other cities, but New York soon became the most prominent center, and its merchants, leading dealers. Most merchants engaged in foreign commerce had long been jacks-of-all-trades, exporting and importing, selling at both wholesale and retail, dealing in real estate and insurance, and handling a wide range of commodities as well as bills of exchange. Many took on securities as well, dealing in them in much the same way that they handled dry goods, groceries, and country produce. Like tobacco and other commodities, securities served as a form of currency, and it is probable that local merchants in the smaller towns were the first transferees of the great bulk of them. However, they soon fell into the hands of large wholesale merchants in Philadelphia, Boston, and New York. As early as 1783 or 1784 some of the latter were sending agents on journeys hither and yon through the country to pick up securities at bargain prices. They also advertised in the newspapers their willingness to purchase them, and by 1789 papers were printing quotations regularly. These years, in short, saw the emergence of the stockbroker's profession.

New York promptly established itself as the country's leading security market. (By 1797 the city would pass Philadelphia and jump into first place in both the import and export trade.) The market for securities was unorganized at first. What converted it into an organized one was the funding and assumption policy of Secretary of the Treasury Alexander Hamilton. In August 1790 Congress approved Hamilton's proposal that the new federal government assume the debts of the states and fund both these and the continental certificates of the old government into three new security issues. The standardization of these securities into three fairly simple types—three percents, six percents, and six percents on which interest was deferred till 1800—tremendously facilitated speculative transactions. The eagerness of the public to purchase securities, however, should not be ascribed to speculative enthusiasm alone. It also means that there was a considerable volume of savings in the country awaiting opportunities for profitable investment on the part of small capitalists.

Fanning the public's interest in securities were those of some of the banks and other new business corporations, especially the shares of the

Bank of the United States. In chartering the institution in 1791 Congress stipulated that three-fourths of the Bank's authorized capital should be payable in United States funded sixes or threes. Within an hour, the capital was heavily oversubscribed. Within days the new bank "scrip," as the certificates for the initial payment of $25 were called, were quoted at an advance of nearly 100 percent. By August scrip had become the subject of a speculation so unprecedented in America as to be reminiscent of the notorious South Sea Bubble of early eighteenth-century England. Issued at 25, scrip reached a high of 280.

The snorting, stampeding bull could not be handled in the old way. Casual response to newspaper advertisements began to give way to public auctions in 1790, and by 1791 regular auction sales were in vogue. In July 1791 more than $180,000 in public securities passed under the hammer of McEvers and Barclay. This firm, with offices on Greenwich Street and a warehouse on Pearl Street, New York City, was one of the first to include securities in its inventory. John Pintard of Wall Street was another, and he was followed by Leonard Bleecker, whose office at 16 Wall Street was one of the finest in the city, and Sutton & Hardy, which was next door at 20 Wall. Pintard & Bleecker appear to have formed a partnership by July 1791, for, like McEvers & Barclay, they too were advertising auction sales that month. After July, the appetites of New Yorkers for securities was so great as to require auctions twice a day, at noon and in the evening, each of them held by a specific firm at a time announced in advance.

Further organization of the securities market proceeded apace. After forming a partnership with Benjamin Jay to specialize in securities, John Sutton joined other Wall Street leaders in organizing a central auction at 22 Wall Street. Every day at noon public sales in securities were held at 22 Wall, and within days this new "Stock Exchange Office" had become the largest auction in the city.

The mode of operation of the office was simple. Sellers would place their securities in the hands of Jay, Sutton, or some other auctioneer, who would then collect a commission on the sale. Businessmen bidding on shares for their customers would similarly collect a commission for their services. Unhappily, the system soon broke down. Some men visited the sales simply to learn the going prices, which enabled them to offer the same securities elsewhere at a lower commission. Their continuing trading after the end of the formal auction also had the effect of reducing the amount of securities available for the next day's sales.

Determined to tighten the organization of their market, Wall Street's leaders proceeded to form a new auction. Two dozen men or firms pledged themselves to buy and sell securities among themselves for fixed fees and not attend other auctions. This was the famous Buttonwood Agreement between securities professionals. In effect, they "organized a broker's guild, whose major function was to exclude nonmembers and maintain rates while minimizing competition." After conducting business on the street for a while, the new organization moved indoors and drew up plans to construct its own building. Incorporating as the New York Tontine Coffee House "for the purpose of a Merchants Exchange," the organization sold 203 shares for $200 each. While membership appears to have been open to any businessman desiring to join, the price was too high for most smaller dealers. In effect, membership in the Exchange was "virtually restricted to the wealthy members of the city's financial establishment." Before long, the Buttonwood Agreement lapsed, but its exclusionary principle served as the foundation of the New York Stock & Exchange Board, organized in 1817. The Board was the forerunner of the New York Stock Exchange.

What of the others, the brokers who for financial or other reasons did not become members of the New York Stock and Exchange Board? The others traded in restaurants or coffee houses, or wherever else they could meet with their clients. In warm weather they traded in the open air, and "since they gathered in the streets, Wall Street thought it best to name them after their condition: they were known as curbstone brokers." These, then, were the origins of the Curb, renamed the American Stock Exchange in the twentieth century. But that lay far in the future. Between the early nineteenth century and that distant future lay economic developments and corporate responses to them that would slowly help shape the size and nature of the securities business.

FROM THE CONSTITUTIONAL PERIOD TO THE CIVIL WAR

Of first importance was population growth and its movement to the West and into the cities. The American people numbered fewer than 4 million when the first census was taken in 1790. Swelling with immigration as well as by natural increase, the numbers mounted with each passing decade, and by the eve of the Civil War totaled more than 31 million. Urban growth, spurred by commercial development and especially by significant industrial beginnings in the 1820s and thereafter, kept pace. By 1860 the 24 tiny cities of 1790 had become 392 in number, with New York's 813,000 people making it by far the largest in the United States.

Corporations to supply water, construct bridges, operate ferries and steamboats, and provide insurance and banking facilities received charters in increasing numbers from state goverments. As before, they were essentially quasi-public in nature. Even the manufacturing corporations chartered in the early years of the century probably fall in the same category. During the troubled years that culminated in the War of 1812, and during the war itself, the stream of manufactured imports declined to a trickle. In this situation some state governments appear to have adopted the view that patriotism required the chartering of domestic manufacturing corporations. Between 1808 and 1815 New York issued more charters (165) to joint stock companies engaged in manufacturing than to all public utilities combined (164)! The phenomenon did not reoccur in any other period before the Civil War.

The field in which the public service corporation took its most distinctive rise was known to contemporaries as that of "internal improvements." These were turnpikes, canals, railroads, and other transportation facilities required in both the settled areas of the East and in the rapidly growing West. Lured by cheap land and constantly expanding urban markets for agricultural produce, settlers poured westward in a torrent following the War of 1812. Ninety-seven percent of the American people had inhabited the East Coast in 1790. In 1860 that percentage was down to 50 percent, and areas to the west that had been almost entirely uninhabited by white men and women were now admitted to the Union as states in the East Central and West Central regions. Thirty-five percent and 13 percent of the population then lived in those two regions, respectively, while another 2 percent had opened up the Far West. The resulting need to bind the newly settled areas of the West to the economy of the seaboard states became the nation's primary economic problem.

Solving that problem required the investment of large sums of capital, and state goverments themselves supplied much of it—nearly three-fourths of the sums invested in canals between 1815 and 1860 for example—by floating bond issues and using the proceeds to purchase the stocks of corporations chartered to undertake the construction. To tap private savings the states had to overcome the natural reluctance of investors to put their money into projects that by their very nature could not promise quick returns. Indeed, almost all of them were developmental in character: returns depended not on exploiting existing economic opportunities, but rather on those that would be created by the settlement and economic activity that the construction was designed to promote. Profits would necessarily be deferred and widely diffused.

The states used the legal system to overcome the reluctance of private investors. "Be it enacted by the Senate and House of Representatives in General Court assembled," reads a Massachusetts statute of 1818, that the following named individuals "hereby are constituted a corporation and body *politic*." As "bodies politic" these corporations were accorded certain exclusive privileges, among them monopoly rights of way, tax exemption, the right of eminent domain, and the right, granted to many nonbanking corporations, to facilitate the raising of capital by engaging in banking operations and holding lotteries. In sum, not private capital alone but public as well—federal, state, and local—joined hands in characteristically mixed enterprises to create the social overhead capital so essential to the development of the nation's resources.

The grant of special privileges to attract hesitant investment was undoubtedly necessary in the early stages of the country's development. The alternatives would have been public construction financed by taxation, no more popular then than now. But the technique was bound to raise opposition once businessmen, attracted to a host of investment opportunities opened up by the country's economic growth, found their paths blocked by the privileged positions occupied by the early investors. The proprietors of the Charles River Bridge between Cambridge and Boston, for example, argued that the Massachusetts legislature had by implication given them an exclusive monopoly and that the legislature's later authorization of the rival Warren Bridge infringed upon that monopoly. Chief Justice Roger B. Taney of the United States Supreme Court disagreed, and his decision (1837) freed new businesses from the fear of claims of monopoly on the part of older corporations with ambiguously phrased charters.

An apostle of corporate egalitarianism, Taney also determined to crack the power of the second Bank of the United States (1816–1836), which Congress had incorporated after the expiration of the charter of the first Bank. "There is perhaps no business more liberal," he remarked, "as the business of banking and exchange; and it is proper that it should be open, as far as practicable, to the most free competition and its advantages shared by all classes of society." As Andrew Jackson's Secretary of the Treasury, he had presided over the removal of the government's deposits in the Bank (1834), and thus deprived it of the power to curtail loan expansion on the part of state-chartered banks. With their profit-making opportunities unleashed, the number of state banks rapidly increased, from 506 in 1834 to 901 only six years later. At the outbreak of the Civil War they numbered 1,601.

These successful attacks upon enterprise restrictions in the corporate field mark the beginning of the transformation of the quasi-public corporation into the private business corporation. In addition, they also necessarily exerted an influence upon securities markets. While it is true that pre–Civil War markets were thin partly because of the ability of partnerships to raise most of the capital required for early development, and partly because of the young nation's heavy resort to capital imports—by 1838 foreigners had purchased an estimated $80 million of state bonds, with an additional $30 million of bank and railroad bonds held abroad by that year—it is also true that the legal roadblocks that we have discussed discouraged incorporation. Their gradual removal was bound to exert a more positive influence on the process.

At any rate, the decade of the 1830s is marked by a rapid flotation of securities. Many of these issues, perhaps most of them, were handled by commercial bankers who combined the investment business with their commercial banking business, and by brokerage houses. It had long been customary for commercial banks, and for the great merchant houses in foreign commerce as well, to purchase large blocks of securities and resell them in smaller lots, or to take the securities as agent for the issuing corporation and sell them on commission—Stephen Girard of Philadelphia and John Jacob Astor of New York often handled government bonds in these ways, and during the 1830s they were joined by many other banking houses, for example, Brown Brothers and Company, and Prime, Ward and King.

The developing securities markets played a role of increasing importance in the 1830s. By bringing together issuers and customers they enabled more and more corporations to attract the funds of savers and to set them working toward the country's economic objectives. They also helped determine which new enterprises were deserving of capital, as well as helping corporations already in existence decide how to make the best use of the capital at their disposal. The list of available securities was a short one in the mid-1830s, but it was growing. Besides reporting various federal, state, and local government obligations, the New York *Evening Post* gave quotations during 1835 for 22 New York City banks, 14 banks outside New York, 21 railroads, 32 insurance companies, and 7 gas, coal, or canal companies. By 1856 railroad issues outnumbered the banks, 42 to 35, insurance companies had fallen to 9, and 20 industrials were on the list. Most of the latter were engaged in mining, transportation, or real estate.

Unfortunately, we do not know which of these companies' shares traded on the Stock and Exchange Board, precursor of the New York Stock Exchange, and which traded on the Curb. The probability is high, however, that older, more heavily capitalized firms gravitated toward the Board. Certainly the Board itself—"the Establishment"—preferred to handle the securities of such firms. As the Establishment usually is, the Board was conservative. It cultivated an aura of respectability. It was reluctant to explore and innovate. It left that to the curbstone brokers. In what appears to have been an informal understanding, the Board acknowledged the brokers' right to "a niche of their own on Wall Street, with a monopoly of those securities not traded at the Exchange." In sum, the curbstone brokers located themselves, at the corner of Wall and Hanover by the early 1850s, "on the street, in the open, good weather and bad," along the cutting edge of the nation's economic development. Because of the Establishment's "limited views on what constituted status, power and economic growth" the curbstone brokers "were able to exploit new industries and securities."

Among those new industries in the years before the Civil War were railroads, gold mining, and petroleum. A speculative boom in railroad shares took place in the securities markets in the mid-1830s, and by the early 1840s there is evidence that securities of large and small lines alike were being traded on the Curb and auctioned at the Board. Typically, new issues came first to the Curb, where trading was two way and continuous, and then, after they had attracted the attention of the Board, they moved to the auctions. As a general rule, Board members were not interested in the thinner, less heavily capitalized issues and left trade in them to the curbstone brokers.

It was the same with the mining shares that reached Wall Street in the early 1850s following the great Gold Rush to California a few years before. The Board did not trust them. Exotic, cheap, and volatile, they "attracted the gaming element," and by the mid-1850s were being traded on the Curb in volumes far exceeding the shares of rails, canals, and banks combined. Such was the feverish interest in them that several non-Board members organized private auctions. Some of the Board's leaders even went so far as to organize a separate Mining Exchange, which in its short lifetime of six months "had more members and traded more shares than did the Board." But the real action was on the street. On a busy day, when 6,000 shares might be auctioned off at the Board, Curb volume might soar to over 70,000. More than a million shares a month changed hands in the outdoor market in some of the months of the boom year 1856.

"The Board's unreceptiveness to new ideas and desire for respectability enabled the curbstone brokers to grow in numbers and wealth." In 1857 Hunts Merchants Magazine described them as "a very large class of speculators . . . composed of the oldest and most experienced operators in the Street." Many of them had previously been members of the Board who had been compelled to vacate their seats because of their inability to cope with the numerous ups and downs of the market. But by no means all of them had failed to fulfill their contracts, for "the contracts of many of the curbstone brokers are infinitely better than many of the Regular Board."

POST–CIVIL WAR EXPANSION

It was these irregulars, these nonestablishment outsiders, who were first to seize the new opportunities opened up by an economic expansion in the second half of the nineteenth century so massive as to dwarf anything that had come before it in American history. Surging relentlessly to the West, farmers settled and placed under cultivation more land in only 30 years (1870–1900) than in all the previous years of the American past. Farmers were joined by cattlemen and miners in pushing outward the frontiers of the economy, making the West the fastest growing region in the United States. In the 30 years between 1870 and 1900 the population of the West rose from fewer than 1 million to more than 4 million. The railroad made it possible for this vast area and its people to become part of a rapidly forming national market. The first great transcontinental line was completed in 1869, and of the astounding total of

200,000 miles of track laid down between 1870 and 1914, nearly half lay west of the Mississippi River.

So too did most of the nation's precious metal mines. The first of the mining frontiers had opened in the Sierra Nevada region of northern California following the discovery of gold at Sutters Mill in 1848. California's gold and, for a number of years after 1859, Nevada's silver and gold were perhaps the most famous of the mining frontiers of the Far West, but they were not the only ones. Contemporaneously or later, silver, and then copper and zinc in Colorado—and in the twentieth century deposits of molybdenum, vanadium, tungsten, and uranium—gold and silver in Idaho and Montana, gold and lead in Utah, gold, silver, and copper in Arizona, gold and copper in New Mexico, and gold in the Black Hills of South Dakota, opened new mining frontiers in both the Northwest and Southwest between 1860 and 1880. In 1897 mining corporations chartered in Colorado exceeded those chartered for all other purposes by a ratio of nearly three to one.

Shallow virgin placer deposits on the western slopes of the Sierra Nevadas were so rich that "mining" was at first any man's game. All the grizzled prospector had to do was to use his knife, hornspoon, or shovel to dig out the gold and then wash it by swirling it around in a pan or bowl to separate it from foreign matter. These easy early days soon gave way to one of more substantial capital needs as river mining, and other more scientific techniques were adopted. Exploration of Nevada's famed Comstock Lode by daring entrepreneurs, who cut drifts, tunnels, and crosscuts far underground and installed costly surface machinery, led by the mid-1870s to the discovery of what was called "the greatest bonanza of all time." Between 1873 and 1882 two mines joined together as the Consolidated Virginia produced a total of $105,168,859. The yield of 60 principal Comstock mines between 1859 and 1882 amounted in all to $292,726,310. The role of rising capital inputs in producing these results is suggested by a calculation that the ratio of total capital to product in the production of precious metals rose from 2.55 to 3.15 between 1870 and 1880, and to 5.41 in 1890.

The curbstone brokers were in the thick of the effort to provide the needed capital. As early as 1864 and as late as 1906 Curb organizations dominated the trading of mining shares. At the earlier date only a half-dozen mines had their shares listed on the NYSE while more than a hundred were traded on the Curb. At the later date mining shares made up the bulk of the Curb's business. It was the same old story of conservative reluctance, on the one hand, and of entrepreneurial enthusiasm on the other. For the precursor of the NYSE, shares had to be seasoned. Had it not been for the curbstone brokers many dozens of small firms would not have had the opportunity to mature, to change from green to gold.

It was the same with the industrials. The second half of the nineteenth century is marked by a phenomenal expansion in the use of the corporate form, especially in such fields as iron and steel, nonferrous metals, textiles, chemicals, and liquor. Indeed, manufacturing corporations make up a large percentage of all charters granted by the states after 1875. What about the size of these corporations? Historians of business incorporation in the United States generally regard as "small" corporations those with less than $100,000 in authorized capital stock. "Medium" ones were those between $100,000 and $1,000,000; and "large" ones were over $1,000,000. In most states, the incorporation of small companies far outnumbered those of medium or large companies. Indeed, the trend in small incorporation was upward and steep until 1918.

The NYSE displayed marked reluctance to deal in the stocks of these small, new industrial companies. (Professor Sobel believes the Exchange's members were "at least a generation behind the times.") In contrast, the Curb concentrated its attention on smaller companies, and most industrials began their trading lives there. Early in the twentieth century the volume of trading in the new industrials and in the growing mining stock list was huge—on some days in excess of 2 million shares. Yet the division of labor between the two exchanges was of long standing, and relations between them were cordial, certainly at this time.

THE CURB

In accordance with that division the Curb functioned as a "proving ground for new securities" while the Exchange concentrated on seasoned issues and on maintaining high standards for listing and trading. When a new company had proved itself and transferred its shares to the NYSE, Curb members almost always stopped dealing in them. That was the unwritten agreement: a member of the NYSE would transmit to his representative on the Curb, a commission broker, orders for unlisted stocks, and the representative would execute them. At the turn of the century, as two generations before, 85 percent of Curb business consisted of executing orders transmitted to it by the NYSE. Thus, for the most part, Curb business was wholesale, its members rarely dealing directly with the public. The two exchanges complemented each other and rarely competed.

Curb members fell into three clearly distinguishable categories. The largest group were the commission brokers, the men whose livelihood depended on maintaining good relations with a member firm on the NYSE, the source of orders for securities not listed on that Exchange, and for whose purchase or sale commissions were earned. The second kind of broker, known as a "two dollar broker," was a marginal figure who dealt on his own account or tried to pick up "whatever business might come along." Often these were men "getting their start on the Curb, or those engaged in shady dealings. The out-of-doors market had many such people, and since there were no regulations, listing requirements, or committees on standing or admission, their members were always being replenished." Such people rarely got very far. They were ostracized and were encouraged to leave the arena.

The third group was composed of specialists. The term means what it implies. Specialists were men "who concentrated their time and money on a few stocks apiece" and controlled the trading in those issues. They were able to do so, to serve as market makers, because of the sizable investments in those stocks that they made on their own account. Specialists stood ready to buy or to sell in small or large lots, their dominant position with respect to an issue insuring that their bid (buy) and ask (sell) quotations established its market price. Such men were necessarily among the more well-to-do in the curbstone community. With the exception of those specialists who made markets in low-priced mining shares, some of which were quoted in pennies, they were the community's leaders.

The arena in which these curbstone workers conducted their transactions is well characterized as "the Broad Street Jungle." To the uninitiated vision in the 1890s it must certainly have seemed so. Telephone clerks perched precariously on the window ledges of the curbstone broker's office would relay to their brokers on the crowded street below buy or sell orders received from the broker's correspondent house at the Stock Exchange. The messages would have been incomprehensible to an outsider for they were delivered in the form of hand signals accompanied by shouts. Fingers were used to spell out the identity of the security and the number of shares to be purchased or sold. To make it easier for a clerk to pick out his broker in the milling crowd below each broker wore some distinctive article of clothing—a colorful jacket or an unusual hat.

By then the brokers were beginning to become distinctive in other ways as well. Earlier in the century the Curb had been "the domain of lower- and middle-class Protestants who could trace their ancestry back to the nation's farms." The huge immigrant waves that broke on the shores of America in the 1880s and 1890s changed all that. Immigrants from northern and western Europe were accompanied in increasing numbers by those from the South and East—Italians, Russians, and others fleeing deprivation and persecution. The latter brought a new tone to New York and its financial district. In the 1870s New York had been essentially a Protestant, native-born city, although one with large numbers of Irish Catholics. By 1890 "some 40 percent of all New Yorkers were of foreign birth, and much of lower Manhattan was in their hands." Eastern European Jews settling in the tenement areas between ghettoes formed by the Irish and the Italians, "fell heir to the neighborhood north of the financial district, and could easily reach Wall Street by taking the Broadway horsecars." The Curb "became a magnet for the new Americans, especially the Irish and the east European Jews, whose numbers there were disproportionate to their representation in the financial community at large."

One of the most prominent Jewish brokers, however, had migrated to New York not from overseas but from the American South. Setting up shop as a curbstone broker in 1872 Emmanuel ("Pop") S. Mendels, Jr., enjoyed a rapid rise in prestige. "He seems to have been prim and stiff-necked on questions of honesty and corruption, while also possessing leadership qualities." Mendels's intelligence and growing reputation enabled him and a few others to form an informal committee on membership, ethics, and listing. The object of the "Mendels Circle" was to cleanse the Curb of marginal brokers and securities, and to regularize transactions, in short, to raise standards, in an effort to elevate the stature of the Curb vis-à-vis that of the NYSE.

Especially troublesome objects of the cleanup drive were "bucket shops." Ostensibly, these were brokerage offices, but in reality they were nothing of the sort. Customers' orders were not actually executed.

Transactions were closed by the payment of gains or losses as determined by price quotations. In other words, bucket shops were places to register bets or wagers. The Mendels Circle, and later leaders as well, took aim at these offenders, but they proved an elusive target, difficult to bar from operating on the Curb. Mendels did succeed, however, in inducing a small job printer to gather and publish daily information on quotations and volume (not very reliable information as it turned out), and in 1904 he and his associates had the first issue of the "Official Curb Directory of New York Curb Market" published. It contained the names, addresses, and telephone numbers of 209 brokers considered reliable by Mendels and his Circle. The two publications "marked the first move toward regulation and organization—feeble though it was—at the Curb."

One large obstacle in the way of success consisted of the NYSE's suspicion that these self-policing, regulatory moves would serve as preliminaries to a formal organization of a competing Curb market. The suspicions were heightened whenever curbstone brokers mentioned the possibility of moving indoors to escape the elements, and sometimes to escape objections by the police to the traffic problems created by the throngs of brokers and onlookers. Somehow Mendels was able to convince the NYSE that his proposed New York Curb Market Agency was not an organization (even if it functioned like one!), and in 1908 he presided over its birth. Actually the Agency—with Mendels its first agent—was a "semi-official extension of what the Mendels Circle had been trying to do at the Curb for the past decade and more." Its manual mentions such functions as issuing a Curb directory and maintaining a bureau of statistics and "a record of Transfer and Registry offices for general information." It would also attend to street sprinkling and cleaning. No threat of moving indoors there!

THE EARLY TWENTIETH CENTURY

The momentum building toward formal organization could not be stopped. By the early twentieth century the success of the Curb, and the power, wealth, and prestige of its leading brokers, were not to be denied. By 1907 well over 400 specialists and commission brokers were operating on the Curb. The number of securities traded there quintupled between 1899 and 1906, rising from 100 or so issues to more than 500. Volume, especially in the new industrials and in mining stocks, swelled more rapidly at the Curb than at the Exchange. From sales of $10 million in bonds in 1900, the figure rose to $26 million in 1907, before soaring to $66 million in the next year. From sales of fewer than 300,000 shares of industrial stocks in 1900, volume rose to 4.8 million in 1908. Mining stocks doubled their 21-million-share year of 1900 just eight years later.

In 1910 the NYSE finally bestowed its imprimatur on the Curb as New York's second securities market. It did so by abolishing its Unlisted Department, switching the increasingly popular industrials on the list to the regular board and encouraging mining shares to return to the Curb. For years the chief threat to the Curb's well-being, indeed, to its very existence, had been the possibility that the NYSE would increase the number of securities on its Unlisted Department, thus depriving the Curb of business. Now it would have even more business, thanks in large measure to strong criticism of the NYSE's historic opposition to the formal organization of the Curb by an investigating committee appointed by Governor Charles Hughes of New York.

Mendels quickly moved to consolidate and organize the outdoor market. Wishing to obtain assurances that the old relationship between the two markets would continue, Mendels sought in advance the NYSE's approval of a Curb transformed from a mere agency into an organized body. The NYSE obliged, its chairman expressing the opinion that "so long as no dealings are had in securities listed at the Stock Exchange, the Curb is justified in making all necessary rulings and laws for their own protection." Shortly thereafter Mendels and his advisers drew up a constitution for the New York Curb Market, and early in 1911 the new organization came into being.

We have sketched here in bare and simplified outline developments that can be followed in all their richly detailed complexity in the work of Professor Sobel. It is only necessary to add to our own brief account two major facts. One is this: The first Chairman of the Curb, John L. McCormack (Mendels declined the honor because of his age) set in motion the machinery provided for by the new constitution. Two of the original eight committees dealt with membership and listing, the latter of which became "the true heart of the new Curb Market."

Members were urged not to trade in unlisted securities, and while some did so they stamped themselves as marginal men who dealt in marginal stocks—"the most speculative securities of the most questionable companies." At the other end of the spectrum of quality were the stocks and bonds usually found on the Big Board. In between were the less seasoned issues of new companies for which the Curb had long been the traditional home. Surprisingly, there also traded on the Curb the securities of companies "unwilling to release sufficient information to receive Stock Exchange acceptance." These included E. I. DuPont, International Salt, Otis Elevator, and Sears Roebuck. American Tobacco traded in the 450 range, Standard Oil of New Jersey in the 600s! (When the Exchange lost the Standard Oil listing at the beginning of the 1930s some of the brokers on the floor draped in black the post at which it had been traded.) The essential task of management of the new Curb was to cleanse itself of the most marginal men and securities and upgrade the list. This was the path that had to be taken if the Curb were to attain the status and respect its leaders knew it deserved.

McCormack's successor in the chairmanship, Edward R. McCormick, set about these tasks with such energy and vigor, requiring that mining and petroleum companies deposit additional information on the quality of their assets as a condition for listing (for example, was the property developed or underdeveloped?), and investigating complaints, that by the end of his seven-year tenure he had elevated listing into an important status symbol. This was not McCormick's only achievement. Indeed, he assigned even higher priority to a second major objective—to move the Curb indoors. His success in achieving his two major goals made him "the most important figure in the Curb's long history."

THE 1920s

And that is our second major fact—the move indoors. The date— 1921; the location—113–123 Greenwich Street. (When the original building was added to in 1930 the old entrance on Greenwich Street was replaced by a new one at 86 Trinity Place, the present-day location of the Exchange.) Leading the brokers to the site of their newly constructed three-story building, McCormick said simply, "The dye is cast. The old order is gone forever." It was indeed. Nearly 130 years after the curbstone brokers had taken to the streets to offer their services, a solid, respected organization was in being. During the boom years of World War I, the stock list had expanded at the Curb, and volume had soared. "In 1913, the list contained 124 mining issues, 34 industrials, and eight petroleum stocks; in 1916 it had 184 mining stocks, 86 industrials, and 19 petroleums." Reported NYSE volume in 1918 amounted to more than 191 million shares, but over 167 million shares changed hands at the Curb, and volume there was rising at an even more rapid rate than on the Exchange. To be sure, higher-priced, more seasoned issues dominated the NYSE list while the Curb's most active stocks usually sold for less than $5 a share. That's the way it always had been and in the main would continue to be—many smaller companies would get their start in competitive life by tapping the resources of capital made possible by a listing on the Curb.

The capital formation process worked this way. It began when an investment banker agreed either to buy the shares of a newly chartered corporation at a stipulated price per share or agreed to dispose of the securities on commission. In either case, the stocks had to be sold, with the banker's earnings dependent upon the selling price of the share. Let us assume the banker applied to the Curb for permission to have the stock listed among the securities traded on that market. If so, he had to file the necessary papers and supply the required information about the assets of the company. Once the Curb's committee on arrangements, one of its most powerful committees, found everything to be in order, it assigned the stock to a specialist. Sometimes, however, the banker might request that the stock be placed with a particular specialist, one known to be particularly talented, or perhaps a friend of someone at the company.

But this is not to imply that most stocks traded on the Curb in the 1920s were listed. Indeed, the exact opposite is true: a large majority were unlisted. A specialist won the right to handle a stock simply by purchasing some shares and applying as a stockholder for what were known as "unlisted trading rights." (They were really privileges rather than rights.) There is on record no instance of a refusal of such an application. And this means that most trading on the Curb took place in the issues of companies about which little or nothing was known.

That's the way it was in the Roaring Twenties. Standards were not of the highest on any of the exchanges. Good times often spawn carelessness and greed, and except for a steep recession in 1920–1921 these were good times indeed. The period was one of high optimism that America had moved into a "New Era" of permanent prosperity. Unemployment was low, averaging 5.1 percent of the labor force between 1923 and 1929, and real incomes were up, both per worker and per capita. The former rose from an average of $629 a year between 1909 and 1918 to $738 between 1919 and 1928, the latter from $517 to $612. A remarkable extension of sales "on time" (installment sales) also took place. Finance companies specialized in providing consumer credit in this form in a volume that rose from $1.375 billion in 1925 to $3 billion in 1929. Extensive use of the technique made possible a wide distribution of such consumer durables as automobiles, furniture, radios, and other electrical equipment for the home.

This large increase in the purchasing power of the public, accompanied by a remarkably low rate of inflation—prices were essentially stable from the end of the 1920–1921 recession to the end of the decade—fueled significant increases in business investment. All the components of gross capital formation—producer durables, construction, change in inventories, and foreign investment—went up, and these increases in capital formation paved the way for a huge expansion in the output of prepared foods, other perishable and semidurable goods, and such durables as refrigerators, vacuum cleaners, automobiles, furniture, and radios.

Needless to say, hundreds of new manufacturing companies were chartered to help produce this output, to help make possible what has been well called the "consumer durable revolution" of the 1920s. And "most of the new issues made their bows at the Curb." Reinforced by so many signs of economic well-being, optimism spiraled upward into a fever cloud of speculation. Volume on the Curb began to rise sharply early in the decade, from 15.5 million shares in 1921 to 21.7 million in 1922, then to almost 51 million in 1923, the *Wall Street Journal* attributing the interest "to a mania for securities in small firms which would do well once recovery [from the recession of 1920–1921] began." Whatever the explanation—"*The New York Times* believed the activity at the Curb to be due to the added trust speculators had in the indoor market"—that activity continued to mount throughout the decade. By 1929 the 15.5 million shares of 1921 had become more than 476 million, and bond trading had risen from $25.5 million (principal amount) the former year to $513.5 million the latter.

An increasing proportion of these securities originated abroad. After relying for more than a century upon foreign sources of capital for its economic growth, the United States emerged from World War I a creditor nation, transformed into the world's prime source of capital for the developing countries, especially those of Latin America. By 1928 European and Latin American bonds were being traded on the Curb in larger volumes than on the Big Board. The Curb overcame the problem of trading in foreign stocks by joining with the Guaranty Trust Company in establishing American Depository Receipts (ADRs). Instead of buying foreign stocks, which were hard to transfer from the registry of one nation to another, Americans bought ADRs. These represented shares of stock deposited in a foreign bank. Theoretically, the purchaser could take the ADRs to the foreign bank and exchange them for the actual shares, but this rarely was done. In the main, ADRs were objects of speculation, and the volume of trading in them was high. "By the end of the decade, the Curb had more individual foreign issues on its list than all other American securities markets combined."

Two other innovations of the decade are deserving of notice—initiation and development of a clearinghouse for Curb transactions (1923) and expansion of the Curb's ticker network. Prices of securities on the Curb were not yet carried by newspapers so that it was all the more essential that an alternative means be pursued to get this information to speculators and investors. Accordingly, Curb ticker service was made available to almost every large city in the nation, the number in operation rising from only 266 in 1921 to 2,643 by 1930.

The volume of trading on the Curb surpassed that of the Big Board for the first time in history in June 1929. Well before then it could no longer be said that "low-priced issues of dubious value" dominated the Curb's list. Once again, determined executives made a difference. Under the administration of President David V. Page (1925–1928), so-called "penny stocks" were removed from the list. At the end of Page's tenure, the Curb's list contained over 1,700 issues, and of these 1,150 paid dividends. Only 25 were priced under a dollar a share.

For this and other reasons the reputation of the Curb rose in the eyes of the Establishment. The tremendous volume of business made Curb brokers "wealthier than ever before in the market's history." (A "key indicator" of this was an astonishing rise in the price of a seat on the Curb, from a high of $6,800 in 1921 to a high of $254,000 in 1929.) Even though maturing companies transferred their shares to the Big Board, "an endless supply of new firms"—life-blood of economic growth— kept coming to the Curb. The Curb did lose ground in one sense: some of its more successful brokers and specialists used their new-found wealth to purchase seats on the NYSE. But while the Curb may be said to have suffered from "too much success," such transfers also elevated the Curb in Big Board esteem, and contributed to the relative harmony that existed between the two exchanges. Smaller than the NYSE and less prestigious, the Curb had nevertheless emerged as the nation's second largest securities market. A change in name provided additional evidence of its new status; in 1929 the New York Curb Market became the New York Curb Exchange.

THE GREAT CRASH AND THE GREAT DEPRESSION

On and on the good times rolled. There seemed no end to it, no cap to the highs. Even after the sickening plunge of the market on "Black Thursday"—October 24, 1929—a distinguished economist at Yale intoned the belief that the market had reached "a permanently high plateau." To him as well as others, sobriety must have come with a jolt. In September the industrial averages had stood at 452. Two months later they were half that. By July 1932 they had sunk to 58. According to the NYSE, the market value of all listed securities was $89,668 billion in September 1929. Three years later, again in July 1932, their value was $15,663 billion.

In the afterglow of the Great Crash people saw things they had missed before—signs of the economy's growing weakness in the form of low farm incomes, the lagging of wages behind productivity growth, and a tailing off in auto output and construction. The upshot of these and other factors was a decline in the net national product in current prices of more than 50 percent between 1929 and 1933, more than a third in constant prices. As of 1932–1933 industrial production was down by more than half; gross private domestic investment, by nearly 90 percent (in constant prices); and farm prices, by over 60 percent. In March 1933 unemployment stood at about 25 percent of the labor force, and the nation was plunged into catastrophic depression, the deepest in its history.

In the 1920s the American businessman had been a popular hero. Henry Ford, possibly the greatest manufacturer of all time, may have been the best known figure in the world. Visitors from abroad made pilgrimages to his auto plant in Michigan as though it were Mecca. In the 1930s the hero became the goat, the figure on whose shoulders was heaped a mountain of blame for everything that had gone wrong in a complex economy linked by trade and investment with the economies of the larger world. Much of the blame was undeserved, but the adoption of stricter guidelines for the operations of the financial community, including those of the securities markets, was undoubtedly essential to the restoration of public confidence. In the short run, however, some of the new legislation may have inhibited economic recovery, as we shall see.

Two circumstances in particular had helped feed the speculative binge of the late 1920s, both of them having to do with the sources of funds available for the purchase of securities. Commercial banks sometimes organized investment affiliates and used funds deposited in the commercial half of the alliance for speculative ventures in the investment half. For example, Charles E. Mitchell was chairman of the board of both the National City Bank and the National City Corporation, respectively, the world's second largest commercial bank and the country's largest investment banking house. The Glass-Steagall Banking Act of 1933 required banks belonging to the Federal Reserve System to divorce themselves from their security affiliates, compelled private banks to choose between deposit and investment banking, prohibited partners or executives of security firms from serving as directors or officers of commercial banks that were members of the Federal Reserve System, increased the authority of the 12 Federal Reserve district banks to supervise and control the amount of credit extended to their members, and empowered the Federal Reserve Board to regulate bank loans secured by the collateral of stocks or bonds. Commercial bank "loan on securities" to brokers and dealers or individual speculators had reached a high of $8.3 billion in 1929.

That was one source of the credit that fueled the upward spiraling securities markets in the late 1920s. But compared to brokers' loans it was a minor source. Brokers' loans enabled purchasers to obtain stock on margin, at some (small) percentage of the purchase price, and the loans were subject to call rather than extended for a given period of time. Attracted by interest rates that rose from around 5 percent at the beginning of 1928 to 12 percent the last week of that year, cash flowed into the call money market not only from such domestic sources as corporations and wealthy individuals but from abroad as well. In the early 1920s brokers' loans ranged between $1 billion to $1.5 billion a year. During the summer of 1929 they increased by approximately $400 million a month, and by the end of that summer the grand total exceeded $7 billion.

Determined to place limits on the capacity for speculation, Congress in 1934 empowered the Federal Reserve Board to set margin rates, obviously having in mind the desirability of much higher levels than previous ones. But unharnessed speculation was only one source of peril to the long-term health of the markets and the securities industry. Another was transactions in the securities of companies about which little or nothing was known. Congress addressed this problem, too. The Securities Act of 1933 (often called the "truth in securities" law) required full disclosure of pertinent information by underwriters. To administer the law, Congress established the Securities and Exchange Commission (SEC) the next year and required that all listed securities be registered with the Commission. Fortunately for the Curb, the business of which was dominated by transactions in unlisted securities, the Act as amended in 1936 "provided that any exchange could admit to unlisted trading privileges a security that had not been fully listed and registered with the SEC provided the exchange could also establish that there was an active market and widespread distribution in the vicinity of the exchange." The law also stated that in order to qualify for unlisted trading under this clause, the issuing company had to be "subject to substantially the same duties and obligations as a fully listed company."

The Curb Exchange was saved, but many of its brokers must have wondered, in the doldrums of the depressed 1930s and later as well, whether the securities business was worth the candle. Did the new legislation make things worse, at least in the short run? Many critics believed so, and they included some Federal Reserve officials. In their view both the Securities Act and the Securities Exchange Act inhibited recovery by increasing the costs and risks of new flotations and by making officers of issuing companies and underwriters reluctant to assume risks for fear of incurring civil and criminal penalties. Critics also argued that the Glass-Steagall Banking Act of 1933 got in the way of recovery in at least three ways. Recovery required broadening, not narrowing the types of loans made by banks, but the Act, by indicating official opposition to loans on the collateral of securities, threatened to restrict them. Secondly, prohibiting the payment of interest on demand deposits led to withdrawals of some correspondent bank deposits from financial centers, thus depriving the latter of funds that they would probably have been able to utilize more effectively than the banks withdrawing them.

Finally, the requirement that commercial banks refrain from investment banking lessened the number of underwriting facilities at a time when the economy needed all the investment that could be induced.

Whatever the configuration of causes of the long-drawn-out depression—the cost of capital was not among them, for interest rates were low throughout the decade—precious little investment could be induced, and the securities markets languished. Annual stock volume on the Curb Exchange declined from 476 million shares in 1929 to merely 46 million a decade later. The market value of all listed stocks fell in the same interim from $25 billion to $7.6 billion. The "highs" for the price of a seat at the Curb followed suit, declining precipitately from $254,000 in 1929 to $12,000 in 1939. Preparations for war in 1939–1940 finally put an end to the economic depression, but depression in the financial district lingered on. In 1942 a seat on the Curb changed hands for $650. Even the ending of the war did not much help things, an upswing in 1945 being followed quickly by another decline. "Not until the early 1950s would a sustained advance take place in the financial district."

THE POSTWAR PERIOD: THE 1950s

By the mid-1950s the greatest bull market since the 1920s was in full swing. The much-feared postwar depression had failed to develop, the Korean War was winding down, and the most popular president in American history up to that time—Dwight Eisenhower—occupied the White House. Even more importantly, innovative products propelled by a new science-led technology were rushing onstream, leading scholars awestricken by such things as automatic production controls to suggest that America was experiencing a second Industrial Revolution. From the nation's factories poured television sets, automatic washing machines, home freezers, room air conditioners, dehumidifiers, electronic typewriters, and small computers. It seemed like the 1920s again, writ large.

Ralph Waldo Emerson said that the world would beat a path to the man who invented a better mousetrap, but he was wrong. The inventor would have to advertise. The stocks of the corporations manufacturing these new products, many of them small companies, did not sell themselves. Investors were shown the way to market by sales efforts on the part of brokerages, news items written by economists and journalists, and market letters like *Value Line*. The American Stock Exchange—the Curb Exchange formally surrendered its old name on January 5, 1953—went the publicists one better. It helped investors reach market by encouraging small investors to join investment clubs. Pooling their funds and knowledge and investing as a group, the clubs grew rapidly in number and purchases in the late 1950s.

The Exchange not only helped investors reach market, but it reached out in ingenious ways to publicize the Amex and to attract new listings. Right after the end of World War II, Fred Moppat, a respected member of the Wall Street community who was also a member of the Board of Governors, succeeded in getting a public relations committee established on the Board. The action led in 1946 to the setting up of a division of public relations under Vernon Lee, an advertising copywriter whom Moppat had induced to join the Exchange. Soon thereafter, however, Lee took over a division regulating relationships with member firms, leaving public relations responsibilities in the hands of John Sheehan.

Open, affable, and a great storyteller—as his Irish derivation might imply—Sheehan had joined the Exchange in 1946. He was only 28 years old when assigned to public relations in 1948. By his own admission Sheehan did not have much background in the news business, but he was intelligent, innovative, and determined to succeed in his new job. He had good reason to want to succeed: when he came out of the service at the end of World War II he had a pregnant wife, no house, and no furniture. Working at the Amex by day and attending Pace College at night, where he majored in marketing and advertising, he soon learned what he had to do to make the Exchange better known.

Sheehan not only formulated a program for accomplishing this, but he badgered President Ted McCormick about his ideas on almost a daily basis. Sheehan lived in New Jersey, and he had gone there one day to address one of the local service organizations when he received a message from McCormick to return directly to the Exchange instead of going on home after completing the afternoon's work. The message said that the president wanted to discuss a couple of important matters with his public relations man.

McCormick came right to the point. "For a long time you have been making a nuisance of yourself about a motion picture," he told Sheehan. "Well, you better get busy." Sheehan was delighted; he had been urging the president to do some kind of communications work with educational institutions to acquaint them with the Exchange's operations, and a motion picture about the Exchange seemed the best way to do this. Sheehan got up to go. "Wait a minute, don't run so fast," McCormick said. "You've also been making a nuisance out of yourself about a visitors' gallery." At that time—the year was 1951—the narrow balcony area at the north end of the trading floor was used principally by members who brought their families and friends there to take a look at the activities on the floor. Sometimes, too, trainees were taken to the balcony and spoken to over a public address system. Sheehan wanted to formalize the viewing area for the public. "Get going on it," McCormick told him.

With two major projects in hand Sheehan got up once more to go, and once more McCormick restrained him. Sheehan had pointed out again and again that the brokerage houses ought to become better acquainted with the listed companies. "You know that magazine you've been talking about for publicizing Amex companies," McCormick said. "You got it. When are we going to have the first issue?"

With his hands as full as his head Sheehan went to work. In time a visitors' gallery was opened on the east wall of the trading floor behind the trading booths. In further time the area would be taken back by an Exchange in need of additional space for expanded operations. But before that happened the viewing area was transformed. A large plastic screen placed at each section pointed out the features of the trading floor. The voice was that of John Daly, "probably the premier voice in the United States at that time." (Daly was host of a popular Sunday night show on which Dorothy Kilgallen and others, blindfolded, would try to guess the identity of prominent guests from Daly's vocal cue cards.) Daly's wasn't the only voice. Tapes explaining Exchange operations were prepared in Spanish, French, Italian, German, and Yiddish. Later, Russian was added.

Sheehan's magazine project culminated in the *American Investor*. Circulated principally among member organizations, to which copies were provided free of charge, the magazine talked about Amex companies in every issue. Undoubtedly the general public's knowledge of the American Stock Exchange was most advanced by the movie. Certainly, Sheehan had great fun in getting it made.

In Hollywood he found keen interest in the small film business, especially in corporate motion pictures, on the part of Universal-International. Twenty- to thirty-minute films were lucrative and kept a lot of studio space working. In addition, the Amex film could be used as an advertising tool in approaches to other companies. U.I. shot the film on its back lot and "did a bang-up job." On being conducted to the set Sheehan marveled at the success of the director in recreating the Amex floor, trading posts and all. He had ordered the posts to be shipped to California, but in truth they had not arrived in time for the shooting of the film. The director had used photographs of the trading floor marked to show the position of the posts and turned them over to the shop. Overnight, facsimile posts had been constructed that so resembled real posts that Sheehan was completely fooled. To create the steel treads on the steps going up to the clerks' telephone booths, the shop made an open frame of wood, laid the two-by-twos down on the floor, painted them with a flat paint, and while they were wet sprinkled them with corn flakes that had been sprayed black. All this during the course of a lunch at the studio commissary! "We create miracles around here," the director had told him. Sheehan believed.

The Amex film was distributed on a free, nontheatrical basis to schools, colleges, clubs, and organizations of all kinds throughout the country. Widely acclaimed, it did much to educate the general public about the workings of the Exchange.

Although the magazine, visitors' gallery, and movie enhanced the exposure of the Amex, the director of public relations acted in still other ways to further that cause. He accompanied President McCormick to London and Edinburgh, and both McCormick and his successors (up to 1982) on trips to all the major cities of the United States whenever media relations were involved. "Whenever we did a major cities trip," Sheehan explained, "I'd always try to get the president on the air or on TV in the morning so that the listed company president in that community would be able to hear or see him while he was shaving. Later in the day when the latter showed up at the Amex luncheon he might say 'Mr., I saw you on TV this morning, you looked great.'" The tactic must surely have strengthened the sense of identity between the interests of listed companies and the Exchange.

Attracting those companies to the Amex in the first place was another area yielding to Sheehan's imaginative tactics. Exchange employees sent as regional representatives to drum up business for the Exchange were far from being household figures. Sheehan devised ways of increasing their recognizability, of giving them presence in whatever city they were visiting. He would call the local radio or TV station and say that the Amex representative could speak eloquently on how the stock ticker system worked, or how stock watch worked.

The representatives began to get publicity, their pictures appearing in local papers. Afterward, when they called on a listing prospect, the CEO would often be able to say, "I saw your picture in the paper." Thus, although Sheehan could not market Amex people as listing salesmen and saleswomen he did improve their level of acceptance.

Finally, Sheehan must be credited with the founding of Radio Amex in the mid-1950s. Using three broadcast booths and the voices of secretaries—Dora Nestor, Mary Cromer, Lisa Kravitz, Norma Bodner, and Maria Earle—the station broadcast stock prices, market index movements, and, whenever attribution to the company president made it possible to do so, an explanation of why a particular stock had moved up or down.

Sheehan devised a surprisingly simple but effective way to get final prices on the air soon after the appearance of the word "close" on the tape. IBM cards were keypunched with numbers from 1 to approximately 200, the number of stocks that could be fitted into a 15-minute broadcast. Each of the cards had been preprinted with the name of the company, the issue, and the post at which it was traded. Each bore a series of blanks for each day of the week, making available a script for the entire week. The cards were then distributed to the trading posts.

At each post a clerk was given responsibility for writing down both the closing price and the amount by which that price was either up or down. A couple of supervisors picked up the cards "in jig time" and handed them to one of Sheehan's people waiting for them on the trading floor. They were, of course, all jumbled up, but not for long. Rushed by elevator to the sorting machine on the seventh floor, they appeared in numerical order 15 seconds later. The key to the success of the operation was this: at the very beginning, the stocks had been listed in alphabetical order on a sheet of paper, with the first stock number one and the last, number 200!

One day a couple of "visiting geniuses" came to Sheehan's office with the news that they had just sold the New York Stock Exchange a system for rapidly obtaining closing prices. They offered the system to the Amex at a reduced rate. After Sheehan patiently explained his own simpler system for doing it, the embarrassed would-be salesmen beat a hasty departure.

Thus Radio Amex was born. "Eight or ten phone calls and maybe a couple of lunches" then succeeded in getting the Associated Press radio to take a couple of the Amex broadcasts each day. "Suppose AP had 300 radio stations in its family. That's 600 broadcasts. UPI was even bigger. Say they had 500 stations and agreed to 3 feeds a day. That's a total of 2,100 broadcasts. And if you add CBS, NBC, ABC and the state networks, which came along later, you multiply to totals to a staggering number." One broadcast to a large radio station in Atlanta, say, which put out a feed to small independent stations all over the state, exemplified the rippling effects of state network systems. Besides disseminating Amex stock prices by radio Sheehan also made use of the press for even larger purposes. "We started off by employing on an after-hours basis when the market closed a couple of youngsters who worked on the trading floor, and we would develop statistical analyses, and the active stock reports which the wire services weren't putting out at the time, the kind of things you see in the Amex market diary in the papers today. I invented a system called "making your own breaks." If you want something to be someplace you have to develop it yourself and then market it to them." Of course, Sheehan added, the Amex services were always free.

Those services consisted of putting the Amex stories together and running them uptown to the AP, UPI, *The New York Times*, the *Herald Tribune, Wall Street Journal,* and the *Journal of Commerce,* "wherever there was an outlet for us. Envelopes would go to the market lead writers in those days till we got them to write their own on the Amex. For many years the *Herald Tribune* ran a daily market lead on the Amex. It was quite a feather in our cap to get them to do this on a daily basis. And then to get the *New York Times* to do the same thing."

Sheehan says that he got tired of seeing Ted McCormick's face in those days. "I'd walk down to the railroad station in Dumont and there Ted McCormick would be on a billboard reading the *Herald Tribune.* On a train at the end of the car I'd see Ted again, quoted as saying, "I read the *Herald Tribune* daily." For a long time pictures of the new listing ceremonies on the Amex trading floor were carried in the *Trib* and other papers. We made it all possible by hiring a photographer to take the photos. I directed the pictures."

John Sheehan indeed made his own breaks. And the Amex prospered, not alone because of Sheehan, of course, but also because of Vernon Lee, the secretary-announcers and other dedicated people. Trading on the Amex boomed, vaulting from a daily average of 264,807 shares in 1949 to 1,947,534 shares in 1961. Partly because the Amex was the historic home of the speculative securities of small new companies, its percentage of total stocks traded on all American securities exchanges—15 regionals, besides the Big Board, and the over-the-counter market in New York (which was not really an "exchange" at all, for it had no trading floor)—rose steadily throughout these years. The number of shares listed at the Amex increased substantially in the 1950s, and so too did the price of a seat on the Exchange. From a high of $10,000 in 1949, the latter rose to $80,000 in 1961.

These were heady years, but they exacted a price. Easy times too often led to easy morals. The ancient temptation to make an extra buck, in combination with administrative inattention to life on the trading floor, led to abusive practices by leading specialists on the Exchange. (The Big Board was also in need of reform in the 1950s.) Professor Sobel tells the story in gripping detail and since our purpose is to pick up the story where he leaves it off (in 1971), we must refer the interested reader to him. It is a story of price manipulation, illegal short sales, rigged markets, fee splitting, sales of unregistered issues, trades made on the basis of inside information, and other forms of wheeling and dealing. The upshot was a rigorous investigation by the SEC and a thorough housecleaning by an Exchange all the more determined to justify self-regulation by the quality of its police work.

THE 1960s

The housecleaning took the form of a series of reforms, carried out largely during the presidency of Edwin ("Ted") D. Etherington (1962–1966), one of the giants in the history of the Exchange. The first was administrative in nature. A new constitution replaced an older one of 1939 in which power had reposed in the hands of brokers (mostly specialists) and their committees. The remodeled constitution eliminated the committee system and shifted most of the power to the president and his staff. Etherington proceeded in 1962–1963 to bring in over 40 new staff members, "most of whom filled newly created positions." The most important new appointment was that of Paul Kolton, an expert in public relations, whom Etherington brought over from a vice presidency at the Big Board, "to restore the Exchange's reputation for honesty and fair dealings." Kolton soon began to work closely with the president on the floor and in the back offices.

Other reforms soon followed. The Amex adopted more stringent listing and delisting rules. To be listed, a security had to have outstanding stock in the hands of the public worth at least $1 million. Other preconditions stipulated minimal net earnings for the fiscal year preceding the filing of the application for listing, and (a somewhat lesser amount) for the past three fiscal years. This represented significant reform—before 1962 Amex had had no such requirements at all. The adoption of *delisting* rules enabled Etherington to remove questionable issues from the Amex in his effort to upgrade the market. The program proved a success. Despite the delisting of marginal securities, the list increased in size every year but one during the 1960s.

Surely one of the most important of the Etherington reforms affected the specialist, the Amex training program for whom was "one of the most thorough in the nation." Besides stressing the importance of this program, the president took other steps to strengthen the specialist system. Recognizing that the success of an auction market depends upon the effectiveness of specialists in stabilizing securities prices in both bull and bear markets, he insisted that the specialists have sufficient resources of both capital and manpower to enable them to do their job. The enlarged markets of the 1960s required that small units of each give way to larger ones. Under Etherington's prodding the average number of specialists per unit increased from 2.9 to 4.8. One-man units, and later those of two men, were eliminated, the minimum number being fixed at three. To strengthen the units financially each was required to have "sufficient funds to handle at least 2,000 shares, or $100,000 in cash, whichever was larger, for each security in which it specialized." As a result, the units were able to handle additional securities, the number per unit rising from an average of 19 in 1964 to 37 by 1971. "To enable the Amex to handle high-priced, high-volume stocks, several extra-large units with large blocks of capital were created. By 1971 the Exchange had 11 five-man units, four six-man units, and one each of nine- and twelve-man units."

Two major consequences flowed from the success of the reform program. In the first place, the Amex's remodeled mechanisms and rejuvenated personnel enabled the Exchange to handle a trading volume of unprecedented proportions. Between 1960 and 1969 average daily volume nearly quintupled, the annual number of shares traded rising from 286 million to approximately 1.2 billion. In 1961 the Amex had its first 5-million-share day, in 1968 it doubled that figure before soaring to over 11 million shares on the last day of 1969. The price of an Amex seat also soared, rising from a high of $60,000 in 1960 to $350,000 in 1969. (In 1967 the price for the first time exceeded that of 1929.)

In the longer run the second consequence was the more important. It took the form of elevated status for both the Amex and its leaders. Historically, the Amex had served as a training ground for young brokers during periods of high volume. Afterward, the best of them would be "promoted" to the Big Board. This scenario was followed in the 1950s and 1960s too, but increasingly, major commission houses assigned to the Amex not only junior people in need of training but also some of their top men. Historically, too, issues traded on the junior exchange had moved over to the Big Board after "seasoning." During the 1960s the automaticity of the progression was arrested when Syntex declined overtures from the larger exchange to apply for listing. It was "the first time an Amex stock that qualified in every way for Big Board listing decided to remain at Amex." In the sequel, many others followed suit.[2]

The rising prestige of the Exchange and its executives was also to be seen in the growing cooperation between the latter and their counterparts at the Big Board. In the 1960s the two exchanges, together with the National Association of Securities Dealers, cooperated with the SEC in trying to overcome problems generated in the back offices of the commission houses by the huge volume of trading. Massive paper work was overwhelming record keeping and accounting and interfering with the prompt transfer and delivery of securities. The president of the NYSE and Etherington's successor at the Amex, Ralph Saul (1966–1971), agreed first to cut back on trading hours (in 1967–1968) to give the brokerages more time to catch up on their paper work, and then to close down on Wednesdays during the second half of 1968. Saul also addressed the crisis by other measures, for example, extending the facilities of the American Stock Exchange's Clearing Corporation to a number of over-the-counter issues that had not previously used them. "The crisis affected the entire securities industry, and could not help but bring the exchanges closer together." The two presidents "often operated as a team," with Saul's views and plans second only to those of the leader of the Big Board in dealing with the situation. The contrast with 1929 was a vivid one. The New York Stock Exchange then spoke for the financial district, but no reporter thought it necessary to ask the Curb president his views. Forty years later, the Amex was part of the Establishment. A succession of Amex presidents would command increasing respect throughout the financial community, not least because of their leadership in automating the operations of the securities industry. (For Amex presidents, see the Statistical Appendix.)

N O T E S

1. Robert Sobel, *The Curbstone Brokers: The Origins of the American Stock Exchange* (New York: Macmillan, 1970), and *Amex, A History of the American Stock Exchange, 1921–1971* (New York: Weybright & Tallen, 1972). Most of the sentences and phrases placed in quotation marks in the following pages are taken from Professor Sobel's studies and are intended as tributes to his insightful formulations. My account depends almost entirely on the Sobel volumes for the facts about the Amex and its predecessor institutions and practices, but I have utilized my own researches in economic and business history to depict the larger environment in which the Amex functioned. Sobel's volumes tell the story up to 1971; the purpose of the present volume is to take the story from 1971 to 1989.
2. In 1981 Syntex transferred to the New York Stock Exchange.

CHAPTER 2

THE BEGINNINGS OF MODERNIZATION

On taking office in November 1966 President Ralph Saul remarked, "It's a new American Stock Exchange." "Now," he added, "we must continue to grow, be prepared to innovate and give better quality and services to the public." A half-dozen years before, another head of the Amex, Joseph F. Reilly, had also sounded a trumpet call to innovation, and his immediate predecessor, Edwin T. McCormick, had done the same. McCormick recommended that the Amex consider emulating the Toronto Stock Exchange by installing a small electronic system to handle quotations, and Reilly's proposals were even more sophisticated. He pointed out that one system, offered by Teleregister, "could provide brokers and other interested parties with stock quotations, ranges, and volumes in a matter of seconds, produce a newspaper stock table every hour, and provide a résumé of the day's trading shortly after the closing bell at three-thirty." Three years later the system had been improved, and according to Reilly, if auxilliary computers were also used, it could handle most of the Amex's paperwork and make it possible to reduce substantially the number of clerks and other personnel on the floor and in the back offices.

Reilly foresaw the inability of the Exchange to function in the enlarged markets that were expected in the 1960s unless a considerable amount of automation were adopted. Unfortunately, many specialists, believing that new sophisticated systems might not only make clerks obsolete but also take over some of their functions as well, looked upon some of Reilly's ideas with fear and suspicion and voted them down. The discussion within the Amex was then subordinated to the need to give priority to the irregular trading practices to which we have already referred.

The automation issue was bound to reemerge. The choice was simple and it was stark: either the Amex equip itself to compete with other marketplaces or wither on the vine of technological obsolescence. A new era had come into being after World War II, an era in which the organization and processing of information and knowledge were being revolutionized. Some called what was going on a second Industrial Revolution, others spoke of a postindustrial world. Still others preferred the "Information Age." Whatever the designation, it is clear that the electronic digital computer was at the center of the revolution and remains there.

Unlike the calculator, the computer has a memory, a set of preprogrammed instructions or mathematical rules that it applies automatically to new data introduced at a later time. Like radar, jet aircraft, and other complex high-technology developments incorporating state-of-the-art scientific knowledge, the electronic computer was a product of governmental need during World War II. The first large electronic digital computer, the "ENIAC," was built during World War II to enable the Army's Ballistic Research Laboratory to calculate trajectories for field artillery and bombing tables, a tedious task previously requiring large numbers of mathematicians using desk calculators. The ENIAC was an enormous contraption, 100 feet long, 3 feet wide, and 10 feet high, and it contained about 18,000 vacuum tubes. Even though technical improvements were soon forthcoming, computers remained very costly after the war; they were difficult to program and were vulnerable to failure because of the dependence of their complex circuitry on vacuum-tube technology. Many companies had both the knowledge and resources to build them, but great uncertainty over the size of the potential market made them reluctant to invest the substantial scientific, technical, and financial resources required if they were to become commercial suppliers of computer systems.

Even IBM held back at first. It was not till 1953 that the computer giant began shipments of its high-performing general purpose machine, the "701," a computer that was 10 to 100 times faster than the ENIAC. It was also much smaller and cheaper; indeed, it was the first general purpose computer that did not have to be built in the customer's own computer room. IBM's shipments of one a month were a production record unmatched at the time by any other company. Then competition, the glory of the American enterprise system, stepped in to do its work. First Remington Rand and Burroughs, then General Electric, RCA, and Control Data, and still later Apple, Wang, Commodore, and Tandy, began turning out computers that were not only smaller and cheaper still, but increasingly versatile as types of uses and users multiplied. Under the whip of competition for market share the technology of the industry changed dramatically. First transistors, then silicon chips, replaced vacuum tubes. Chips no larger than the head of a thumbtack could hold the equivalent of 100,000 transistors, and work on a far larger integration of circuitry was proceeding apace.

Aware of many of these developments and devoted to their institution, Amex executives one after another successfully urged the Board of Governors to support plans to equip the Exchange with the products of the new technology. To see more clearly how it would be used, and how its use would enable the Amex to function more efficiently as a central marketplace, let us briefly review the nature of the stock exchange business as it was conducted in the early 1960s, before the beginning of modernization. Before we do so it is important to emphasize that almost all the steps in the process to be described must still be taken today. It is just that thoroughgoing automation permits them to be taken more efficiently and quickly, and with a much reduced risk of error or loss.

Let us begin by making it clear that brokerage firms who are members of the American Stock Exchange have booths on the trading floor from which to conduct their transactions, that they do so with the help of their clerks and through the medium of floor brokers in their employ, and that the actual buying and selling of securities is done by specialist units charged by the Amex administration (its Allocations Committee) with the responsibility for maintaining a continuous and orderly market in designated securities—all stocks traded being handled by one or another of such units. Specialists are market makers. By buying or selling for their own account as well as for others they provide a market where none may have existed, or raise or lower a price for the purpose of narrowing the spread between the last sale and a quoted price. Their activity is essential to the smooth working of a two-way auction process, a process in which numerous buyers (bidders) and sellers (askers) determine the prices at which securities change hands.

All right, let's go. We are in the pre-automated age of the early 1960s. The member firm's booth clerk receives a sell order either from the firm's order room or branch office via telephone or teletype. The clerk relays the customer's limit order—that is, to buy or sell at a designated price—from the booth to the floor broker. To do so he uses a hand signal or writes the order—to sell 100 shares of CMF at 25 1/4 or better—on an order slip and places it on a conveyor belt that carries it to the edge of the trading floor. The floor broker acknowledges the order and walks to the post where CMF is traded and hands it to the specialist. The specialist stamps the order with date and time and files it in the trading post rack until ready for execution. He executes the order when the market price of CMF reaches 25 1/4 or better, and records the volume, price, and clearing name (more on this in a moment) of the contra-broker on the order slip. (If the specialist executes the order for his own account he enters the sale in his trading book.) The specialist's clerk then reports the execution of the order to the member-firm booth clerk via a pneumatic tube system. And in the meantime the data clerk at the trading post has checked the accuracy of the stock symbol and sale price on the sales slip. The sale is then entered into a key set, the data clerk verifies the entry, and the sale of 100 CMF at 25 1/4 or better appears on the ticker.

We shall see how automation gradually changed life on the trading floor. But the story we have told is incomplete. We have yet to talk about "back office" operations, which are no less essential to the working of the securities industry. The broker who sold CMF on behalf of his customer had to compare his record of the transaction with the buying broker to make sure that the two were in agreement on the terms of the trade. The former had to deliver stock certificates to the latter, who, in turn, had to pay for them. A transfer agent—a firm specializing in that function, or one of the New York banks that are members of the New York Clearing House Association, (clearinghouse banks)—had to record the change in the identity of the seller to that of the buyer.

And there was the rub: just who was the buyer? We are no longer talking about the single customer of our description but rather about the hundreds of customers served by numerous brokers on any given trading day. On any given day Broker A might sell 100 shares of CMF stock to Broker B, who in turn might sell them to C, who might sell them to D, who might sell them to E, all on the same day. In this series of transactions A's obligation to deliver the stock was *initial* and had to be met. Similarly, E's right to receive was *terminal* and could not be canceled. But the rights and obligations of B, C, and D were *intermediate* and canceled out since each was obligated to deliver and had a right to receive the same number of shares of CMF stock.

Who was to do the canceling and how was it to be done? If only Broker A knew about Broker E's claim he could deliver the shares to him directly. Unfortunately, he dealt only with Broker B and knew nothing of E's terminal right. The solution: each broker reported all his obligations and rights to a central agency—a clearinghouse—and this agency eliminated the intermediate obligations and rights and informed the broker with the initial obligation of the identity of the broker with the terminal right. Only at this point was it possible for the transfer agent to record the change of title from the initial to the terminal owner.

Now, as we have seen, Amex executives resolved many years ago to keep abreast of the most recent technological advances. President Etherington, Reilly's successor[1] viewed automation as a refinement of the specialist system rather than as a threat to it, and in 1965 persuaded the Board of Governors to adopt a long-range program.

The first step would be the mounting of electronic keyboards at every trading post for use in transmitting information from the floor to the stock tickers. This program was completed in 1966. Computers would also be used to take over operation of the ticker systems. A "talking computer," called Am-Quote, would receive price and volume information from the tickers. A broker wanting the latest information on a particular stock could dial a number on his telephone, and the computer would relay the information by means of special prerecorded tapes.

The Board charged an eight-man committee with the task not only of putting the plan in operation but also with preparing for additional changes in the future.

President Saul continued the work begun by Etherington. In July 1968, for example, the Board approved a contract with Ferranti-Packard Electric Limited for the purchase of three electrically operated systems for the display of last sale price, and tick and bid offer prices at the trading posts on the floor of the Exchange. (A "tick" represents the difference between the last-sale price and that of the previous sale.) A contract with IBM to supply and provide technical support for computers to implement the Exchange's Odd-Lot Automation Program, approved the following month, affords insight into the nature of the Amex's long-range automation program as of mid-1968.

The basic purpose of the plan was to automate the nonauction processes on the trading floor. Computer execution of market orders for odd lots (less than 100 shares) represented its initial phase. A computerized system would automatically store and execute trades in odd-lot market orders, simultaneously sending execution reports to the originating firm. In the course of development the system would acquire the acronym MOLE (Market-Order Odd-Lot Execution service). The objective of the second phase was to enable member firms for the first time to send round lot limit orders and cancellations (lots of 100, 200, etc., shares to be bought or sold at a designated price rather than "at the market") into the computer system to be read and switched to the proper trading post. When instructed to do so by the specialist, the computer would execute the orders and report both to the tape and to the brokerage houses concerned for confirmation. This service came to be known as LOS (Limit Order Switching service).

The third phase of the long-range plan had to do with various execution and reporting aids for round-lot market orders, including an input device at the post that would read the original order after its execution and satisfy all the various reporting requirements for the ticker network, and for confirmation report and clearing. At this point substantially all outgoing booth operations could be eliminated, with material reductions in incoming traffic to booths since odd lots and limit orders would be received directly by the Exchange. These various steps would provide for the "locked-in trade," and this in turn would permit the final step in the plan to be taken, that is, implementation of the floor-derived clearance. A locked-in trade, it should be made clear, is one in which all pertinent trade data are captured at the moment of execution. Capture of the data assures a compared clearance, activates the ticker, and furnishes execution reports to the firms involved in the trade. Traditionally, the uncompared trade had hampered clearance operations and impaired the overall efficiency of the market. "Locking in" therefore promised a higher level of productivity for the marketplace.

These were plans for the future, and we shall see how they were modified and implemented. Meanwhile, more modest measures already taken in the direction of modernization, for example, the creation of larger posts and the improvement of traffic flow, helped the Amex cope with the big bull market of the later 1960s. Trading volume surged, especially in 1967, 1968, and 1969, when a total of nearly 4 billion shares changed hands on the Amex. But the problems generated by those heaving markets drove home the lesson that automating the floor of the Exchange, however desirable and important in itself, was not enough. For those problems turned out to be industrywide. As we have seen, a massive paperwork log jam developed in the "back offices," where trades were processed, arrangements made for legal transfers, and certificates transferred and delivered. Many of the houses performing these operations failed, victims of their inability to cope with the record-keeping, accounting, and most especially, financial reserve requirements of the heavy volume. According to Ralph Saul, errors in handling orders were costing brokerage houses "some $100 million a year."

The Amex president saw the problem whole. Brokerage firms, he pointed out, are not alone. "We are dealing with a financial community. Banks are intimately involved. So are institutional investors, retail customers, transfer agents, the exchanges and their clearing and depository operations, and corporations. It follows that remedies to the major operating problems must be resolved in concert." The Amex decided to sponsor a major study of the entire securities industry by the North American Rockwell Corporation. The resulting study was what the Exchange called "the first *total* systems analysis of securities industry operations."

The North American Rockwell proposals partly overlapped the plans already set in motion by the Amex. Like the latter, the new proposals were designed to provide an orderly flow of data from the inception of an order to its receipt and execution, and thereafter to reporting, clearance, settlement, and transfer operations. The report made five major recommendations: (1) that errors at the very source of a transaction be reduced by on-line copy editing of orders, and by a monitoring system to speed trades to market; (2) that a locked-in trade procedure be developed to capture, at the point of trade, all data necessary to report transactions simultaneously to the ticker network, originating broker offices, and clearing and surveillance functions; (3) that a centralized system be set up for clearing securities by automation, more specifically, that a new National Clearing Service be established and linked by computer to regional clearing centers in major market areas; (4) that the flow of securities through most of the system be eliminated by placing them in Transfer Agent depositories electronically tied to the clearing service; and (5) that delays in the transfer and registration of securities be overcome by establishing standardized, high-speed and consolidated facilities using both man- and machine-readable stock certificates, attachments, and instructions.

Implicit in the North American Rockwell study was the desirability of close collaboration between the two national exchanges, the New York Stock Exchange and the Amex. That collaboration was soon forthcoming. Two executive vice-presidents, Paul Kolton of the Amex and R. John Cunningham of the Big Board, began in the late 1960s to explore "methods by which their operations might be coordinated, and in some cases joined."

> Shared computer time seemed a natural area for cooperation. Another would be the introduction of Amex securities into the Stock Exchange's Block Automation System, a computerized network aimed at facilitating large block transactions [10,000 or more shares]. A unified clearing house was also considered, and Kolton and Cunningham saw little reason why the exchanges could not cooperate in the establishement of a central depository for all exchange securities.

The latter suggestion was one that the Amex had taken the lead in forwarding since early 1969. More specifically, it had been urging the establishment of an organization, representing both the banking and securities industries, to plan, design, and implement changes in operating systems that cut across industry lines. It had in mind such desiderata as those of building an expansible depository system and standardizing documents.

Essentially, the goal was to reduce the amount of paper as much as possible and to standardize the irreducible minimum. There was even a good deal of talk, which some thought at least premature and even a bit irresponsible, of a "certificateless society." If securities, preferably in large "jumbo" denominations (to minimize their number) could be housed physically in a central depository, the accounts of the brokerage firm owning them could be debited or credited by the depository to reflect purchases or sales made by those firms. The firms, in turn, would keep their own records of securities owned by the individuals and institutions who were their customers. The system was envisioned to function in the manner of the Federal Reserve banks, which held the required deposits of their member banks, while the latter maintained their retail relationships with customers.

The New York banks had gone along with the idea, but the New York Stock Exchange hesitated because of its uncertainty over the extent of the authority to be granted the full-time director of the proposed organization. By March 1970 this problem had been resolved and a committee formed to represent New York clearinghouse banks and securities industry groups. Known as BASIC (Banking and Securities Industry Committee), the committee proceeded to propose "the creation of a Central Securities Depository System, which would incorporate the Big Board's Central Certificate Service (CCS). The new facility would provide services for both exchanges, as well as the regional markets and the over-the-counter market." Agreeing that the new system would "go far toward the goal of 'immobilizing certificates,' ending abuses and losses, and automating the district," the presidents of the New York Stock Exchange and the Amex entered all eligible Amex securities into the Big Board's CCS in 1971. In that same year the exchanges also joined the commission houses in adopting "better standardization procedures on clearances."

By 1971, in short, the year in which Paul Kolton succeeded Ralph Saul in the presidency of the Amex, "automation and standardization had become key words in the district," and "strong ties and common bonds" had been established between the Big Board and the nation's other major exchange, the Amex.

Kolton was quick to give credit to his predecessor. "Mr. Saul," he wrote in his first "President's letter" to the Exchange and its membership, "was among the first to see the need for a systematic revision of the industry's operating structure, the necessity for a formal inter-industry approach to processing problems, and the importance to the Exchange of pushing ahead with a broad automation program." The credit was deserved, but not a small share of it belonged to Kolton himself. Kolton's early business career had been marked by achievement. A graduate of the University of North Carolina, he joined the Amex in 1962 as executive vice-president after a decade in advertising and seven years of service on the New York Stock Exchange as director of public information. In the years before being elected to the presidency of the Amex he strongly supported the development of cooperative solutions to interindustry problems, participated actively in such major industry studies as that by the North American Rockwell Corporation, and played a key role in launching the Exchange's comprehensive automation program to modernize the trading floor.

One consequence of the latter was his ability to announce in the fall of 1971 that development work on the MOLE and LOS projects had been successfully completed and that both services would be inaugurated early the next year. In addition, a pilot test would be made of the use of a cathode ray tube (CRT) in a member firm's booth to display limit orders. Hopefully, the experiment would enable floor members to gain experience in visually monitoring all incoming orders and in deciding how to enter them in the execution process. The new president—the first professional staff member to be so elevated on any of the nation's major security exchanges (but not the last!)—emphasized that the new programs were "designed to maintain and improve the Amex as a competitive marketplace by lowering the costs of order execution." When fully operational, the Amex automation system was intended to capture member firm orders as they entered the floor, store them electronically in computer memory files, display limit orders in automated specialists' books, and capture the necessary price, volume, and related data at the point of execution. In essence, the system would link the Amex market to an electronic network of over 4,000 main and branch offices and ultimately eliminate many manual steps not part of the auction process.

The drive to automate the Exchange continued to move in high gear during Kolton's first year in office. As expected, both MOLE and LOS went on-line in 1972, but these were not the only achievements. Adopting a new market data input system, the Amex installed the first two of thirty electronic optical mark-sense card readers at trading posts. Particular credit for overseeing these and other advances belongs to Richard M. Burdge, who had been appointed senior vice-president in charge of operations in June 1969.

One of Kolton's first moves on assuming the presidency had been to secure Burdge's promotion to executive vice-president in a major restructuring of the Exchange's administrative organization. To centralize administrative controls, staff responsibilities in the Amex's 13 divisions and 32 departments were gathered into 3 groups. While two senior vice-presidents, James W. Walker, Jr., and Winsor H. Watson, Jr., were made responsible for legal, regulatory, and governmental activities (Walker) and for direction of a new marketing services group (Watson), Burdge was asked to head up operations, administration, and finance. In a memo to the Amex membership Kolton spelled out the meaning of "operations." The term embraced several functions—market operations, data systems, automation, communications, and continued planning in all those areas. Kolton made it clear that Burdge would "concentrate on the Amex's expanding automation program which includes several key firsts for the securities industry."

With day-by-day operational responsibility to oversee the development and implementation of the Exchange's long-range program in the hands of Burdge, Kolton was free to turn his attention to other pressing issues. The most important of these was the increasingly significant challenge to the specialist system offered by the National Association of Securities Dealers Quotation System (NASDQ). Using computers, scanners, and telephones rather than the floors of an exchange—and thus bypassing the middleman—over-the-counter dealers formed a "third market" in Big Board stocks. Pension funds, insurance companies, and other institutional investors were patronizing this market in increasing numbers. These organizations had attempted to purchase seats on both the New York Stock Exchange and the Amex, where their large transactions could be conducted without going through the commission houses. The tactic would have saved them sizable fees but at the expense of the bypassed brokerage firms.

The two exchanges rejected the institutional overtures under the terms of their constitutions, and the suitors turned instead to the third market. The Amex was only affected indirectly by this development (in 1971, only one Amex stock was covered regularly by third-market firms), but the threat to the specialist system was "the greatest . . . Wall Street had ever known." Responding to the threat, the two major exchanges moved closer together than ever. On the street there was even talk of a merger.

While no merger took place, two important things did happen. The first, an outgrowth of the paperwork crisis, was the coordination of operations between the two exchanges. Operational cooperation, already represented by the introduction of Amex securities into the Big Board's Block Automation System, and the creation of the Central Securities Depository System, was extended still further by the organization of the Securities Industry Automation Corporation (SIAC). Owned and financed jointly by the Amex and the New York Stock Exchange, SIAC was formed to consolidate ultimately the communications, clearing, data processing, and automation facilities of the two exchanges.

In 1972, when SIAC began operations, one of its major projects, originally funded and operated by the Amex, was transferred to the new corporation. The Securities Industry Telecommunications Organization (SECTOR) had been formed by the Amex as a service to brokerage houses. By using low cost bulk voice facilities and a device permitting the standard telephone-grade line to be divided into a number of teletype lines, SECTOR was saving its more than 100 participants in the program nearly $130,000 a month. In a move toward industry cooperation, SECTOR's eligibility was expanded to include regional exchanges and their members.

A second program, expanded in 1972, was designed more specifically for the benefit of members of the Exchange. To senior executives of nearly 500 brokerage firms, the Planning Division of the Amex distributed an operations report and a financial report under its Feedback and Analysis of Control Statistics (FACS) program. The former report was designed to pinpoint areas of strength and weakness in the firm's securities processing and control. The financial report compared the firm's financial performance for the previous month and year with that of firms of similar size and business mix. The purpose of the program, in short, was to develop standards by which member firms might measure their operational and financial capability.

As we shall see, this was one of the many services developed by the Amex over the years for the benefit of its member firms and listed companies. Not the least of these was to be the mutually beneficial interplay between the Exchange and the listed companies, which was made possible by the formation of the Listed Company Advisory Committee. Made up of nine chief executives whose chairman met with the Exchange Board, the members of the committee gathered for the first time in March 1972 to discuss matters vital to the interests of their companies, their shareowners, and the market for their securities.

THE MARTIN REPORT

The second important consequence of "the complex of Wall Street problems" was a major study of the securities markets by an unusually well-qualified student of the financial markets. A former chairman of the Federal Reserve Board, William McChesney Martin was at the time the president of the New York Stock Exchange. Martin acknowledged in the opening sentence of his report, "The Securities Markets," that the study had been made "against a background of crisis in the securities industry." The "old familiar patterns" of that industry had been "disrupted by the appearance of two new forces: institutional investors and computers." By mobilizing capital, the former had acquired the power to influence the way markets were made. The latter, because of the communication system they offered, made it possible to execute many transactions in Big Board listed securities on various other exchanges and in the third and fourth markets.[2]

The dispersion of trading away from a central auction market had begun to fragment that market, and while some lauded the resulting competition, Martin insisted that competition "must exist under similar rules and in the same arena" if it were to be beneficial. But the rules differed. Dissimilar regulatory policies made for differences in disclosure of information about activity in these markets and in access to them. In consequence, it was "increasingly difficult for the public and fiduciaries alike to obtain the best prices available at any given time."

Computers, however, provided the means to improve radically the way markets operated, and Martin commended the progress in automation the exchanges were making, citing in particular the "consolidation of certain computer facilities of the New York Stock Exchange and the American Stock Exchange," which would "provide maximum economy in their use." Computers offered a solution to the operational and competitive problems of Wall Street. They made possible a centralized national market that is nationwide in scope. That market should be an auction market. Such a market, in Martin's judgment, was best suited to provide both maximum liquidity and "a continuous, fair and orderly market with centralized disclosure of all executions of buy and sell orders and other material facts." The Big Board, the Amex, and the regional exchanges should be linked in a national exchange system "which would have the same rules for all members." Martin opposed institutional membership on stock exchanges because of the concentration of economic power that might result. (It was "imperative that the market should be designed to serve the public, to serve the small investor equally as well as anyone else.") But he would "preserve and defend the specialist system."

There has been a great deal of criticism of the role and function of specialists. However, no better system of maintaining a continuous and responsible market has been suggested. The capital resources of specialists, however, should be increased to meet the requirements of today's trading, and methods be developed to encourage and enable specialists to improve performance of their functions in instances where securities are offered in unusually large volume.

In addition, the rising trend toward public ownership of member firms should be encouraged as a means of providing capital on a permanent basis.

The reaction at the Amex was to appoint a 14-man committee, headed by Board Chairman Frank C. Graham, Jr., to make a detailed study of the Martin Report. In addition, Amex officials took part in discussions of a national exchange system with a committee representing the New York, Midwest, Pacific Coast, and Philadelphia-Baltimore-Washington stock exchanges. The Graham committee's study permitted President Kolton to make the following major points in testimony before the Securities and Exchange Commission (SEC) in October 1971. The proposed integrated national system of exchanges, Kolton said, ought contain three essential parts: (1) independent market centers made up of existing SEC-registered exchanges, with competitive market makers operating under equal regulation; (2) a national communications network, with a consolidated ticker tape, to link all market centers in the system into an electronic network for inputting, disseminating, and displaying bids and offers, and capable of switching public orders to whichever market provided the best execution; and (3) a policy-making, self-regulatory governing authority made up equally of exchange respresentatives, broker-dealers, and the public. Each participating exchange, Kolton emphasized, should retain its separate identity.

The recommendations of the Martin Report were controversial and would be discussed on all the exchanges for months. Eventually, some of them would feed into congressional debate culminating in a major revision in 1975 of the Securities Exchange Act of 1934. And one day the consolidated tape would become a reality. Computers had indeed disrupted the "old familiar patterns" of the securities industry. But really fundamental change in the organizational structure of the industry was bound to meet proper principles of territoriality, so to speak, and was bound to encounter deserved resistance on the part of organizations proud of their past and confident in their ability to adjust to changed conditions while preserving their own identities. And so the bold new proposals were earnestly discussed and then for the most part set aside until future technology made dramatic change inevitable.

The present and its demands were turbulent enough. Trading volume for 1971 had gone over the billion share mark for the fourth time in the previous five years, and volume for 1972 exceeded that of the previous year once more. The number of securities listed on the Exchange continued to grow, new stock and warrant issues during 1972 approved for original listing (179) being "the second highest in recent history," bringing the total number of securities traded on the Exchange to 1,419. Exchange revenues, principally from listing fees, clearing charges, and investment income, kept pace. Block transactions (10,000 shares or more) in 1972 numbered 3,237, up nearly 20 percent over the previous year's, and while these represented only a very small percentage of all transactions, they appear to have begun to exercise an intimidating effect on the smaller investor. At any rate Kolton believed the first imperative of the securities industry was to "reattract" the individual investor by continuing to improve services and investment opportunities. Institutions needed the active participation of individuals if the pricing mechanism and viability of the securities markets were to be preserved.

Both years recorded memorable events at the Amex. In 1971 the Exchange celebrated the fiftieth anniversary of its move indoors, named a new president (Kolton), and incorporated. And late in 1972 the Amex reorganized its governing structure to provide equal representation on the Board of the securities industry and the public—ten being chosen from each sector. The new Board met for the first time in November and as its first order of business elected Kolton to serve as the first full-time chairman and chief executive officer of the Exchange. The governors then approved Kolton's recommendation that Richard M. Burdge succeed to the presidency. The change in structure had been recommended by the Martin Report, and a similar change was made by the NYSE. In the perspective of time, structural reorganization was to be seen as an event of extraordinary importance. The exchanges thereby shed many of the remaining vestiges of "private clubs."

1973–1974

Good times don't last forever, but neither do bad times. The near-record exchange business of the opening two years of the 1970s gave way to a pair of years that pressed hard in the other direction. Despite the fact that the SEC had gone along with an upward revision of commission rates the previous year, the first since 1958, Chairman Kolton reported in his annual letter to the Exchange membership that 1973 "was a most difficult year," with volume, prices, listings, and income "down significantly." As the Exchange that "principally serves individual investors and as the market for maturing companies," he added, "the Amex reflected the inactivity of the former and the market problems of the latter."

Those problems were severe indeed. At the beginning of 1973 the economy was humming along near full capacity, but after the dropping of controls by the federal government, farm prices exploded, followed by a general commodities boom, soaring inflation, tightened credit conditions, a jump in interest rates to record levels, and, at the end of the year, a fourfold increase in oil prices by the Organization of Petroleum Exporting Countries (OPEC). From an annual rate of 3.3 percent in 1972 (CPI), inflation surged to 11.0 percent in 1974. The confidence of businessmen and consumers turned to fright, and 1974, with real GNP falling by 2 percent, became the worst year for the American economy since the end of World War II. The fortunes of the Amex reflected those of a nation whose economy appeared to be heading into depression. In his report to the membership at the end of the year, Kolton stated that both stock prices and volume had plummeted, and the profits and capital of brokerage firms had been hit hard, forcing some to either merge or go out of business. In short, what had been endured was "the worst year for the securities industry since the Great Depression." The Exchange's Market Value Index, introduced in 1973 to replace the Price Change Index, closed at 90.33, down from the base of 100.00 set at the end of August.

At the Amex as elsewhere throughout the business world, retrenchment and vigorous cost controls were put in place. These were necessary measures, but they were not taken at the expense of the Exchange's long-range commitment to automate order processing and the clearing functions of the marketplace. This too would lower costs, of course, but Kolton and the Amex had another set of reactions to the downturn. Barrons magazine hinted at what was going on in an article published in the late fall of 1973:

> Weep not for the Amex. Thanks to a revamped management team, aggressive marketing, and hard-nosed cost-cutting, the nation's second largest stock exchange is alive and well and busily planning for the better days that hopefully lie ahead.

"Aggressive marketing" took several forms. The first order of business was to address the needs and interests of listed companies, present and prospective, and those of member firms. Amex representatives reviewed industry developments with officials of its nearly 600 listed companies, went over individual company trading records and then responded to questions about market activity. Under the Exchange's new "Major Cities" program, Kolton and other executives traveled to a half-dozen cities to confer with senior officers of companies in all three categories. The Exchange also adopted a new program to increase personal contact and discussions with the corporate finance departments of member organizations, and held meetings with a dozen underwriting groups in various cities to describe the services of the Amex and the advantages of listing on it.

Meetings of this kind were especially desirable in view of the sharp drop-off in the underwriting of stock issues. According to *UnderWriters Performance Record*, the number of new industrial issues fell from 991 in 1972 to 160 in 1973. (In 1974 the number was to hit bottom, a mere 38 being recorded.) Stock prices were so depressed that companies were discouraged from looking to the equity markets for new capital needs. Finally, in 1973 the Amex initiated the first advertising campaign in its history to promote the unique qualities of the Amex market and the special characteristics of the Exchange. The series appeared in the *Wall Street Journal, The New York Times*, and in a group of leading national magazines, each of the ads reaching an estimated circulation of 4.4 million people.

The *Barron's* article also contained another striking phrase. The Amex, it said, was "busily planning." It was indeed. The downturn had sharpened competition between marketplaces for a dwindling amount of business. The NASD was making a determined effort to persuade companies to remain in the over-the-counter market, and the New York Stock Exchange had lowered its listing standards for warrants. To make matters worse, 35 to 40 companies listed on the Amex were transferring each year to the Big Board.

What about the possibility of compensating for the lost revenue by permitting continued Amex trading in those issues? To be sure, the constitutions of both exchanges barred trading in the other's stocks. Perhaps the Amex ought to amend its constitution? But if it did so, if it adopted a system of dual trading, how would the historic mission of the Exchange be affected?

Traditionally, the Amex had functioned in a *dual* role—as a major marketplace and seasoning mechanism for new growth companies and as a primary market for the issues of established corporations. Would a regime of *dual* trading enhance that role? More broadly, what might the Amex do to widen its appeal to the investing community and those who served it? To probe these questions the Board established a Special Committee to Study Amex Future Markets. Board member Robert C. Van Tuyl was named its chairman.

It took only a few months to dispose of the dual trading possibility. Aware that serious legal and operational matters would have to be considered, the Committee first solicited the views of the general membership and then most particularly those of 19 large firms holding memberships on both the Amex and the Big Board. When the latter group overwhelmingly opposed the repeal of the ban on grounds of "potential cost pressures and operational and best execution problems," the Committee first put the issue on the back burner and then allowed it to expire quietly. (Later, as we shall see, it was to be resuscitated.)

It had plenty else to do. Before the end of 1973 the Committee had reviewed, and the Board had approved, proposals to encourage a broadening of the Exchange's domestic list. The companies for which the new policy was devised were real estate "cash flow" firms and those engaged in exploration, development, and research, companies that did not have the immediate generation of net profits as their principal objective and that therefore could not meet existing net income requirements for listing. (The real estate companies referred to used accelerated depreciation to take advantage of favorable tax treatment and normally did not report net income.) Quality firms in these categories had substantially larger net worth than that required to meet Amex listing standards and could be depended on to meet their financial obligations. The Exchange adopted higher delisting criteria for these companies as well.

The Board also approved an important new program to attract additional overseas security listings and to further strengthen the Amex role as a major international stock exchange. This effort met favorable responses not only from the SEC but also from the State and Treasury departments in Washington. With the government's removal of the Interest Equalization Tax early in 1974, the position of U.S. capital markets relative to most other markets became a stronger one. The Big Board joined the Amex in efforts to reduce remaining obstacles in the way of growth in foreign listings by urging repeal of the federal withholding tax on dividends and interest earned on U.S. securities held by foreigners. For its part, the Amex prepared a brief to the SEC recommending that the Commission exempt qualified foreign companies from SEC registration, as required under the 1934 Exchange Act, provided those companies contracted with the Exchange to fulfill the obligations of a listed company.

The Amex went even further—not only did it wish to encourage participation in U.S. markets by an ever-widening class of foreign investors, but it also favored broadening foreign broker-dealer access to those markets, provided their American counterparts were accorded reciprocal privileges abroad. Accompanied by Vice-President Bernard Maas, who had witnessed the Crash of '29 as an Exchange employee, Kolton met with listing prospects, merchant bankers and government officials in England, France, and Germany in 1973, and in June of the following year the pair traveled to London and Basel. Although the trips did not yield the hoped-for results, they testify to the Amex's determination to become a leading exchange in the international arena.

Chairman Kolton and President Burdge had some other things up their sleeves as well. Both were determined to position the Exchange for the tougher and even more competitive era that lay ahead. Trade in equities was off—so why not adopt a policy of product diversification? Why not develop new products? One possibility was that of trading mortgage futures on the Exchange. A mortgage futures market would stabilize the availability of money for residential mortgages by establishing a forward market similar in concept to the type used for many commodities. The instruments involved would include mortgage-backed securities guaranteed by the Government National Mortgage Association (GNMA, or "Ginnie Maes") and by the Federal Home Loan Mortgage Corporation (FHLMC). Such a market would serve the interests of home builders as well as lending institutions.

A second possibility was that of establishing a market on odd lots ($1,000 to $99,000) of U.S. government and federal agency securities. The originator of the idea that the Exchange might provide such a market was Michael Dritz, a principal in the registered bond specialist unit on the trading floor. The idea seemed a good one. In the past, virtually all dealings in government securities had taken place in the institutionally oriented over-the-counter market. Their availability on the Exchange in odd lots seemed well calculated to appeal to the individual investor, whose interest was already being piqued by current yields. Finally, preliminary discussions with nonmember odd-lot dealers in such securities had evoked an active interest in specializing in them on the Exchange.

A third possibility arose out of federal legislation enacted in 1974 that would permit Americans to own and trade gold on or before January 1, 1975. Should not the Exchange establish a central secondary market for the trading of gold certificates? and silver too? Last, but far from least, there was the possibility of trading options. The Amex was abuzz with excitement as President Burdge announced in April 1974 that the administration would centralize and coordinate the study and evaluation of these and other possibilities by setting up a New Products Division, whose head would report to him personally.

Eventually, after careful planning by the Exchange and scrutiny by the SEC, all of these innovations came on-line, their revenue-enhancing results naturally varying from product to product. The "big enchilada" was the trading of options, both before and after implementation of the concept. Not that options on equities were something new. "Puts" and "calls" were traded over-the-counter in New York in the early 1800s, and in Europe long before that. What was new was the idea of trading them on an exchange. Credit for originating that idea belongs to officials at the Chicago Board Options Exchange (CBOE), an affiliate of the Chicago Board of Trade, who persuaded the SEC in February 1973 to allow the CBOE to set up a pilot program.

Acknowledging that the CBOE had "pioneered options," Chairman Kolton saw no reason that the Amex should not be permitted to mount a pilot program as well, especially since competition among markets had long been recognized as an important objective of the Exchange Act. Kolton had another good reason for advocating options trading on the Amex: in contrast with marketmaking by broker-dealers at the CBOE, the Amex auction system—"with the paraphernalia of trade reporting, specialist systems, audit trails and the ability to reconstruct the market"—offered distinct advantages to the investor. After considerable preliminary discussion and review, the Amex Board in July 1973 approved plans for developing a pilot project, and at its first meeting that September the Special Committee on Future Amex Markets agreed that the project should receive the Exchange's "highest priority."

Nearly ten months later, in July 1974, Kolton informed the Board that "the Amex's resources were being fully devoted to getting options trading on-line." And it took another six months before Kolton was able to inform members and member organizations in December 1974 that the "American Stock Exchange's plan for the trading of call options has been declared effective by the Securities and Exchange Commission." Why the long year and a half lapse of time?

Looking back on these events some years later Kolton provided some answers. "Getting the thing on-line," he told an interviewer, "was the single most extended and difficult period that we had in terms of satisfying the various constituencies."

The principal constituencies were the SEC, the CBOE, the city and state of New York, and the community of Exchange members. An "enormous number" of legal problems came to the surface. The SEC was concerned about the potential for abuse. Could the Exchange give assurances that the "whole unregulated put-and-call market" would be brought under control and public responsibilities fulfilled? It could, and did. What about clearances: Would the Amex set up its own clearing corporation or buy a piece of the CBOE clearing corporation? The SEC thought that there should be only one of the latter, but the CBOE was reluctant to allow a competitor to get its foot in the door to its monopoly. Not that the CBOE president thought that a monopoly was right. "I don't believe in monopolies philosophically," Joseph Sullivan told the SEC, but "when you have a monopoly," he added, "it's a pretty good thing." Kolton recalled that Sullivan "was nifty at deflecting our proposals."

The Amex chairman countered with some niftiness of his own:

> I was on the phone yelling, pleading, cajoling, calling the SEC, calling our senators, calling our friends in the street (who were all interested, but kind of bemused at the struggle going on).

Pressure on the CBOE from the SEC itself finally brought this phase of the struggle to an end. The CBOE would not get any more options to trade unless it went along. And so it did.

One additional hurdle had to be cleared: New York City and New York State discovered the stock transfer tax and decided that it applied to options. Had the decision stuck, the cost differential in favor of the CBOE would have kept options trading out of New York. Kolton explained: "For low-priced options, given what they were trading at—sixteenth and thirty-seconds—you multiply that by 100 and add $5 transfer tax and you're out of the box." The cost of the transfer tax could be greater than the cost of an options contract. Once again the Amex argued its case before authoritative groups: ". . . we went to the governor, we went to the mayor, we went to the New York State Attorney General, we went to the city council of New York." And the upshot was a determination by New York State Attorney General Louis Lefkowitz that options were not equities and hence were not subject to the transfer tax.

1975: NEW PRODUCTS ON THE AMEX

A few other problems remained to be worked out—development with the CBOE not only of a common clearing system but also a common last-sale tape, standard options terms and conditions, and provisions for making quotations available to qualified nonmembers—and the Amex was off and running. On January 15, 1975, the many months of planning, testing, and waiting culminated with the opening of call options trading on the Amex in the stocks of six leading U.S. corporations. The following week, 14 more classes of options were phased in, the underlying stocks being those of Digital Equipment, American Cyanamid, Burroughs, Chase Manhattan, and other major companies. To oversee further development of the new program, the Amex Board approved appointment of the 17-man Special Options Committee, and a new vice-president, Paul M. Blair, was placed in charge of Options Trading.

The first month of the new year also saw the beginning of trading on the Amex in U.S. Government securities in odd-lot amounts. By year's end a total of 181 issues, including those of most federal agencies, were being traded. Among agency issues were those of Federal Land Banks, Federal Home Loan Banks, and the Federal National Mortgage Association (Fannie Mae). The Exchange planned to round out the program with the addition of U.S. Treasury bills in 1976. It took pride in the fact that continuous trading in an Exchange market environment was now available to the small investor. In addition, the existence of a communications link between the Depository Trust Company and the Federal Reserve Bank of New York made certificateless trading possible, thus affording more efficient and much less expensive clearing, settlement, and custodial services.

Although new listings remained down, the economy finally turned the corner in 1975, bringing higher volume trading in Amex securities, and increases in price for nearly 84 percent of them. With stock volume at 541 million shares, up over 12 percent from 1974, and corporate bond volume $303,672,300 (par amount) as against $279,864,000 the year before, revenues were also up by $4,796,000. Best of all, Exchange operations yielded net income of $316,000, which compared nicely with a net loss of $1,089,000 in 1974. (See Statistical Appendix.) The new products made increasingly important contributions to this result. (Trading in U.S. Government notes and bonds came to $44,269,000 in principal amount, the daily average rising from $154,000 in February to $360,000 in December.) A total of 3,482,258 call options contracts, representing 348,225,800 underlying shares, changed hands, and before the year was out the options list increased to 44 underlying stocks. From a daily average of 4,233 options contracts in January volume rose to 15,673 in December.

As a result of its successful introduction of call trading the Board moved to broaden the Amex's options program by submitting to the SEC a package of rules designed to permit trading in puts as well. Competition between exchanges for the increasingly popular trading in options was growing, and the Amex was persuaded that competitive advantage would fall to the exchange able to offer both. Much of recent interest in puts appeared to stem from their use in investment and speculative strategies in combination with listed calls, for example, hedging long stock positions or writing "straddles" (a put and call with the same strike and expiration date on the same stock). It followed that if one exchange traded only calls and a second exchange traded puts and calls in the *same* security, the great bulk of the options business would flow to the latter.

The logic was impeccable, but for reasons we shall later examine, SEC approval was long delayed. So too was the SEC's approval of a Board plan to establish a special category of memberships for the sole purpose of trading options, as principals, on the Amex floor (Options Principal Memberships, or OPMs). The plan envisaged a payment of $15,000 for each OPM, with the money being added to the Exchange's capital improvements fund and used to help finance an expansion in capacity. Not only had demand grown for additional booth space and off-floor support personnel since the last floor modernization program in 1968, but the new products, especially options, were creating a need for additional floor space to accommodate personnel, and input and display equipment as well.

They also created a need for administrative reorganization at the Amex. Early in 1975 the Exchange was realigned into four major divisions. While Norman S. Poser and Winsor H. Watson, Jr., continued as executive vice-presidents for Legal and Regulatory activities and Marketing Services, respectively, Robert T. Eckenrode was appointed senior vice-president, Administration and Planning, and Robert J. Birnbaum executive vice-president, Trading and Markets. Birnbaum, a future president of both the Amex and the NYSE, had come to the Amex in 1967 after six years with the SEC, where he served as branch chief of Regulation and Inspection. With a B.S. in business administration from New York University and a law degree from Georgetown University Law School, Birnbaum was well equipped to play a leading role in the Amex's adjustment to a sharply more competitive environment created by major change in the country's securities laws.

NOTES

1. Except for the brief interim presidency of Edwin Posner in 1962.

2. The most important of the fourth market firms at this time was Institutional Networks ("Instinet"), formed in 1967. For the relationship between Instinet and the Amex, see below, pp. 65 and 133.

CHAPTER 3

THE NATIONAL
MARKET SYSTEM

In June 1975 Congress enacted legislation—the Securities Acts Amendments—designed to remove impediments to competition throughout the nation's securities industry. Calling the securities markets "an important national asset which must be strengthened and preserved," the new law directed the SEC "to facilitate the establishment of a national market system for securities" and to promote "fair competition among brokers and dealers, among exchange markets, and between exchange markets and markets other than exchange markets." New data processing and communications techniques made it possible for all exchange members, brokers, dealers, and securities information processors to have "access on reasonable and non-discriminatory terms" to quotation and transaction information, and for "a national system for the prompt and accurate clearance and settlement of securities transactions" to be established. The linking of all clearance and settlement facilities and the development of uniform standards and procedures for carrying

61

out those functions would reduce unnecessary costs and better protect investors.

A number of developments help explain why Congress passed this law. Surely one was the inadequate preparation of the securities industry for the large expansion of investment in equities in the 1960s by such institutional investors as pension funds, bank trust departments, insurance companies, and mutual funds. In the resulting paperwork crunch, some 100 brokerage firms went to the wall. In addition, the resistance of these big investors to fixed commission rates led the institutions to turn to the regional exchanges and to the third market and, partly as a result, induced the SEC to begin a phasing out of fixed rates in 1970 by prohibiting any minimum commission to be charged on portions of orders over $500,000. On May 1, 1975, the SEC required that all commission rates paid by public customers be subject to negotiation, and the Securities Acts Amendments passed the next month ended fixed rates for transactions between exchange members by May 1, 1976. Finally, some observers believed that the interests of the investing public would be better served by a national market system in which the New York Stock Exchange played a less predominating role.

But just what did the Congress mean by "national market system?" It never defined the term, and neither did the SEC. Was its purpose a wholesale restructuring of the nation's securities markets? If so, no one had asked for it. A restructuring would have altered business practices and market relationships that had evolved over 175 years. A central market would have affected the economic interests of many groups, for example, those of public commission houses, specialists, and floor brokers on both national and regional exchanges, as well as market makers in the third market.

At the Amex, the Board of Governors agreed unanimously that consideration of a national market system focus on two essential issues: "the unique characteristics of Exchange markets in general that should be preserved within the context of a national system, and the special qualities of the Amex, in particular, that serve a public purpose." The New York Stock Exchange was no less determined to preserve the unique characteristics of exchange markets. In short, while there was widespread agreement within the securities industry that a national market system would be a "good thing," opinion differed just as widely on what that system should look like. The grand design was attractive on paper but might well be interpreted in such a way as to invite strong resistance on the part of the interests of the real world.

If the architects of the design had in mind a central electronic repository and display system that eliminated the need for an exchange by having buying and selling done directly by brokerage houses through a central computer system—"black box" automaticity—not only "interests" would be affronted but common sense as well. While a fully automated market is technically feasible, automation does not itself create a market. Norman S. Poser, explains:

> In the overwhelming majority of stocks, public buying and selling is often insufficient to ensure that the order of a willing buyer can always be matched with that of a willing seller. For that reason, markets are created or their quality is improved by professional dealers (specialists or market makers) who put their own capital at risk and thereby supply liquidity to the markets.

When, inexplicably, the SEC, despite what the Amex Board said was that agency's "professed intention not to proceed toward automated execution systems designed to replace existing exchange markets," allowed the Cincinnati Stock Exchange in the spring of 1978 "to implement an electronic trading system in which agency and principal limit orders could be entered and automatically executed through the system by brokers and dealers from terminals in their offices," the Amex fired off an indignant letter of protest. As it turned out, only limited use was made of Cincinnati's National Securities Trading System (NSTS). "Ninety-seven percent of the NSTS share volume in 1980 was accounted for by five participating firms. One of these, Merrill, Lynch, Pierce, Fenner & Smith, accounted for about 75 percent of this volume. In July 1983, Merrill Lynch withdrew from NSTS, citing the lack of business of the Cincinnati Stock Exchange."

There is a good chance that many if not most congressmen who voted in favor of a national market system understood by that term a system in which the nation's securities markets would be linked by maximum use of computers and communications technology. If so, they merely wished to encourage the acceleration of a process already well under way by having the SEC remove impediments to its further development. In the early 1970s, well before the enactment of the Securities

Acts Amendments, several organizations, including both the NYSE and the Amex, were trying to develop the technology that would be necessary for central market receipt and execution of orders. Under the direction of Senior Vice-President Eckenrode, the Amex committed substantial resources to the effort. Indeed, a model of the system showing how it would work was set up at the Amex and a number of people from the industry invited to view it.

Unhappily, the technological underpinning of the system was not yet available. In the words of Gordon Nash, a man destined to become the Exchange's chief legal officer in the late 1980s, "The thinking was ahead of the state of the art at that point." The effort to establish the Amex as a leader and central player in creating the technology of the national market system, however, "added to the Exchange's credibility" when discussion of such a system accelerated in Congress and in the industry in the mid-1970s.

The linking of clearance facilities was another necessary component of any national system. Linkage would ultimately reduce clearing costs significantly to users, consolidate the various clearing funds, and bring about a single unified set of rules. As early as December 1974, seven months before the amended securities laws, the Amex had joined the Big Board, the NASD and five regional exchanges in signing a memorandum of understanding. The plan called for the creation of a single processing and clearing facility in the New York area by merging the New York and Amex Clearing Corporations, with subsequent participation of the NASD in the proposed new entity. Unhappily, President Burdge was obliged to say in a subsequent report to the Board, this objective had been "materially set back" as a result of the NASD's having entered into a separate agreement with the Bradford Computer Company to act as processor and manager of the proposed facility. By the end of 1976 Chairman Kolton was able to announce that the SEC had approved the merger of the clearing corporations of the two national exchanges and of the NASD into the new National Securities Clearing Corporation (NSCC). Even then, the "effectiveness of the merger" had to be postponed because of objections raised by the Bradford Computer Company. These overcome, the merger finally became effective on January 20, 1977.

Owned by the New York and American Stock exchanges, the NSCC contracted with the Securities Industry Automation Corporation (SIAC) to serve as the processor for the new facility. Following the consolidation, interfacing arrangements were developed to link up all major clearing organizations into a truly national clearance and settlement system. In consequence, a broker may select a single clearing organization to clear all his transactions, no matter where the purchase or sale occurs, or who the opposite side broker may be. The system permits single-account clearing by broker-dealers in the clearing organization of their choice and eliminates unnecessary duplication of post-trade activities. The trading, surveillance, and market data compiled by the SIAC are made available not only to the NSCC but also to three other agencies made possible by the new technology, that is, the Consolidated Tape Association, the Consolidated Quotation System, and the Intermarket Trading System.

The Consolidated Last-Sale Reporting System (Consolidated Tape) was already being worked on while Congress was considering the 1975 Securities Act Amendments. Started on June 16, 1975, the Consolidated Tape reports nationwide trades in all common stocks listed on the New York, American, and some regional exchanges. Managed jointly by all the participating exchanges and the NASD, the tape captures all last sale prices of securities listed on the primary exchanges, as well as selected issues on other exchanges, and disseminates them nationwide in the sequence in which they are reported from the various markets, including trades effected in the over-the-counter market in such listed securities. The tape has two parts, Network A and Network B. The former reports transactions in NYSE-listed securities that take place on the New York Stock Exchange or on any of the participating regional stock exchanges and other markets, including the New York, American, Boston, Midwest, Pacific, Philadelphia, and Cincinnati Stock exchanges, the NASD, and Instinet (Institutional Networks Corporation, a system tailored for institutional investors). Network B does the same for Amex-listed securities. Norman Poser has called the Consolidated Tape "the first solid step" in the development of the National Market System.[1]

Surely the Composite Quotation System (CQS) represents a second solid step in the same direction. As early as 1973 the SEC viewed the then-proposed CQS as being "at the heart of the central market system." No wonder. One of the fundamental building blocks of a national system is a means for enabling brokers to obtain and compare quotations from various competing market centers. In contrast with the Consolidated Tape, which provides data on completed transactions, the CQS "displays nationwide the prices currently bid and offered on any of the seven participating exchanges and in the over-the-counter market for the same stocks, and the number of shares sought or offered at these prices." CQS became fully operational in August 1978.

Perhaps the main cog in any national market system is an electronic linkage between competing market centers that enables brokers to send messages back and forth and to effect executions between those centers. The Intermarket Trading System (ITS), which began functioning in the fall of 1978, provides such a linkage. Essentially, ITS consists of a central computer facility, a network of interconnected electronic terminals in all the participating market centers, which provides a two-way communications capability, and also quotation displays of bids and offers in all competing markets. Thus, a broker in any one of the markets can determine whether a better price is available in another market and, if so, he can use the electronic network to reach into that market and take advantage of the better execution opportunity shown to be there.

The administrations of both national exchanges are in agreement that while a great deal of progress has been made toward the achievement of a national market system, that system will continue to evolve as increasingly effective technologies are applied to existing market institutions. Technological innovation will continue to broaden the scope and increase the availability of information about security market transactions, and increased competition between the exchanges, and between them and the NASD, will continue to lower the costs of those transactions.

MERGER?

A very real possibility existed that competition between the securities exchanges would be lessened by consolidating the NYSE and the Amex. As early as December 1974 a committee of the Securities Industry Association, established to explore that possibility, had recommended a merger on the ground that initial savings alone from abolishing duplicative administrations and facilities might run from $2 million to $3 million a year. With merger talk in the air, both national exchanges appointed committees to study the question, the ten-man Amex Special Merger Committee being composed of "present and past governors and former exchange chairmen." David S. Jackson, a former president, was named chairman. The assigned study, Chairman Kolton explained, "would be undertaken in the context of developing a central market system."

Six months later the committee was ready with its report, and the Amex board, after meeting in executive session to discuss it, unanimously determined that a merger would not be "appropriate." In a detailed memo to Amex employees, Kolton explained why. "Fundamental" to the decision reached was the important and unique role of the Amex in providing markets for smaller, growing companies, which facilitated their capital-raising ability. The fact that the Amex focused on the special needs and concerns of such companies and actively competed to attract and retain listings, brought a number of major benefits to the companies, their shareholders, and the investing public. In the event of a merger, these advantages might be lost. In addition, it was felt that many Amex companies would be deprived of the recognition and attention they enjoyed as important companies on the smaller exchange.

The Board also believed that a consolidated exchange might have less incentive to be innovative in providing markets for new types of securities. In the past the Amex had initiated exchange trading of such securities as warrants, ADRs, and securities of REITS and savings and loan associations. If the innovative impulse were diminished significantly, the capital-raising ability of new enterprises might be affected.

The Board noted the active competition between the two exchanges to improve services to member firms and to the public, to attract volume, to persuade over-the-counter companies to list, and to provide orderly and liquid markets. That competition gave Amex specialists a "particular incentive" to maintain performance at a high level in order to retain listings. Were the exchanges to combine, the incentive to improve performance provided by competition might be lessened, or lost altogether. Kolton concluded his discussion of the possible impact of a merger on public companies by noting that the representation of Amex companies on the governing board of a combined enterprise would in all likelihood be reduced or eliminated, in which case, smaller companies would be unlikely to have a voice in determining exchange policies affecting the markets for their securities.

Kolton next turned to public interest considerations. Over the years, he pointed out, "the Amex has introduced new products, established new procedures for dealing with operational and regulatory matters, and developed advanced technology capable of handling substantially higher volumes efficiently." Such innovations, like those initiated by other self-regulatory organizations, were often adopted throughout the industry once their value was proven. Clearly, the public benefited from having two primary exchanges rather than just one.

Kolton also voiced the Board's concern over the effect of consolidation on the system of self-regulation. That system, with government oversight, had worked well over the years. But if the major exchanges were to consolidate, self-regulatory organizations would probably play a significantly reduced role, and in consequence, there would be an increase in government control. The Amex did not believe that would be in the best interests of either the investing public or the securities industry.

Finally, Kolton questioned the realism of projected savings to be achieved through merger. Such savings "frequently prove to be illusory. In fact, the opposite is often the case." Anyway, the most significant duplicative costs borne by the member firms had already been eliminated. The Securities Industry Automation Corporation (SIAC), established jointly by the two exchanges to conduct their data-processing, clearing, communications, and operational planning programs, had reduced costs in 1974 by $9 million in comparison with 1972, when SIAC was organized. And over the years the Amex and NYSE had developed methods for reducing or eliminating duplicate regulatory activities in such areas as member firm inspections and qualifying examinations.

While these considerations argued powerfully in mid-1975 against the wisdom of consolidation, other considerations, as we shall see, were to put the matter in a different light in 1976–1977, when, once again, the Amex Board took up the question of merger. In the meantime, the two primary exchanges continued to compete vigorously with each other.

Within a year of the passage of the Securities Act Amendments, Chairman Kolton attributed to that legislation the development of "intense competition throughout the industry." In the listed options market competition intensified as the number of options exchanges expanded to five with the addition of the Pacific Stock Exchange and the Midwest Stock Exchange. Competitive trading between the two largest options markets, the Chicago Board Options Exchanges and the Amex, began on December 14, 1976, when calls in MGIC Investment Corporation were dually traded. And in January 1977 the NYSE announced its intention to initiate options trading.

The competitive blockbuster, however, took the form of constitutional changes recommended by the Amex Board in July 1976 and subsequently approved by the membership. The changes repealed the so-called "New York City Rules," rules which had been part of the Amex constitution since the organization of the New York Curb Exchange in 1911. Matched by corresponding provisions in the constitution of the New York Stock Exchange, they required the Amex to delist and cease trading in securities that transferred to the Big Board. Their repeal pitted the two national exchanges in head-to-head competition.

While the Amex decision was responsive to instructions to both exchanges by the SEC that they review the ancient prohibition in the light of the 1975 Securities Acts Amendments, it was not a decision taken lightly. In a long, carefully considered memorandum to the Board, Executive Vice-President Norman S. Poser in charge of the Legal and Regulatory Affairs Division weighed the pros and cons of the move. The dual trading prohibition, Poser pointed out, had operated as a basic structural feature of the Amex market by framing its traditional role of "seasoner" of the securities of newer and smaller companies. Once those companies had grown to the point of eligibility for listing on the Big Board they had moved there in "a steady flow." While the rate of transfer tended to vary with market conditions, and was influenced by the relative success of the Amex's listed company retention program balanced against the NYSE's new listing efforts, an average of 26 companies had done so each year in the 11-year span 1965–1975. In fact, the shares of more than 50 percent of NYSE listed companies were once traded on the Amex.

Automatic delisting meant that Amex specialists, unable to continue making markets in the securities of those companies, were debarred from the competition for earnings. Those same specialists, though, themselves faced competition from the third market and the regional exchanges, which together commanded 5 to 6 percent of the total trading volume in Amex-listed securities. The losses hurt the Amex as well, since slightly over 20 percent of its revenues came to it from listing fees.

There were additional reasons for opting for change in the status quo. The Amex equity volume had continued to decline as a percentage of the Big Board's. In 1967 through 1969 it had been roughly 40 percent, but in 1973 the percentage had dropped to the 15 to 20 percent level. By 1976 it had fallen still further to 13 percent, although adding options volume brought it to over 28 percent. The continuing institutionalization of the securities markets was another unfavorable factor since the Amex had historically served the individual investor. Repeal of the dual trading prohibition would, at a minimum, enable the Exchange to continue trading in securities transferring to the NYSE.

On the other hand, the views and interests of the Amex member firms required careful consideration. Over 90 percent of them were also members of the NYSE. A threat of counteraction by the NYSE might force dual members to choose between the two exchanges. Furthermore, within the framework of its traditional role as a "seasoning ground," the Amex had "frequently been regarded by major dual member firms as innovative and as taking a leadership role in industry matters." Might it not complicate the Amex's ability to retain the support of its member firms if it mounted so significant a challenge to the basic structure of the exchange markets? Yet the fact was that the two exchanges were already engaged in strong competition, and the move toward a national market system promised to intensify it, and bring the Amex under growing competitive pressure from the regional exchanges and the third market as well. Given these prospects, Poser concluded, the Amex should maximize opportunities for growth.

The Board and the membership, as we have seen, agreed. The historic step was taken, and dual trading began on August 23 when Varo, Incorporated, an Amex-listed stock, began trading on the Big Board. By the end of 1976 four more corporations that transferred to the NYSE chose to continue having their stocks traded on the Amex, the companies involved expressing their satisfaction with the tighter markets produced by the competition. To further encourage this development, the Amex adopted a simplified listing procedure and revised initial listing fees for NYSE-listed companies opting for dual listing, and for those companies wishing to list their securities on the Amex and NYSE simultaneously. These moves soon proved unavailing. In each case, trading volume in dual listed securities gradually evaporated on the Amex, and one by one the half-dozen companies involved filed applications with the SEC to delist their stocks from the Amex. Although repeal of the New York City Rules did not result for long in increased competition, the SEC had another string in its bow.

Technology and dual listings were not the only sources of increased competition. Some of the rules of the nation's securities exchanges did not appear to comply with the Securities Acts Amendments. After reviewing the rules and constitutional provisions of the Amex, the SEC listed 194 of them alleged to impose unjustified restraints on competition, to deny "due process," or to impede development of efficient clearing and settlement by tying those functions to markets where the trades occurred. While to the Amex administration it was "unclear, in the case of many of these provisions in what respect the SEC believes them to be defective," the Exchange carefully studied the allegations, accepting some as justified and rejecting others.

Amex Rule 126 (g), for example, provided that in transactions in particular securities the Exchange might in its discretion give priority to orders based upon size rather than upon the normal time priorities. To the SEC suggestion that the rule might discriminate unfairly among customers, the Exchange responded by agreeing to delete it on the ground that the power to invoke size priority was "rarely if ever used by the Amex." The Amex response was quite different to the SEC charge that the Exchange's Rule 6, which restricted members from executing transactions in listed bonds on the over-the-counter market, presented an obstacle to the goals of fair competition among brokers and dealers, and to economically efficient executions of transactions. The Exchange agreed to amend the rule to the extent that it restricted members from executing orders off-board with a nonmember market maker or "block positioner" (a dealer who takes the opposite side of a trade in order to give liquidity to the market). It did not believe it appropriate, however, to amend it with respect to principal transactions or "in-house agency crosses" executed by members.

When a broker completed a transaction in a listed security within his own firm instead of transmitting it to the exchange floor, he completed it "in house," on the "upstairs market." A "cross" occurred when he acted as agent for both a buyer and a seller in a completed transaction. The Amex deeply believed that restrictions on such practices were "necessary for the proper functioning of the Exchange markets in the public interest," that "a reasonable off-board trading rule, reasonably administered, serves to protect investors, maintain fair markets, provide an effective pricing mechanism, enhance best execution possibility, and provide the framework for a national market system."

President Birnbaum, who had succeeded Richard Burdge in May 1977, was emphatic in his statement before the Joint Hearings of two House subcommittees on the development of a National Market System. The Amex, he said, considered the elimination of off-board trading restrictions that prohibited exchange member firms from crossing customer orders in their offices and from effecting off-board principal transactions in listed securities, "the most serious and far-reaching problem which remains to be solved in connection with the development of the national market system."

> We believe that the principal threat not only to existing markets but also to the national market system as conceived by Congress, is the potential for internalization of order flow within large brokerage firms once off-board trading restrictions are removed. Such internalization of order flow has the potential for preventing a significant amount of buying and selling interest from being reflected in the marketplace, thus increasing market fragmentation and decreasing price efficiency. This would deal a crippling blow to our auction markets as we know them today and would likely make a national market impossible of achievement.

After considerable vacillation, the SEC in June 1980 finally adopted a rule (19-c-3) that precluded application of off-board trading restrictions to stocks that became listed on an exchange after April 26, 1979, or that were traded on an exchange on that date but did not remain listed thereafter. The rule appears to have had little effect on the trading patterns of the stocks affected by it.

COMMODITY OPTIONS ON THE AMEX

What did affect trading patterns was the deepening entrepreneurial response of the Amex to the challenges and opportunities presented by the competitively charged national securities market. One such response took the form of a question: Could the Amex develop a commodity options market capable of competing successfully with other commodity option markets? The Exchange had first examined the feasibility of trading commodity options in 1974, but the Board subsequently decided to give priority to the development of a put options program, to adding call options in additional underlying securities, and to the possibility of options in fixed income securities. In June 1975 it approved exploring options or futures on commodities and mortgages only as "low level efforts."

Then something happened. At a Board meeting on February 12, 1976, the Options Committee raised the question of the desirability of trading commodity options on the Exchange; Board member George Reichhelm suggested that a higher priority be assigned to a study of the question, and the Board, after discussion, agreed that this should be done. The ensuing study, prepared by an Assistant Vice-President in the New Products Planning Division, Lee R. Steur, sounded a note of caution, warned of difficulties ahead, and raised a number of questions.

First, there was the question of legality. Congressional legislation in 1974 had charged the Commodity Futures Trading Commission (CFTC) with responsibility for determining whether to legalize or prohibit the writing of commodity options in the United States. (Attorney General Lefkowitz of New York urged their prohibition.) Second, if permitted, should exchange-traded commodity options be allowed? Third, should the CFTC allow or even require the trading of options and futures on the same exchange? Even if the answers to these questions were affirmative, and the Amex were permitted to develop a program, it would face strong competition from the commodity exchanges, from the Chicago Board of Trade, the Pacific Commodities Exchange, and the Comex (the primary futures market for silver, gold, and copper in New York), which had also expressed an interest in commodity options. Would the Amex be able to compete successfully, especially with a commodities market trading both options and futures? Would commodity dealers help sponsor Amex commodity options by participating in its market?

There was only one way to answer a number of these questions, and a rising crescendo of interest appeared to demand that it be taken. In June 1976, twenty-seven members of the Exchange signed a petition requesting that two of their fellow floor members be permitted to speak to the Board on "why the Exchange should start trading commodity options." Three months later in a detailed presentation to the Board, Senior Vice-President Eckenrode made a strong case for doing so.

The Amex, he pointed out, was continually looking for ways to diversify, "much as major firms have done," continually searching for products that were countercyclical to the equities market. Those products, of course, must have economic value and be attractive to member firms. Commodity options met both criteria, for owners of commodities, gold for example, needed a means of hedging against price declines, a means of transferring downside risk at the price of foregoing some upside profit. While futures did this, for many buyers they transferred too much risk—"the buyer of a future who's holding it at delivery month must accept delivery of the commodity at the price specified in the futures contract; and if prices continually move the limit he may not be able to get out of the contract by selling it." Futures, therefore, were largely a professional market. The buyer of options, in contrast, faced a limited risk. The most he could lose was the premium paid to buy the option, while the seller's risk of owning the gold was reduced by the amount of the premium he received for selling the option. Gold options would be very similar to stock options, "which now many people understand."

Eckenrode proceeded to describe the way in which the Amex proposed to operate the new market. The Exchange would set up a separate organization for trading in commodity options, and a separate subsidiary to issue, be obligor, clear and settle options, and supervise exercise. Membership would be open to all qualified Amex members and associate members at nominal prices, and to bullion dealers and commodity brokers—"enough commodity experts to make a viable market"—at a higher price. Trading would begin with puts and calls in gold and silver bullion, with other nonagricultural products to be added later. Contracts would expire every other month and correspond with delivery months for futures contracts so that joint settlement would be possible.

On August 26 the CFTC had paid a visit to the Exchange, had responded favorably to the proposed program and had been "impressed with Amex and its regulatory capability." SEC representatives had come five days later, and in a subsequent letter had "indicated that the meeting was very worthwhile." And so at the Board meeting on September 9 Eckenrode asked for approval of "initial development and funding of a three-part pilot project for the commencement of trading in put and call options in selected commodities, starting with gold and silver bullion, under the aegis of a new exchange organization created for that purpose." Development costs would amount to approximately $200,000 of an estimated total cost of $985,000 if the program were carried to completion. The motion to approve was carried unanimously, and in December the Exchange announced that the Amex-developed options clearing system would also largely be usable for commodities options clearing, and that before the year was out Nathan Most would be on board as director of Commodity Options Development.

Founding director of the Pacific Commodities Exchange (1970–1976) and its president (1974–1976), Most came to the Amex from Washington, D.C., where he served briefly as executive assistant to the chairman of the Commodity Futures Trading Commission. In May 1977 the Amex Commodities Exchange was organized as an independent corporation to trade futures, options, and "spot" (cash) in bullion and financial instruments, and Most was named its president. Actual trading (in GNMA futures contracts) began on September 12, 1978, and the next day volume rose from an initial day 137 to 282 contracts. Everything seemed to point to the successful introduction of an innovative program.

Alas! It was not to be. Barely six months later, Eckenrode reported that there was "concern over low trading volume and attendant losses." Even more ominous than a continuation of loss was the news, conveyed to the Board in April 1979, that "Standard & Poor's has indicated that it plans to grant an exclusive license to the Chicago Mercantile Exchange to trade futures on its S&P 500 stock index." The Amex's American Commodity Exchange (ACE) began trading futures in U.S. Treasury bills on June 26, but by October Eckenrode was obliged to report that volume in the new product was "virtually nil." ACE losses continued to mount month after month, and by October 1979 they totaled $952,000 for the year. The Exchange developed an agressive marketing campaign, but it seemed to help little. And so in the fall of 1979 the Amex appointed a special committee to evaluate the future of the ACE. By the early spring of the following year that future appeared bleak, and the Board voted unanimously to accept the recommendation of its special committee that the existence of ACE as an independent agency be terminated.

What had gone wrong? Almost from the beginning of the experiment ACE had been obliged to confront the serious problem of insufficient depth and liquidity. Despite the fact that 87 percent of the respondents to an informal survey of eligible voters among the membership of the Amex had gone on record in the fall of 1977 as in favor of the proposed Commodities Exchange, too few of the Amex floor members had participated in its markets. Trading volume in the new products had been thin almost from the beginning, and by March 1980 had fallen "well below the break-even" point. Moreover, the proposed program to trade gold and silver options, the "original impetus for the development of a commodities program," had been "deferred indefinitely."

In all probability, the most fundamental reason that the new market failed to outgrow its fledgling stage had been identified by Lee S. Steur in his lengthy initial report on the Amex proposal: the existence of older and more experienced commodities exchanges. The Amex's special evaluating committee explicitly acknowledged that "the Chicago commodities exchanges have proven to be strong competitors," and when a new player, the New York Futures Exchange, a subsidiary of the NYSE, appeared ready to enter the game, the Amex decided to trim its losses.

In "its current form," the committee argued, ACE would not be able to compete successfully. It therefore recommended that the ACE administration carefully consider merger proposals from both COMEX and NYFE. A month later, in April 1980, the ACE board voted to accept the NYFE proposal "on a strong consensus that NYFE represented the most effective potential competition to the Chicago futures markets." The Amex board agreed unanimously to the Big Board for $245,000, losses on the operation having already been pared by the sale of its market data, surveillance, and clearing system, which the Exchange had developed for ACE's use.

The experiment had not worked out, but this was hardly cause for distress on the part of Amex executives. They knew full well that the very *raison d'être* of the Exchange was to serve as a proving ground for innovative, risk-taking entrepreneurs, that it was willingness to take risks that propelled the economy forward. A risk was just that, a chance to win and a chance to lose. The one implied the other, and both were indispensable to progress. From the perspective of the American economy, loss was never absolute. It always entailed a learning process, whose value reduced or even erased the loss. One could not preach from such texts without knowing that the sermon applied as much to the minister as to his flock. And that Amex executives deeply believed in the truth of its texts was evident from what they had said and done in the past, and from what they were on the very threshhold of reiterating in the present.

They had learned from their recent entry into the options markets as well. Determined to succeed in it, they mounted a costly surveillance system that would track every trade. These procedures enabled them to discover in March 1976 that nearly two dozen of its specialists had reported fictitious transactions. The Exchange notified the SEC and launched a comprehensive inquiry that revealed that inexperienced traders had engaged in the fictitious reporting in order to bring last sale prices of options —usually inactive ones—into line with the then current quoted market and the current price of the underlying stock. The exhaustive investigation, on which the Exchange spent nearly $750,000, turned up no evidence that the specialists had engaged in the practice for profit, or that the public had sustained injury. The public may have escaped damage, but the Exchange did not.

More than a dozen years after the options scandal of 1976, old timers were still reacting with expressions of pain at the mention of it. The Exchange was polarized, with the floor accusing the administration of having overreacted, of not having protected their interests. Mutual suspicion hung heavily in the air, with some traders accusing others of tape recording people on the floor. To make matters even worse for a supposedly self-regulating organization (SRO), the state as well as the SEC and the Exchange itself launched an investigation.

Some who lived through those days describe an environment that was "horrible," "terrible." There was the spectacle of state police handcuffing and photographing specialists and hauling them to court to be booked. Even the senior floor governor had to excuse himself from the Board because of his own involvement. One prominent Board member thought the polarization probably more severe than at any time in the previous history of the Exchange. With a substantial portion of the floor population under investigation and having to retain counsel at their own expense the institution approached unmanageability.

Although some Board members attributed the behavior of the specialists to a desire to outperform the CBOE, that behavior could not be condoned. The Board voted to punish the persons involved by imposing fines and/or censures and took immediate steps to prevent a recurrence. In the long run, the most important effect of these events may well have been the lessons drawn from them by a Board member who was soon to become chairman of the Exchange. As we shall see, the style of Arthur Levitt, Jr., was to promote mutual trust and to govern by consensus.

THE YEAR OF THE BICENTENNIAL

The investigations and the punishments meted out to the guilty specialists appear to have had a good effect in the short run, too. Undoubtedly reassured by the Exchange's reputation for integrity and vigilance, trading in options continued to mount, as did that in equities. Total revenues in 1976 rose from $9,058,000 the year before to $33,624,000 "due to substantial growth in options trading and increased equity volume during the year." The number of call options contracts traded more than doubled, rising from 3,482,023 in 1975 to 8,828,456, average daily volume increasing over the same interval from 14,155 to 34,895. The number of options classes traded also jumped from 44 to 59. Not only did new stock listings (36) go up, reversing a three-year down trend, so too did trading volume in stocks and other securities. Stock volume rose by nearly 20 percent from 540,934,210 to 648,297,321 shares, volume in corporate bonds, from $259,395,000 in principal amount to $301,054,000. Odd-lot trading in Treasury bills had begun on December 9, 1976, completing the full range of government securities available for trading— notes, bills, bonds, and various agency issues. Odd-lot trading in these various securities more than doubled, rising from $44,401,000 to $97,516,000 in principal amount. (See Statistical Appendix.)

Gains of these dimensions promised more for the future and induced the Exchange to expand its floor facilities over a two-year period and to modernize still more its physical plant. At the same time it began to plan for its longer-range facilities' needs as these were likely to develop into the 1980s.

EXPANSION AT THE AMEX

The rising volume of trading in both equities and options had prompted the Board in June 1975 to authorize a major study of the Exchange's trading floor capacity requirements under a series of assumptions projecting market activity to the end of the decade. Ready in preliminary form in January 1976, the study compared then extant capacity with potential needs. At the beginning of 1976 the trading floor covered approximately 20,000 square feet, of which about 13,000 square feet were used for trading space and 12 trading posts. The rest was used for 81 machine booths and 171 telephone booths occupied by members and member firms, for administrative and equipment space, and for rest areas. The floor population of 1,230 people was divided into the following four groups: approximately 500 active floor members, 300 member firm personnel operating booths, 200 specialist clerks, and 230 exchange personnel (reporters, data clerks, and messengers).

Trading at that time took place in about 1,250 equity issues and 44 options classes. Over the year 1975–1976 the floor population and floor configuration comfortably handled average daily trading volume of about 2 million equity shares, and, over the six-month period from July 1975 to the end of that year, about 20,000 option contracts (equivalent to 2 million option shares), or a combined volume of 4 million average daily shares. The study estimated that the extant configuration could handle an average daily combined volume of 4.8 million shares, surges of several days duration of up to 9.6 million, and one-day peaks of up to 12 million shares.

Whether or not that configuration would require altering, as well as the nature and extent of the alterations, depended on one's assumptions about future volume, and here the study presented four scenarios. The most pessimistic described declining volume in a framework of slow real economic growth, with high inflation and high interest rates, fewer member firms, restricted growth of the options market and diversion of stock trading away from primary exchange markets. The most optimistic reversed these assumptions about economic growth and inflation, adding for good measure "declining unemployment, improved investment tax policies, and wide use of an expanded list of call and put options, as well as other options instruments," a context in which both stock and options volume might rise rapidly.

After estimating combined volume in 1976 and 1977 under each of the four scenarios, the study concluded that only the most optimistic one would exceed "the present capacity of the floor, fully manned, of 7.6 million daily combined shares." Prudent planning therefore suggested exploring means of augmenting trading capacity without incurring the substantial expense and dislocation of a major facilities expansion program. For the near term—1976–1977—"automation enhancements" offered the best solution. The "volume-sensitive" operations of the Exchange fell into four categories: trading; trade reporting (execution reporting to members and public reporting); trade comparison, clearance, and settlement; and surveillance. Except for the trading process itself, "which involves the factor of human decision making," all of these areas had been subjected extensively to techniques of automation in recent years.

The Common Message Switch (CMS), for example, serving both the Amex and the NYSE, had been operational for about a year. CMS offered brokers an electronic communications link to the trading floor and was used to direct odd-lot orders from member firm offices to the correct trading post. CMS could be further developed to provide a switching service for appropriate options orders and round-lot stock orders. Building on CMS, which handled incoming orders, a turnaround capability could be added for Post Execution Reporting (PER). PER would enable single round-lot execution reports of orders entered through CMS to be returned directly to member firms, bypassing the pneumatic tube system and floor booths. By saving the time and manual effort of member firm booth and floor broker personnel involved in reporting executions, PER could effectively increase floor capacity by an estimated 7 percent.

In addition to upgrading CMS and developing PER, the study also recommended enhancing automation of the Amex options comparison system to raise capacity to 50,000 daily contracts, and the completion of automation of the Amex surveillance programs for equities and options, major portions of which were already well under way. Completion would dramatically reduce the labor intensity of surveillance and permit the capacity to keep up with increases in trading volume at minimum cost.

So much for shorter-term (1976–1977) capacity requirements. In addition to continued automation, requirements for the longer-term (1978–1980) involved space planning. The Amex called upon the architectural and engineering firm of Kahn and Jacobs/Hellmuth, Obata, and Kassabaum for a variety of alternatives relating to the reconstruction of the trading floor and adjacent areas. One alternative was to construct a balcony above the existing booths on the west wall of the trading floor and to move the booths to the balcony. If this were done an additional 4,000 square feet—representing a 31 percent increase of the existing 13,000 square feet of trading area—would become available. And since the construction would permit the floor to accommodate an additional 200 members and attendant support personnel, floor capacity would rise by about 25 percent. A second alternative was that of constructing a second trading floor in the air space above the present trading floor. Other alternatives involved purchasing other properties, the most feasible being the adjacent building to the northwest of the Exchange (22 Thames Street).

The following month, February 1976, the Board approved the proposed two-year program to expand the Exchange's capacity by increasing both automation capabilities and available space on the trading floor. Specifically, it approved an expenditure of $50,000 to prepare automation plans for Post Execution Reporting of multiple round-lot executions by 1977, $50,000 to prepare detailed architectual and engineering plans for raising west wall member firm booths to a balcony level, and an additional $150,000 to redesign current trading posts. Displays required for options required streamlining the posts, and so did equity information displays. Both interfered with lines of sight for hand signaling by members between posts and booths.

The story of the modernization of the Exchange has a beginning but not an end. In time, PER came on-line (in March 1977), only to be expanded from 100-share day orders to accommodate up to 200-share market orders, and up to 400-share limit orders. PER provided a means for member firms to send orders directly to the specialists' posts and to receive back execution reports in electronic form. Conceived as a way of increasing the capacity of the floor to handle increased order flow by facilitating the transmission and reporting of routine orders requiring minimal brokerage skill and judgment, the system eliminated the need for an incoming order to be received by teletype, or written out at a booth, walked to the post, and then walked back to and reported from the booth after execution. Instead, orders were sent directly from a member firm's main or branch office, printed on a high-speed printer at the trading post, and presented to the specialist for execution. Following execution, the specialist clerk marked a computer readable card that was used to report the execution back through the PER system to the member firm.

In time, other systems, such as OARS (Open Automated Reports System), also came on-line. OARS stored and tabulated electronically market orders entered prior to the opening of the market, and by matching them, calculated any imbalance between buy and sell orders in each stock. Initially, the system handled up to 200 shares in equities; its expansion accommodated up to 500. Then there was AMOS—Amex Options Switch—designed to automatically route one to five contract market and limited-price option day orders and reports between member firm offices and the trading posts. Approved for development by the Board in December 1977, AMOS was successfully tested in February 1979. In July of the next year the Board voted to expand the system to enable it to accept market and marketable limit orders.

The story of expanding capacity by altering the use of space is more finite. The Board decided to accept the recommendation of its consulting firm to increase the size of the trading floor by raising the west wall booths to the balcony level. More explicitly, those booths would be demolished and the area thus made available would be used for additional, improved trading posts. It soon became clear, however, that if the balcony were constructed over the west end of the floor, the restaurant would be wiped out. In terms of cost, minimum disruption, and sight lines to the floor, balconies on the north and south walls would be best. Even so, certain problems would have to be solved. The "biggest problem," an Exchange official jotted down on his copy of "Automation and Facilities Planning," a document prepared as a basis for a formal presentation to the Board, "will be communication between floor brokers and booth clerks—we're working on various systems of moving paper and voice communication between these two."

He was right. After delays caused by labor strikes, shipping problems, interference with trading floor operations, and the need to redesign certain aspects of the project, construction of the north balcony was completed but only partially occupied in the spring of 1979. Some member firms were reluctant to move because "problems have been encountered with balcony communication and tube systems." By mid-summer, however, those problems had been corrected, firms scheduled to move had done so, and construction of the south balcony had begun. By the end of the year that balcony was also completely occupied, and the west wall booths were demolished. Installation of new trading posts in the freed-up space was scheduled for the spring.

Facilities expansion for the needs of the still longer run is another story, and since it principally involves another Amex administration in the telling of it we shall reserve it for the pages ahead.

NOTES

1. Recent volumes, of course, have far exceeded the ability of the eye to "read" the tape as trades are reported. The terminal devices that appear in brokerage offices everywhere can keep up to date and have effectively replaced the old-fashioned "tape" in most instances.

CHAPTER 4

NEW REGIMES,
NEW CHALLENGES

After the resignation of Richard Burdge early in 1975 to accept the executive vice-presidency of INA Corporation, the Philadelphia-based financial conglomerate, the Board allowed the office of president to remain vacant for two years before naming Executive Vice-President Robert Birnbaum as his successor in May 1977. (It did so to counteract the CBOE's offer of the presidency to Birnbaum that same month.) Then in July 1977 Paul Kolton announced his intention not to seek renewal of his five-year contract as chief executive officer. Kolton's administration had truly confronted "a period of change and challenge unprecedented in the securities industry." Who would succeed him?

On November 2, 1977, the *Wall Street Journal* listed nine "persons being seriously considered," and quoted unnamed "sources" as indicating that "there isn't any single person who could be said to have an inside track." Perhaps not. But one candidate was to emerge in front of the pack surprisingly soon. He was Arthur Levitt, Jr., who just a month before the *Journal* article had been chosen vice-chairman of the Exchange.

Kolton very much wanted Levitt as his successor. Their relationship was one of mutual respect and strong friendship. But Levitt was not sure he wanted the job. When Kolton paid him a visit one day at his home in Connecticut and asked if he would consider chairing the Exchange Levitt promised only to think it over seriously. He then proceeded to discuss the possibility with a number of people, almost all of whom advised him against it. They reminded him of the major scandal in options pricing, pointed out that the Exchange had been losing listed companies, and argued that the trend of the country was away from exchanges, anyway. Indeed, they thought it likely that the Amex would merge with the NYSE, that it therefore had no future at all, and that if he took the job "it would swallow me up and spit me out."

Levitt is a great lover of the open country of America, of its forest-land, mountains, and wild rivers, and it was then and remains his habit to maintain equilibrium and perspective by going to Colorado on an Outward Bound trip. Not long after Kolton's visit he decided to under-take an Outward Bound "solo, where they put you out by yourself for 24 hours," and when it was over he had made up his mind. He would not be content to hope the job would fall in his lap; rather, he would seek it aggressively.

It was the summer of 1977. Levitt returned to New York and began waging a vigorous campaign in favor of his candidacy. He found that the listed companies had their own candidate and that the floor had another. As summer faded into fall and fall to winter more and more members of the nine-man selection committee let it be known that Levitt was the person they wanted. Scarcely more than a week after the *Journal* finding that no candidate had the "inside track," the committee announced its choice. "It was really among the happiest moments of my life," Levitt said.

He reminisced about the morning in November 1977 on which the Board was to meet to formally elect him. Jenifer Stanley, who was the wife of a member of the selection committee and in charge of the South Street Seaport, had invited him to see the Fulton Fish Market. After visiting the market at 4 A.M. he decided to go right to work. It was then that he noticed that not all his followers were at the Exchange. Walking to his office on Wall Street he saw that a procession of cats had picked up the odor of the fish by which he had just been surrounded!

The Wall Street office was that of the president of a major brokerage and investment banking house, Shearson, Hayden Stone, of which Levitt had been president and director since 1969. Son of the distinguished long-term and warmly remembered comptroller of New York State, Levitt was an energetic, charismatic man who had served on the Amex Board since 1975 and on a number of other boards and directorates as well. Surprisingly, his collegiate background lay in neither economics nor law. He was a Phi Beta Kappa graduate of Williams College, where he majored in English and wrote an honors thesis on Lillian Hellman! From earlier ventures into journalism (he worked for awhile on *Life Magazine*), and the cattle business (in Kansas City, Missouri) he entered the brokerage business. One of his clients had told him that if he could sell livestock he could sell live stocks. The client's son-in-law was starting a brokerage firm, and Levitt was invited to join. He was to make securities his principal concern for many years, together with the problem of how best to govern the nation's second largest securities exchange.

Levitt's first official act was to accept the office of chairman and to ask the Board to recess its monthly meeting so he could go down to the trading floor to greet the Amex specialists, brokers, traders, and staff members. The polarization created by the options scandal of 1976 very much on his mind, he was determined from the outset to restore the confidence of the floor and the administration. He would not deal in surprises but would discuss with both elements any program he was considering initiating. Indeed, he would invite them to participate in his deliberations on all matters affecting them, and he would try to be as open as possible.

But neither floor nor administration would have very much to do if listed companies continued drifting away. Their confidence had been shaken by the options scandal too. Realizing that the listed companies were vital to the success of the Exchange, he determined to restore their confidence in the Amex. Indeed, he viewed this objective as the most important single item on his agenda.

Levitt worked out a plan. If the listed companies were allowed to play on a broader stage, one on which they could exert greater influence on public decisions affecting their economic destiny, they would realize that the Amex stood for a good deal more in American life than stock exchanges normally do. From the outset he determined to embrace in the name of the Exchange a much more aggressive and creative legislative agenda than ever before.

Levitt also decided to expand the services offered to Amex-listed companies. "I was determined," he reminisced, "that even though we were smaller and less well capitalized than our big sister across the graveyard of Trinity Church we would offer such an incredible array of services that those CEO's who cared about bottom line performance rather than imagery would almost be compelled to stay with us." We shall soon see what those services were and trace the steps of the vigorous and imaginative new chairman as he acted to realize the goals of his tripartite agenda.

Behind action plans and agendas lie beliefs, lie convictions. Whether in business or government, or in cultural and intellectual life, successful people are both led and driven by a vision. In Levitt's case the vision was clear—it was the historic mission of the American Stock Exchange, the role of the little guy, of David, in the capitalistic system. Time and again he reiterated the importance of facilitating the capital formation process for the small- and medium-sized companies whose risk-taking entrepreneurship located their activity along the cutting edge of the country's technological leadership and economic growth. Perhaps he said it best in his annual message to the Exchange membership in 1979:

> This has long been the prime market for newer, smaller risk-taking corporations. Numerous companies first receive national recognition by investors who trade on the Amex. Many companies that now populate the Fortune 500 list had their start here. They were nurtured in the auction market, moving from narrow, or regionally-based, shareholder populations to national prominence. It is a continuing dream. Not only have individual companies grown and contributed to the economy, but newer industries have emerged, supported by the capital of millions of investors who shared in the dream.

The problem was that too many of these "millions of investors" had drifted away from the marketplace. Frightened by the rising prominence of the institutional investor, whose purchases and sales of millions of shares strongly influenced price movements, they had abandoned investing in equities. Traditionally, the Amex had been a "peoples' market," and while it remained true when Levitt assumed the chairmanship at the beginning of 1978 that "about 70 percent of the business brought to the Amex floor is for individual investors," it was also true that "many other individuals [had] forsaken stocks."

Levitt believed that a course of positive action was needed. "Most importantly," he told the Exchange membership in March 1978, "we have to convince the individual investor that the market system is fair and that the same kind of investment opportunities that are available to institutions are also available to individuals." He proposed that an alliance be forged between individual investors, listed companies, municipal leaders, and member firms "to urge Congress and Administration to treat capital formation as the nation's most compelling priority." He believed that tax reforms, more specifically, reduction in the capital gains tax, would "spur investment by individuals in smaller companies."

Suiting the action to the word, Levitt, accompanied by a number of Exchange governors, listed company executives, and members of the Administration, journeyed to Washington in March and testified before the House Ways and Means Committee. The Committee, he later reported to the Board, expressed interest in the Exchange's "proposals for bringing the individual investor back to the market to aid the capital formation efforts of small companies." The Exchange also hosted a luncheon with two prominent senators "to discuss the capital formation needs of smaller companies," and a dinner with members of the Ways and Means Committee and representatives of the Small Business Administration.

One tangible result was the decision of the Senate Select Committee on Small Business to hold hearings at the Exchange in May 1978 on the capital formation problems of small business. A second, even more important result was the signing of a tax bill in the fall of that year that included a significant reduction in the capital gains tax.

The Amex, of course, was by no means alone in pressing for action of this kind to be taken. It was, nevertheless, "increasingly identified as a spokesman for small, developing companies." Not surprisingly, its chairman soon won national recognition of his leadership role in the cause, and in the fall of 1978 President Jimmy Carter appointed him chairman of the White House Conference on Small Business (the conference was held in January 1980). In the fall of 1980 the President also appointed him advisor to the Administration "on implementing small business initiatives."

The accession of Levitt thus coincided with a major effort on the part of the Exchange not only to keep abreast of national legislative and regulatory initiatives but also to influence the contours of public sector developments. Levitt and other Exchange officials regularly appeared before key congressional bodies to testify for or against pending bills affecting the securities industry, especially those touching upon the affairs of the small- and mid-size firms dominating the Amex list, and they met with key congressional delegations to present the Exchange's position on significant legislative proposals. The Exchange's Listed Company Advisory Committee, furthermore, mobilized the listed company community "as a potent political base to lobby for legislation in the areas of capital formation, taxation, and finance."

Exchange officials also stepped up the pace of activity in the private arena. Amex clubs were organized in cities around the world. Retail brokers, as club members, sponsored weekly meetings at which listed company executives gave presentations before an audience made up of leading brokers, analysts, and money managers. In time Levitt came to view the Amex clubs as "perhaps the most successful marketing effort in the Exchange's history." In addition, the Exchange organized a "Little Roundtable" as a mid-range company counterpart to the large-firm membership of the Business Roundtable, and formed a Member Firm Advisory Committee. Finally, the Amex in July 1980 sponsored the formation in Washington, D.C., of an organization destined to exert significant pressure on behalf of the legislative interests of mid-range companies while also serving as a major forum for study and discussion of leading issues in the forefront of American economic life. We shall later discuss in more detail the American Business Conference and the part it continues to play in elevating the public image of the American Stock Exchange.

MERGER—ONCE AGAIN?

None of these things could have taken place, of course, had the Amex failed to retain its independence as a major Exchange. Despite Chairman Kolton's powerful assembly of reasons that the Amex should reject the idea of a merger with the Big Board, that idea was by no means dead. The principal factor in its revival in 1976–1977 was the pressure that the SEC continued to exert on the exchanges to push the development of a national market system. However, several additional factors probably contributed to the Amex's new willingness to entertain the possibility. Start-up costs in getting the options program on-line yielded a loss of $2.8 million to the Exchange in 1976 (although the Amex estimated that on an incremental basis option revenues would exceed direct costs by $140,000). To make matters worse, the continuing expansion of the options program that year was delayed by the SEC "as a result of various options trading investigations." (Much to the annoyance of the Amex, the investigations dragged on and on, the SEC in July 1977 imposing an informal moratorium on exchange listing of any new option issues pending the completion of its broad study. The moratorium lasted three years.) Adding to a long-term outlook that must have appeared less than bright despite the recent pickup in business was a fall of 50 percent in stock share volume on the Amex in comparison with the boom years of the late 1960s, relatively low growth in new listings in recent years, and the Amex's anticipation of only "modest additional revenues" from the dual listing program. The "increasing trend" of orders for securities of dually listed companies, Robert Birnbaum reported to the Board in November 1976, was for them "to be sent to the NYSE for execution."

Finally, options competition from the CBOE, and prospectively from the Big Board, in the opinion of a staff reporter for the *Wall Street Journal*, threatened to "overwhelm the exchange." "The Amex's ability to survive without a merger," the *Journal* reporter continued, "is a big question mark, some key Wall Streeters say."

Whatever the constellation of factors, Amex and NYSE committees were holding joint meetings at the end of 1976 to discuss broad issues posed by the emerging national system, and among those issues was whether or not to consolidate the two exchanges. Out of these discussions came a plan for a merged market in which the NYSE would handle all stocks, and the Amex bonds and options. However, if the plan were adopted, the Amex insisted on assurances that "the smaller companies of the type traditionally listed on the Amex . . . would continue to be provided with an effective market for their securities, at reasonable costs."

1977

On May 12, 1977, the Amex Board voted in favor of the merger. Also in favor of consolidation were "many large firms." These firms realized that if the NYSE went ahead with its independent plan to become a major factor in the options market, it would be they who "would have to foot much of the expected $60 million bill to prepare the New York floor for full-scale options trading." Despite their pressure, the NYSE wavered, the *Wall Street Journal* reporting on May 23 that the Board of the Exchange "decided against taking a vote at this time to endorse the merger in principle." Privately, a number of Amex Board members "expressed indignation" at this outcome. But that was only a first reaction. "I leave it to you to figure out where it stands," Birnbaum told a newspaper reporter the next month. "But we cannot sit around and wait for a merger to be achieved."

Instead of sitting around, the Amex would compete more vigorously than ever. In June the Amex began trading put options on five underlying common stocks, adding, in the words of an Amex news release that month, yet "another chapter in the Exchange's development of new products and services for public investors and member-brokers." Calls in those same five stocks were also among options being traded on the Exchange. The Amex options market had experienced rapid growth since the introduction of calls on six underlying common stocks in January 1975. By June 1977 the Exchange provided a call market in nearly 500 series in 64 underlying issues, and the SEC had authorized increasing that number to 80 once the moratorium was lifted. Trading volume had averaged only 4,000 contracts a day in the first month of the program. By June 1977 the average was 10 times the earlier one—40,000 daily.

On the day puts began trading, the first representatives of a new class of Amex membership appeared on the floor. Options Principal Members (OPM) were permitted to trade options for their own account only; they were not allowed to handle agency transactions for public or brokerage customers, nor could they engage in equity or bond trading on the Amex floor. Recently approved by the SEC, OPMs were sold by the Exchange for $15,000 each to 138 individuals and firms. Eleven OPMs traded on that first day, with the others scheduled to be phased in later that month and early in the next (July).

The growing importance of the Amex options market prompted the Board to reorganize its Options Division. Robert Birnbaum had been the

Some "curbstone brokers" on Broad Street take a moment to pose for the camera, while others carry on business as usual.

Traders in the open air often stood head-to-head. It was especially challenging to get one's voice heard above the din of the crowd.

The heyday of the outdoor Curb market, prior to the move indoors. The abundance of flags flying seems to indicate a national holiday or celebration.

*Using a sharp whistle was one way for a phone
clerk to get his broker's attention.*

The original trading floor of the Amex, much as it appeared in 1921 when the Curb market moved indoors. The trading posts were topped with lights to resemble the outdoor lampposts to which the traders were accustomed.

In 1930, the trading floor of the "New York Curb Exchange" was enlarged to more than twice its original size. Shown here are the "modern" trading posts that became the Amex's logo.

The Curb Exchange's Securities Clearing Corporation, where stock certificates were physically delivered or picked up after being purchased or sold.

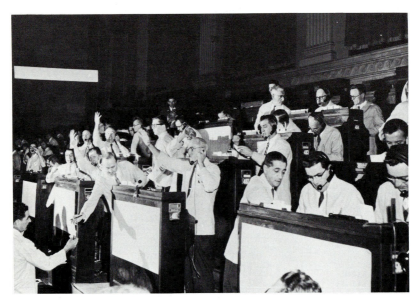

After the move indoors, brokers and clerks found that hand signals were still the fastest way to communicate. The system is still in use today.

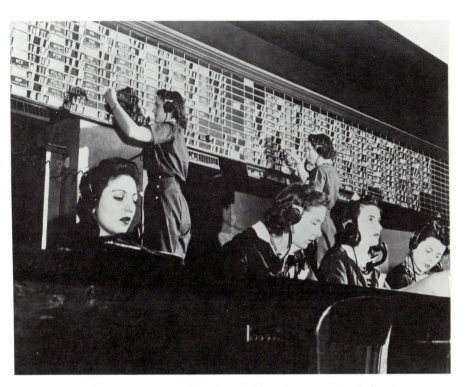

*Telephone operators working the switchboard were constantly busy
routing calls from subscribing brokers.*

The facade of the New York Curb Exchange, the Amex's official title for more than 20 years.

*The word "curb" was dropped completely in 1953, at which time
American Stock Exchange became its permanent name.*

During the 1960s, the introduction of technological advances and new products began to change the appearance of the trading floor.

In the late 1970s, a mezzanine level was added to the trading floor to provide badly needed space, and display terminals were installed above the trading posts.

October 1989: James R. Jones (right), the newly appointed Chairman and Chief Executive Officer of the American Stock Exchange, pictured with outgoing Chairman Arthur Levitt.

chief administrative official for the Exchange's options market, but he was now president, and so two areas he had previously directed, Trading and Markets, were assigned to Vice-President William J. Brodsky. Vice-President Paul G. Stevens, Jr., was placed at the head of the Options Division. In a move foreshadowing the future, Kenneth Leibler was promoted to a vice-presidency and assigned to options marketing.

"Not so long ago the Amex was looked upon as simply a stock and bond market," Chairman-elect Levitt remarked during a visit to Chicago later that year. "We've already added successful markets in put and call options and odd-lot Government securities," and more was yet to come. On Friday, November 11, options trading on the Amex reached a new daily high of 81,804 contracts, surpassing the old record of 77,911 contracts traded on April 14, 1977. Amex brokers attributed the heavy activity to a broad-based advance in the stock market. Fueling that advance was an economic boom that, beginning midway in 1975, would continue through Jimmy Carter's election to the presidency in 1976 and last until 1980.

MORE EXPANSION AT THE AMEX

The onset of the boom, as we have seen, had prompted the Exchange not only to enlarge its trading floor but also to draw up plans for the space requirements of the more distant future. (Indeed, Arthur Levitt served as chairman of the Committee on Facilities in 1976–1977.) One alternative was to construct a second trading floor in the air space above the present trading floor, which would double (to about 41,000 square feet) the available space for trading floor and booths. Another was the purchase of the building northwest of the Exchange (22 Thames Street) and the undertaking of certain renovations to conform it to city building code requirements. (The Exchange was already renting five of the ten floors of the building at the beginning of 1976.) A third alternative was the most radical of all—to move the Exchange itself to another location.

To New Jersey? To Connecticut? Elsewhere in New York? A move of the Exchange to another state was a real possibility in the year of America's bicentennial. Periodically during the Kolton years both New Jersey and Connecticut had made attractive offers in an effort to lure the Exchange. And there was a second consideration, namely, the possibility that either New York City or the state itself would enact a transfer tax or other legislation that would impact adversely on Amex members and customers. Levitt therefore decided to initiate contacts with various state bodies. Soon thereafter he and Paul Kolton were glad to accept an invitation from Governor Brendan Byrne of New Jersey to accompany him by helicopter to an attractive potential site for the Exchange in that state. At the same time the Amex chairman took care to inform Governor Hugh Carey of New York and newly elected Mayor Ed Koch of New York City of the Exchange's possible move.

Both New York officials voiced concern and expressed the hope that they would be permitted to make a competitive proposal. Levitt of course was agreeable and entered into numerous discussions with state legislators in an effort to persuade them that the Exchange was seriously considering alternatives. At the same time, he encouraged them to dissuade the city from adverse tax legislation and to package an offer that would compare favorably with an attractive proposal received from New Jersey. In the meantime, New York administrative officials discussed with their counterparts at the Amex a plan to have the state legislature pass a law that would provide the Exchange with sufficient funds to build its own facility at Battery Park City. Some members of the legislature opposed a subsidy as a massive giveaway, but in the sequel a majority voted to appropriate $40 million to pay for the new construction.

Levitt and the Amex administration then considered with care a proposal from Connecticut as well as those made by New Jersey and New York, and in November 1978 decided in favor of the latter ("The choice of new facilities in New York," the Board of Governors concluded, "would better position the Amex to maintain its key position in securities trading and to be a major force in developing the national market system"). The Exchange proceeded to enter into detailed negotiations with both state and city to develop a lease and the associated agreements made necessary by the appropriation, and after screening the country to locate the finest architects, had design work and performance specifications prepared.

It all came to naught. The essential problems were financial in nature. The head of the Battery Park authority, with whom Amex officials worked closely, advised the Exchange that no more than $40 million would be available and if for some reason that sum should prove insufficient to complete the building, the Exchange would have to pick up the difference. On the face of it, that seemed a reasonable position to take. The state, after all, had provided a subsidy of $40 million. The rub was this: While the state would do the construction work, it would not guarantee either the completion of the building or its satisfactory performance. Even if the new building began to sink in the sand at Battery Park, the Exchange would have to foot the bill for restoration work.

And that was not all. Both city and federal urban development officials demanded that the Amex "provide security, in the form of a letter of credit or other legally binding documents for $13.8 million of tenant's work" on the new facility. Compliance with that demand, the Exchange pointed out, "would tie up virtually all of its working capital, making it impossible for Amex to operate."

Privately, Levitt could not avoid wondering whether the authority and the state were glad to be out from under the deal. When negotiations with the authority first began, Battery Park was in serious financial difficulty and land was virtually being given away. By the time the Amex was ready to go ahead with the project Battery Park had become "one of the hottest real estate areas in the state." Since the Amex had been assigned premium property right on the water, Levitt came to believe that the terms of the deal had deliberately been made onerous to discourage the Amex from consummating it. The property assigned the Exchange could then be sold to someone "who would develop it and bring more revenue to the state than we would have brought."

Following the Exchange's decision in October 1980 not to proceed with the Battery Park project, the Board of Governors decided it had no recourse other than to expand trading floor and booth capacity at its 86 Trinity Place headquarters. In September 1981 it authorized a capital expenditure of $6,980,000 for the construction of an expanded mezzanine trading level that would include four trading posts and approximately 140 clerical support booths. Some of the money was earmarked for safety and environmental improvements. By the end of November 1982 the job was done. The new mezzanine floor had increased trading space by 8,000 square feet and post capacity by nearly 40 percent. The Amex had additional office space, too, thanks to its purchase of the adjacent building at 22 Thames Street in September 1981. When, five years later, the Board approved extending the trading floor into the adjacent second floor of that building, it took advantage of the last feasible opportunity for expansion at its headquarters site.

The decision to make additional space available at headquarters was not the only consequence of the Battery Park fiasco. To obtain bridge financing to cover costs in excess of the $40 million appropriation, the

Exchange had turned to Citibank to obtain the funds. The approach was successful, but the whole episode produced in Levitt a determination to build up the capital of the Exchange. As we shall see, he would emphasize that the Exchange was itself a business seeking every penny of profit it could earn. Its bolstered capital resources would then give it flexibility in the future to determine its own economic destiny without having to look to other sources of financing.

MARKETING THE AMEX

Facilities expansion and the consolidation issue, while demanding of time and attention, by no means absorbed all the energies of the chairman. In early February 1978, barely a month after assuming his new duties, Levitt made it clear that he would pursue with renewed vigor policy initiatives that President Birnbaum had announced the previous July. "The Amex," he told the Board, "has embarked on a major effort to attract new listings to the Exchange in cooperation with its Listed Company Advisory Committee, member organizations and members of the Board of Governors." As part of that effort, Bache Halsey Stuart Shields, Incorporated, assigned a member of its corporate finance department to the Exchange's Market Development Division for one year to work on new listings. And in April, the Board approved the chairman's appointment of John O. Byren as executive vice-president of the Market Development Division.

In July 1978 the Amex launched an "aggressive marketing campaign" in which priority was given to the sponsorship of educational seminars, and of meetings between listed companies and financial analysts; to continued expansion of the Major Cities Campaign; and to the provision of research on listed companies. The main thrust of these efforts, noted Executive Vice-President Eckenrode late in 1978, was toward "retention of existing listed companies, and modest growth in new company listings." "On a long-range basis," he added, the marketing effort was "expected to result in a significant decrease in the number of companies which delist from the Amex." The Amex's Press Relations Division announced at the same time the Exchange's "first continuous advertising program" designed to focus public, corporate, and industry attention on newly listed Amex securities and options and other developments. An Amex advertisement would appear on the Amex stock quotation page of the *Wall Street Journal* every Monday.

These kinds of activities could not be expected to bear fruit overnight. With the passage of time, programs would surely require adjustment in the light of experience. Systematic provision for change in the longer run must be made, and accordingly the Board established the Long Range Planning Committee in 1978. Its mission was to draw up plans 12 to 18 months in advance, and it was to put special emphasis on marketing the Exchange's products, furthering the interests of listed companies, and developing improved governmental relations. In November 1978 the Board named the permanent Committee on Strategic Planning "to monitor industry conditions and make recommendations to the Board relating to long-range planning on a continuing basis."

Levitt himself took an energetically active part in the quest for new listings. After visiting the headquarters of one new acquisition, Texas National Airlines, he announced in April that he "intended to establish an ongoing practice of meeting with such companies as part of the Exchange's marketing effort." In May he visited "several attractive listing prospects" in California, adding Boston, New Haven, and Houston the next month. He by no means confined his frequent trips across the country to prospects alone. He met also with listed companies and their representatives to let them know what his plans were and to learn firsthand about their problems. He wanted them to know that the Exchange was more than bricks, mortar, and wood, more than a domicile for the trading of their stocks. The Amex cared about the well-being of these companies, about their relations with their customers, employees, and executives. It would do everything in its power to help enhance those relationships. To raise the quality of the advice offered by their boards, Levitt acted to recruit former Cabinet members and university professors willing to serve on the boards of directors of Amex companies. Ultimately, a pool of 200 was established.

Levitt also wanted to convince listed company executives of the importance of the specialist function at the Amex. All too often these executives tended to fear, dislike, and even mistrust the handling of their securities by the specialists. To demystify the role of the specialists he encouraged them to meet with company executives at every opportunity to explain what they did and how they did it. The program was well received.

Other measures taken in the early months of the new administration were a meeting of a group of Amex specialists with members of the corporate finance department of Dean, Witter Reynolds, Incorporated, "concerning the Exchange's marketing programs;" a listing presentation before the corporate finance department of Kidder Peabody & Company, and meetings between Levitt himself and corporate finance personnel of E. F. Hutton, Lehman Brothers, and Merrill Lynch; and the deliberate design of the Exchange's 1977 Annual Report (published in the spring of 1978) as a marketing aid to be mailed to the chief executive offices of each listed company, accompanied by a letter from the Exchange specialist in that security. Levitt personally hosted a dinner in April for the Listed Company Advisory Committee and announced that from then on the group would meet six times a year.

Meetings and travels by the chairman continued all through 1978 and 1979, the Exchange expanded its Major Cities Program and gave dinners in New York, Chicago, and elsewhere for listed companies and listing prospects, and, in time, prospects became realities. But not at first. New stock and warrant listings remained remarkably constant at 45 a year through 1977, 1978, and 1979.

GOVERNANCE OF THE EXCHANGE

What was the problem? Surely, in part, the short-run failure to make headway in the campaign for new listings was owing to unfavorable publicity accorded the Exchange's "Governance Report" of 1979. Some of the members of the Board and of the Exchange, opposed to the recommendations of the Report, leaked the story of their opposition to the press with the claim that the changes proposed would place the reins of Amex management "in the hands of a small, self-perpetuating control group." Certainly Levitt himself was persuaded that the action had "cast the Exchange in a bad light." The Board agreed—the matter had been "detrimental to the Amex marketing effort." The tempest had its origins in a somewhat normal difference between the interests of "floor" traders and their employers, "upstairs" firms. The former group is largely concerned with revenue maximization, the latter with cost containment. At the Amex this common source of disagreement had been sharply augmented by the polarization of floor and upstairs forces during the options scandal.

Still smoldering two years later, differences between the two groups threatened to burst into flame almost as soon as Levitt took over as chairman. About two months after assuming office the Exchange nominating committee decided to meet with him and to tell him whom its members were thinking of nominating for positions on the Board of Governors. In doing so, the committee surrendered its traditional independence from the chairman and president of the Exchange, a departure which, in the sequel, Levitt would have reason to regret. At the time, however, he saw himself as responding to forces that had already politicized the committee. The evidence took the form of the committee's consideration of a candidate who would be representative of a floor view rather than an upstairs view on the Board. Allen Gordon had spent most of his career working on the floor of the Exchange and had had less than two years experience upstairs. The committee agreed with Levitt and nominated instead a man with a long history of exposure to the larger context in which the Exchange operated.

There ensued a political campaign viewed by Levitt as "the most aggressive in the history of the Exchange." The chairman took an active part in it. While Gordon funded and ran what amounted to "a primary campaign," Levitt called up members and repeatedly went to the floor in an effort to win membership votes for the committee's candidate. When the ballots were counted, Gordon was found to have won overwhelmingly. And for the next two years the dissident governor made Levitt's life miserable.

> He caused every aggravation that one dissident director or governor could cause. He challenged everything I did, from my strategy to my expense accounts. He suggested malfeasance; he pushed for me to fire Gordon Nash as counsel to the Exchange. He disrupted meetings with constant attacks and criticism.

It was a difficult two years for Levitt, and he breathed a deep sigh of relief when a partner at Goldman Sachs, Robert Minuchen, was nominated and elected at the end of that period to replace Gordon.

The experience had been so disruptive that Levitt decided to have a careful study made not only of the way the nominating process was conducted, but, mindful of the need for assurance that the Amex's structure of governance would enable the Exchange to cope with the complexities of rapidly changing times, the way in which the institution was run as well. In May 1978, with the approval of the Board, he appointed the Advisory Committee on Governance of the American Stock Exchange under the chairmanship of former SEC Chairman William J. Casey. It was a committee of distinguished membership. Besides Casey, it was composed of the president of Fordham University, the chairman of the Hospital Corporation of America, a former U.S. district court judge, the chairman of one major Wall Street firm and a partner in another. A former dean of the Stanford University Law School served as committee counsel, and a former chairman of the Council of Economic Advisers as consultant.

In a letter of May 24, 1978, to Casey, Levitt explained his thinking. The capital market, the securities industry, and the Exchange itself, he wrote, had experienced "revolutionary challenges" since the last reorganization of the Exchange in 1972. At the Exchange, new trading instruments and a new class of membership (Options Principal Memberships) had been introduced. The Securities Act Amendments of 1975 had altered the relationship between the self-regulatory organizations and the Securities and Exchange Commission. The introduction of negotiated rates had "profoundly changed the profile of the securities industry." Finally, the congressional mandate of a national market system had far-reaching implications for the future structure of the securities industry. In view of these changes, and the vital role of the Exchange in the nation's securities markets, he asked the Committee "to take a fundamental look at the Exchange's system of governance and to recommend any possible changes that may help serve the public interest, the needs of publicly owned companies, and the requirements of the nation's securities industry as well as the Exchange itself." The important role of the Amex in the nation's economy, could "best be fulfilled if the Exchange's governing structure is continuously fine-tuned for efficiency, fairness and accountability."

Levitt then laid down his specific charge: "I ask the Committee to consider the role and structure of the Board of Governors and the procedures for its selection. The Committee should also consider the functions and responsibility of the committees and officials that are charged with the supervision of the Exchange's activities, as well as the procedures for their selection." He hoped the Committee would be able to report its recommendations for possible changes to the Board by June 1979.

In its year-long inquiries, the Committee made an effort to "provide the widest possible opportunity for knowledgeable and interested persons to inform [it] of their views of problems in the Exchange's governing structure and procedures and their recommendations for solutions." It invited not only written comments from every member of the Exchange, every listed company, and every present or former member of the Board of Governors, but also oral expressions of their views before informal "hearings" held by panels of the Committee. The information obtained from these sources, and from reading and consultation with the Amex staff, formed the basis for the Committee's Report, rendered in June 1979.

The significance of the consequent recommendations for change is clarified by contrasting them with the constitutional arrangements for the governance of the Exchange prior to the Committee's inquiries. Under the Amex constitution, as amended in 1972, the governing body was identified as the Board of Governors, consisting of 21 members—10 from the securities industry, and 10 from the public—and the chairman, the full-time chief executive officer of the Exchange. Public governors could have no affiliation with a broker or dealer in securities, but might be officers of companies whose securities were traded on the Exchange, as well as representatives of the broader financial community, and other community leaders. No more than 3 of the 10 were required to be registered specialists. Of the minimum of 7 who were not to spend a substantial part of their business time working on the floor of the Exchange, persons known as "office" or "upstairs" governors, 4 had to be associated with firms doing a substantial business with public customers.

The Committee, and witnesses before it, devoted much of its attention to the subject of public members of the Board, to persons unaffiliated with the securities industry. A few witnesses saw public governors as "primarily cosmetic and a time-wasting burden on their more technically informed Board colleagues from the industry." The Committee disagreed. First, there was the record. Reports on the performance of the 20 men and women who had served as public governors since 1972 were uniform: some had done a superb job, many had been good, and a few only fair. (The Report might have added that some had chaired important special committees, and even served on the Exchange's Executive Committee. Economists from university backgrounds, like Raymond J. Saulnier of

Barnard—Saulnier had also served as chairman of the Council of Economic Advisers under President Dwight Eisenhower—and Burton G. Malkeil, chairman of the Economics Department at Princeton, had from time to time been called upon by the Amex chairman to brief the Board on current and projected economic conditions and the forces affecting them. Another former council chairman, Charles Schultze, would soon do the same as a public governor.) The key determinants of performance were individual, a mix of professional background, personal qualities, and dedication.

Second, the Report pointed out, most technical and operational questions arising out of the work of the Amex did not come to the Board for resolution. Rather, they were handled by the administration, or by Exchange committees composed of experienced members of the securities industry. "In a period of rapid flux like the present, the Board of Governors is faced with a host of much wider issues involving the Exchange's relations with the federal government, the New York community, other parts of the financial industry, the media, the investing public, and the public at large, to say nothing of difficult issues of capital commitment, technological development, facilities construction and the like." On issues like these, the Report concluded, the contribution made by public members of the Board could be invaluable. Certainly they were at no judgmental disadvantage because of their limited technical knowledge of the daily workings of the Exchange.

The Committee added a final point. The public, the media, and the SEC perceived the role of the public governors as critical. "A return to a Board of Governors controlled by members of the industry would carry with it at least the image—and perhaps the reality—of the 'private club' environment that gave rise to the difficulties of earlier days and to the successive waves of reform that the Exchanges have experienced." The Committee concluded that the role of the public members of the Board of Governors was "indispensable" and that their number should remain equal to the number of governors elected from the securities industry.

Turning next to the latter, the Casey Committee acknowledged that some of the strongest and most contributory members of the Board had been, and continued to be, from upstairs offices rather than from the floor. But it saw no reason that the number of seats allocated to them (a minimum of 7) should be so much greater than the number allocated to the floor governors (a maximum of 3). Indeed, the Committee found "a pent-up sense of exasperation, or worse," among the people working daily on the floor of the Exchange, people who made their livelihood there and actually made it operate—indeed, the very people (rather than Exchange officials or floor officials) to whom day-to-day operating problems on the floor were brought. The addition of trading in stock options and in government securities had diversified work on the floor and enhanced the need for an increased number of floor governors to give the Board the expertise needed within its own body about these subjects.

Putting together its views on the three constituent components of the Board of Governors, the Committee reached the judgment that the number of both public and industry governors should be 11, but that a better balance within the latter category would be achieved by reducing the number of office governors to 6 and raising the number of floor governors to 5. Overall, the changes would increase the number of Board members by two, making, with the addition of the chairman, a total of 23.

The system for nominating governors, however, was viewed by the Committee as a "serious defect" in the machinery of governance. The system was designed to ensure the independence of the 8-person Nominating Committee (4 from the public and 4 from the industry), but it did so at a heavy cost. By creating a one-year term and forbidding consecutive service, the system condemned the Nominating Committee to "a condition of permanent inexperience." And since the Committee was wholly severed from the Board,—to keep the latter from perpetuating itself—it had no basis for knowing what the Board's needs were, what credentials or qualifications best equipped a candidate for membership, or the particular professional skills or backgrounds needed at a particular time to round out the collective capacity of the Board. In the judgment of the Casey Committee, these disadvantages could be overcome if three of the eight members of the Nominating Committee were members of the Board of Governors (one floor governor, one office governor, and one public member); if the remaining five members were made up of one floor member, one office member, and three public representatives of companies whose securities were listed on the Amex; and, finally, if all members of the Nominating Committee served a three–year term.

As in the past, the Exchange's regular members—650 as of April 1979—should have the sole right to vote for members of both the Nominating Committee and the Board itself. Persons might be nominated either for the Board or the Nominating Committee by written petition signed by 25 or more regular members of the Exchange. (As of the spring of 1979, 307 of the seats on the Amex were owned outright, predominantly by floor members; 315, under agreements whereby a member firm financed the purchase price of an Exchange membership for an individual who was a member of that firm; 8 seats were held by estates or were otherwise temporarily not votable; and 20 seats were held under a recently developed plan allowing a regular or option principal member to lease his membership to another person.)

Finally, the Casey Committee recommended a number of specific procedures relating to the nomination and election processes. Among these was the suggestion that the chairman meet with the Nominating Committee "to review the overall profile of the Board and indicate areas of specialty or of representation which he believes should be given particular consideration at that time." The chairman, too, with Board approval, was to be empowered to select the three Board members to serve on the Nominating Committee.

Naturally, not every member of the Board or of the Exchange accepted every jot and tittle of the Casey Committee recommendations. Board member Admiral Elmo Zumwalt, for example, unable to attend the meeting scheduled to discuss the Report, expressed reservations on one or two particulars in an otherwise "superior piece of work." Zumwalt believed the independence of the Nominating Committee might be compromised if the chairman selected three of the members of the existing Board to serve on the Nominating Committee. He suggested selecting ex-Board members instead. That very feature of the Casey Committee Report, and others as well, was also criticized by dissident members of the Board and of the Exchange, who proceeded to go to the press with the accusation that enactment of the Report's recommendations would convert the Amex into a private club controlled by the administration and its friends.

After reading the inflamatory article, Board member Zumwalt wired Levitt to express his "regret that someone has seen fit to go public on a matter that ought to have been a matter for deliberate and calm discussions within the Board of Governors." Levitt, too, was "dismayed" by the publicity, and so was the Board, which proceeded to emphasize that the role of the chairman as official spokesman for the Exchange "would, in the future, be carefully respected by every Governor." Surely the chairman was consoled by Zumwalt's testimony, which Levitt read to the Board, that he, Zumwalt, had been "subject to no pressure from you or your staff nor the Casey Committee concerning the Casey Report on Government." In fact, Zumwalt reminded that he had initiated a conversation with Levitt after issuance of the Report and found him "quite willing to accept my recommendations for change."

Changes were made indeed. The chairman himself presented alternate proposals, and these, along with those put forward by the Casey Committee, were "extensively discussed and commented on by each Governor." Unanimous approval was given the following major provisions: The size of the Board would be increased to 25 governors, two more than the Committee had recommended, and the members would continue to represent equally the public and the industry. While three of the former were to be principal executives of listed companies, a no less important change elevated the influence of the floor sector, as the Committee had strongly recommended. The office sector retained its representation of seven members, but the number of those who spoke for the interests and needs of the floor was increased from three to five. Overall, the Board was reclassified into three classes of eight governors each, with one class being elected each year for a three-year term; governors were limited to serving two consecutive full terms.

While the current size and basic composition of the Nominating Committee—eight members: four public representatives and four industry representatives—were retained, approved changes reflected both the Casey Committee's concern over lack of continuity in experience, and the concern of Zumwalt and others that the Nominating Committee's independence be preserved. The term of service was lengthened from one year to two, with four members elected each year for a two-year term. One of the four public members was to be an incumbent (the Casey Committee had suggested three) in his second term of office and was to be chosen by the other public governors on the Board. (And at least one public member was to be a principal executive officer of a listed company.) At least one industry member would be a former governor who had retired a minimum of one year before—with a maximum of four years. Finally, the Nominating Committee was to nominate all the members of its successor committee except for the public governor or member. The membership of the Exchange would then elect all individuals nominated to serve on the Nominating Committee. With the subsequent adoption of the requisite constitutional amendments—the changes were not to take effect till 1981—and Board agreement on procedural suggestions made by the Casey Committee—for example, that the Nominating Committee be provided with a written mandate specifying its responsibility for nominating persons of the highest competence and standing and to seek a balanced range and diversity of background and experience among the members of the Board of Governors—the Levitt administration completed its work of refining the machinery of the Exchange to improve its ability to cope with the needs of the 1980s.

AMEX BUSINESS, 1977–1981

Because of the determined vigor with which the new listing campaign was pursued on several fronts, the constant number of 45 new stocks and warrant listings a year between 1977–1979 gave way to 65 in 1980 and then soared to 97 in 1981. (Change in new corporate bond listings was much less dramatic, the numbers recorded for the five years 1977–1981 being 14, 22, 32, 39, and 32, respectively.) Volume in both equities and options also soared, a surprising development in view of the double-digit inflation of the late 1970s and early 1980s, which should have encouraged investments in bonds. Between 1977 and 1981 daily stock volume on the Exchange more than doubled, annual options volume more than tripling. Amex revenues rose from $25 million to $57 million over those years, with net income jumping from $0.8 million to $5.2 million. The price of an Amex regular seat rose from a low of $21,000 in 1977 to a high of $275,000 in 1981. (See Statistical Appendix.)

SURVEILLANCE ON THE AMEX

The rising volume of business in options, a relatively new product on the Amex, accentuated an ongoing problem on any exchange, that is, that of policing its brokers and dealers and the manner in which transactions were made. Not surprisingly, the SEC, wishing to reaffirm the self-regulating tradition in which exchanges operate in this country (i.e., the so-called SROs, or self-regulating organizations), saw the relevance of adequate surveillance and compliance mechanisms to the maintenance of that tradition. And so in 1978 Richard Teberg, the director of the SEC's Options Study Group, conducted what President Birnbaum characterized as an "in depth review of the Exchange's surveillance and compliance procedures." The Board's response was to appoint in October 1978 a Special Committee "to conduct a periodic review (at least annually) of the Exchange's compliance activities." The review would embrace equities as well as options.

Then the Amex decided to go further; existing surveillance systems would be subjected to a "major overhaul" in 1979. The primary need was to reduce the clerical workload "and to satisfy SEC requirements for a complete audit trail on options." Executive Vice-President Eckenrode explained to the Board how this would be done:

> All existing data plus additional data to be made available on each order will be centralized in a data base controlled by a management information processing package. This new approach to surveillance processing will enable the Amex to react quickly to all future SEC surveillance requests in addition to satisfying various deficiencies that exist in today's systems.

Eckenrode added that the "one time effort" would cost $350,000 but because of reduced clerical requirements would result in annual savings of about $300,000.

Despite the steps taken by the Amex and by other exchanges as well to improve their surveillance procedures, the SEC decided in 1980 to develop its own computerized market surveillance system (MOSS). Specifically, MOSS would monitor trading activity (trade watch), reconstruct markets (audit trail), use computer data to determine the impact of trading regulations, provide advance information concerning firms on SROs prior to an inspection, and alert the Commission to potential problems with SRO/SEC investigation/enforcement procedures. The Commission believed MOSS necessary because of the rapid development of options trading and also of the national market system. In addition, MOSS was expected to upgrade SEC oversight of the SROs.

The congressional response was highy critical of the SEC plan, not only because the Commission had failed to disclose details of the system in advance either to the Congress or to the SROs but also because of its concern that MOSS would usurp the traditional role of the SROs and perhaps even lead to an electronic "black box" market. The SROs were at least equally critical. The Amex, for one, expressed its concern that the confidential trading information required for the operation of MOSS be protected from public disclosure. Equally important, a central SEC-operated computer system capturing current trading, clearing, and other surveillance information from all SROs would essentially duplicate the existing surveillance facilities and capabilities of the SROs. In a word, MOSS would increase direct federal regulation of the securities industry.

The SRO response was to form an Intermarket Surveillance Group, composed of the exchanges and the NASD, to work out procedures that would permit the SROs to accomplish the goals of the MOSS system. The Group committed its respective organizations to perfect an intermarket surveillance system and to provide the SEC with the surveillance information that would enable the Commission to discharge its own regulatory responsibilities. In addition, the Amex and the NYSE accepted the need to implement an audit trail for equity securities.

Persuaded that these commitments would enable the industry to develop an effective self-regulatory surveillance program as an alternative to direct daily surveillance by MOSS, the SEC promised not to request funds to enhance the modest pilot program authorized by Congress. And when the chairman of the House Commerce Committee, John Dingell, upset by unfavorable SEC reports on the surveillance capabilities of the NYSE and the NASD, objected to the SEC's acceptance of the alternative plan of the SROs, President Birnbaum reminded the congressman that it was the Congress itself that had established the self-regulatory system.

Working committees of the SRO's Intermarket Surveillance Group proceeded to define the various types of intermarket trading violations that could occur in equities and options, to specify the market data necessary to conduct surveillance for such violations, and to share this information among themselves. Pleased by this progress, and by the SRO's commitment to an effective intermarket trading system, the SEC decided to defer expansion of the MOSS system.

Periodically, of course, it monitored that progress by conducting inspections of operations on the exchanges. SEC inspections at the Amex in 1980–1981 resulted in two reports. The first spoke of the Exchange's equity trading operations and regulatory procedures and focused primarily on the need to adopt an automated audit trail for equity surveillance. The second focused on stock/option market surveillance procedures, including the computerized report that monitored the trading and order activity of Amex specialists and other market makers in the securities underlying Amex options. The SEC voiced concern about the accuracy, and hence the reliability, of the information used to create the report, and the Amex promised to institute spot-checking and automated data editing procedures. Improvements were in order, but the SEC, President Birnbaum told the Board, was "highly complimentary concerning the Amex surveillance staff, particularly the Trading Analysis Division."

A follow-up SEC inspection of the equity surveillance and investigatory procedures employed by the Exchange's Stock Watch and Market Surveillance departments produced a different result. The SEC was "complimentary of the Amex staff and procedures." In the commission's judgment, the Exchange was making "effective use of its automated surveillance data."

A final report followed an SEC inspection of the Exchange's options surveillance program in 1982. The Commission found Amex procedures "adequate and comparable in scope and effectiveness to those in place at other options exchanges." To be sure, there was room for improvement. The Commission asked the Exchange to "adjust some of its violation parameters," and mentioned such weaknesses as the lack of routine surveillance to detect substandard market making by options specialists. It suggested that the Exchange adopt a comprehensive automated program for the conduct of such surveillance.

Actually, the Amex had been considering installing an automated program for some time, but the derivative nature of the options product made the undertaking an extremely complex one. That perhaps explained why no other options exchange had such a program. Amex procedures were not automated, but the Exchange did monitor and evaluate options specialist performance. The administration was willing to undertake to make recommended improvements, but only "to the extent justified."

The Exchange's confidence in the essential soundness of its surveillance techniques appears to have been warranted. Their effectiveness in detecting possible misuse of nonpublic information, and long-term manipulation of Amex listed stocks or options, would subsequently be revealed in several cases referred to the SEC by the Exchange in 1984—the Exchange itself lacking jurisdiction to follow them up. A number of the investigations that followed resulted in indictments by federal grand juries for securities fraud, and in permanent injunctions obtained by the SEC. Amex surveillance procedures were also responsible for discovering several instances of insider trading, including the *Wall Street Journal/ Winans* case and the Searle Options/CBS case, both in 1984, the Exchange working closely with the SEC on the investigations. Early in the next year, Strategy Associates completed a study of the areas in which the Amex had a unique competitive advantage. One of the areas cited was the Exchange's "reputation for integrity and surveillance." The Amex made its reputation the old-fashioned way—it *earned* it.

AMEX DISCIPLINARY MACHINERY

Effective surveillance to uncover wrongdoing was essential if the exchanges were to remain free to regulate themselves. But so too was effective disciplining of wrongdoers. In making the following recommendation in June 1979 the Casey Committee on the Governance of the American Stock Exchange could not have been more clear:

> In order to enhance and ensure the effectiveness and credibility of the self-regulatory aspect of the Exchange's system of governance, the Chairman should periodically obtain an outside evaluation of the Exchange's disciplinary machinery by an ad hoc advisory panel on investor protection and professional responsibility, which would be charged to examine all aspects of the operation of the disciplinary system, and to make recommendations for its improvement if any is needed.

While not accepting the advice that the panel be an "outside" one, the Amex Board proceeded in October 1979 to appoint a Special Committee to Review Exchange Disciplinary Procedures. Chaired by Madeline McWhinney, a public governor of the Exchange, the panel consisted of Exchange officials, members of the Board of Governors, and members of the securities industry. Some had served on Amex disciplinary panels or committees, thus enabling them to provide firsthand knowledge of how the Amex procedures operated.

After an eight-month investigation in which the Committee met with large numbers of people familiar with the workings of the disciplinary process and able to provide opinions about its strengths and weaknesses—for example, members of the Amex staff from the compliance and surveillance areas, both past and present; representatives from specialist firms at the Amex; members of the Exchange who had served as chairmen or members of Amex disciplinary panels and committees; and representatives of regulatory agencies—the Committee issued its report. It was a fully documented report of 80 pages, plus 11 appendices, which analyzed the Amex disciplinary process (prehearing, settlement, hearing, and review procedures), compared it to the rules and procedures of the NYSE, NASD, and CBOE, and also analyzed all Amex disciplinary matters from October 1978 through December 1979, 148 cases in all, which resulted in the issuing of admonitory letters (86), the preferring of formal charges (34), or the decision to close cases without disciplinary action (27). (In one other case, an individual accused by an Exchange floor official demanded a hearing before a disciplinary committee and was found not guilty.)

The Committee's overall conclusion was that the Amex disciplinary process "effectively discharges the self-regulatory responsibilities of the Exchange." The Committee was "particularly impressed with the dedication of the administrative and staff personnel at the Exchange who carry out their duties with a high degree of professional competence."

It did find some investigative shortcomings, however, and recommended changes to improve the system. For example, in certain cases that were closed with no disciplinary action being taken, the records did not adequately describe the reason for the decision to close. The Committee recommended more thorough and comprehensive documentation. In order to facilitate the monitoring of closed cases, the Committee also recommended that periodic reports be prepared by the executive vice-president for Legal and Regulatory Affairs commenting upon investigations closed by the Compliance Department. Such reports would facilitate the work of the Compliance Review Committee. In addition, the McWhinney Committee urged greater utilization of the advice of outside counsel at an early stage of investigations involving "novel or difficult issues."

There were other recommendations too. The Amex, the Committee felt, "should adopt certain measures to enhance further the balance, independence, and experience" of panels selected for the hearing process. For example, a special category of Exchange officials whose sole function would be that of chairing disciplinary panels should be created. And the role played by the Panel Services Department during the hearing process should be strengthened.[1]

But the Committee found no "pattern of unjustified uneveness or unfairness in the sanctions imposed by disciplinary panels or committees that would require a recommendation for improvement." The "future of successful self-regulation," the panel reminded, "rests on the ability of organizations like the Exchange to anticipate the problems and needs of the communities which they serve. In the past, the Amex has shown its appreciation of these goals both by initiating investor protection measures and by engaging in a continuous process of self-examination." "For this," the Committee concluded, "it should be commended." Indeed, the Committee's report was itself "one facet of this self-examination process."

In March 1981 the Board responded to the Committee's Report by approving constitutional and rule amendments relating to hearings before disciplinary panels and to the selection and appointment of hearing officers. The Board also voted in favor of selecting a new Disciplinary Committee each month to hear all summary charges (unlike plenary charges, these were cases involving less serious violations) scheduled during that month. While expressing reservations concerning some of the recommendations of the Report, it was clear that the Amex believed its disciplinary house to be in good order.

The SEC disagreed. After an inspection in mid-1981 of the Amex rule-enforcement program, the Commission, while noting progress by the Exchange in the disciplinary area, nonetheless criticized the Amex staff for failure to bring certain close cases to a disciplinary panel "when, in the SEC's opinion, probable cause existed." But if the SEC disagreed with the Amex, it was no less true that the Amex disagreed with the SEC. And it disagreed "strongly." In the opinion of the Amex, probable cause was "not the proper standard for bringing charges." That standard was "used primarily in criminal law." It did not appear in the securities laws, nor had the SEC defined it in relation to disciplinary proceedings by SROs.

In close or difficult cases the Exchange was reluctant to bring charges against members, especially after a thorough investigation led to serious doubt whether a case could be successfully argued before a disciplinary panel. In an effort to sort out their differences, members of the Amex administration met with the associate director of the SEC's Division of Market Regulation and members of his staff in July 1982. And after a lengthy discussion the SEC staff "appeared to agree that the Amex's standard for issuing charges was appropriate."

Nevertheless, the SEC maintained that charges should have been brought in five particular cases "even if Amex had applied its standard." On this, too, the Amex strongly disagreed. The SEC simply "exhibited an incomplete and fundamentally inaccurate understanding of the specific cases it criticized." The meeting with SEC staff had accomplished some good, however. Although differences in judgment about the strengths or weaknesses of particular investigations might continue to exist, "philosophical differences between the Exchange and the Commission had been narrowed as a result of the meeting on this issue."

Other differences with the SEC arose out of the changed environment for equity securities created by the developing national market system (NMS).

DEVELOPMENT OF THE NATIONAL MARKET SYSTEM

More and more in the later 1970s the objective of linking the nation's market centers, laid down by Congress in the Securities Act Amendments of 1975, was being realized. A consolidated transaction reporting system had been adopted in March 1976 (Consolidated Tape System, or CTS), a consolidated quotation reporting system in August 1978 (Consolidated Quotation System, or CQS), a national clearance and settlement system in January 1977 (National Securities Clearing Corporation, or NSCC), and a comprehensive linkage of competing market centers in April 1978 (Intermarket Trading System, or ITS). ITS, developed and supported by the Amex and NYSE, and by the Boston, MidWest, Pacific, and Philadelphia exchanges as well, soon became the primary mechanism for linking exchange markets. A member of any participant exchange could effect executions against the displayed bids and offers of any other participant exchange.

As of the fall of 1980, however, the NMS was as yet technologically incomplete. At almost the same time that ITS was initiated, the Cincinnati

Stock Exchange's (CSE) National Securities Trading System (NSTS), a computerized automated trading facility, was approved by the SEC and began operating. Thereupon, the SEC and Congress began to press the exchanges to enter into an agreement to interface ITS and NSTS—and also to link the third market makers of the NASD with ITS. If these interfaces were achieved, a comprehensive linkage of all markets would be in place. After intermittent discussions over a two-year period, the CSE in late summer 1980 finally asked to be admitted as a participant in ITS, and the Amex supported the request. The NASD was another matter.

Several times the NASD rejected proposals put forward by the NYSE to bring NASDAQ dealers into ITS. The NASD preferred an automated interface of ITS with an order switching system that it was developing under the acronym CAES (Computer Assisted Execution System). The Amex and the other exchanges, however, strongly opposed a linkage between ITS and CAES unless the SEC adopted an anti-internalization rule. In the absence of such a rule, the exchanges anticipated the possibility that "upstairs," or off-floor market makers, might execute the orders of their own customers without exposing those orders to market makers throughout the system.

Reluctantly, as we have seen, the Amex had supported the SEC rule (19c-3) prohibiting restrictions on off-board agency transactions (except in-house crosses) in stocks first listed on any exchange after April 26, 1979. The Exchange acknowledged that the abolition of such restrictions would encourage competition between the market centers, the prime objective of the 1975 Securities Act Amendments. But if the SEC did not first promulgate an anti-internalization rule there would be a fragmented, rather than a national, market system. *All* orders, the Amex believed, must be executed *within* the linked system. Encouraging the development of dealer markets and the internalization of order flow would permit the execution of orders *outside* the NMS, and hence fragment the NMS.

When the SEC nevertheless ordered an experimental linkage between ITS and CAES in April 1981, the Amex Board briefly considered litigation to block the order. Instead, it decided to join the other exchanges participating in ITS to urge, even more vigorously, the adoption of an anti-internalization rule prior to implementation of the order. The SEC, however, failed to see why a pilot program linkage between ITS and CAES should not be run, and with the passage of time the Amex decided to acquiesce. "It would be difficult," President Birnbaum acknowledged in May 1982, "to demonstrate that Rule 19c-3 [has] thus far substantially harmed the securities markets." Given the available evidence, he added, "it would be difficult . . . to persuade a court that a linkage with upstairs markets without an anti-internalization rule [is] likely to cause such catastropic injury as to justify reversal of the Commission's decision to implement a pilot phase to evaluate the impact of a linkage."

The pilot program, involving 30 stocks,—7 of them listed on the Amex—got under way on May 17, 1982. After being extended, the program was terminated by the SEC on September 15, 1983. All 19c-3 securities then became eligible for trading within the linked system. Because of a low OTC volume environment at that time, however, the SEC decided that the benefits of a public order exposure rule would be outweighed by its costs, and it "deferred action" in the matter. For its part, the Amex went on record as determined to continue to urge the SEC "to assure that linking upstairs market makers with traditional listed markets does not seriously damage the pricing mechanism, liquidity, and basic fairness of securities markets." Noting that the Commission had "in the past committed to take affirmative action to prevent any adverse effect on markets resulting from Rule 19c-3 or the linkage, including the adoption of an order exposure rule, if necessary," President Birnbaum said that at the present time "we do not propose to recommend any action to the Board."

PROTECTION OF PUBLIC LIMIT ORDERS

The unfavorable consequences that the exchanges feared would ensue in the absence of an anti-internalization rule do not appear to have developed. Protection of public limit orders against executions at inferior prices in a linked national environment was another matter. A major component of a national market system, public limit order protection was established by the SEC in March 1979 as a matter of "highest priority." The ITS group, including the Amex, proceeded to draw up a plan for the enhancement of ITS by introducing a component that would serve as an information display system depicting the location of superior priced orders reachable through ITS. The group then proposed a 15-month pilot test of its Limit Order Information System (LOIS), and in September 1980 the Amex Board gave its conditional approval to the plan. The condition was a significant one: the Exchange would not participate in LOIS if that system was not functioning effectively at the time Amex securities were scheduled for inclusion in it. (Since neither the president nor the board ever commented on LOIS again, the presumption is that the Amex condition was not met.)

Differences with the SEC over such matters as disciplinary standards and the lack of an anti-internalization rule, while serious, were to pale in the onrushing 1980s before those with rival exchanges, especially in a national competition for the lion's share of the booming business in options. That competition was so intense that it resembled a feeding frenzy.

N O T E S

1. That role depended on whether or not the issue of guilt had been settled in the hearing process. If so, the panel approved or disapproved the penalty assessed and decided the issue of publicity. If the charges were contested rather than settled, the panel would itself determine guilt and sanctions to be imposed, and, once again, decide whether or not to inform the press about the case.

CHAPTER 5

THE ENTREPRENEURIAL EIGHTIES ON THE AMEX

Before the coming of Black Monday—October 19, 1987—the 1980s were a decade of extraordinary growth for the Amex. (After Black Monday would come a time of extraordinary challenge.) Daily and annual volume in both equities and options broke record ground year after year, and gross and net revenue responded accordingly. (See Statistical Appendix.) The Amex Market Value Index crashed through the 300 mark for the first time in 1980 and reached an all-time peak of 370 after setting new highs 51 times during the year. The $270,000 paid for an Amex seat that year was the biggest price since 1969. In mid-December, an options seat brought an unprecedented $160,000. It was a year, Chairman Levitt conceded, of "dramatic growth."

Even the deep recession of 1981–1982, induced as a matter of high policy by a Federal Reserve Board intent on bringing down double-digit interest rates, failed to halt the spiral. "During 1981," the chairman reported, the "Amex experienced dramatic growth in earnings." Despite recession and stock market volatility in 1982, volume and net income were the second best in Amex history. And so it went, as we shall see, year after year.

OPTIONS EXPANSION ON THE AMEX

The opening of the new decade saw an end at last to the long three-year moratorium (July 1977–July 1980) informally imposed by the SEC on options expansion. Thereupon, the four options exchanges—the Amex, CBOE, and the Philadelphia and Pacific Stock exchanges—proceeded under a lottery plan approved by the SEC to allocate among themselves the underlying stocks for 60 new call options. By the end of 1980 the Amex was trading a new total of 80 call classes and 80 put classes, making it the first listed options exchange to offer to the investing public both puts and calls on its complete options list. Trading had been brisk from the start—indeed, President Birnbaum reported "record volume" in equities as well as options in the fall of the year—but the Exchange "continued to perform well operationally."

Competition between the exchanges to develop and win approval for new options and other products was sharp, but this was all but inevitable given the congressional mandate to create a national market system. Competitive forces had been held in abeyance by the options moratorium, but even before its end in the summer of 1980 the SEC and CFTC had been deluged by exchange applications to offer new investment vehicles. Now that it was over it was more important than ever that the Amex position itself for the struggle ahead. Aware of "the importance of careful planning, the substantial investment any new program would entail, and the fierce competition for these products which was likely to develop," President Birnbaum decided in the spring of 1981 to name a Special Committee on New Product Development. Chaired by Public Governor Burton Malkiel, its mandate was "to evaluate the potential for new product development at the Amex, to provide detailed policy recommendations for the introduction of proposed new investment vehicles, and to outline priorities and schedules to guide the expansion effort."

By July 1981 Dr. Malkiel was able to present an interim report to the Board on behalf of his Committee. To maximize the chances of success, he recommended that the administration develop options in four product areas simultaneously. Malkiel listed them in the following order of priority: precious metals, Treasury securities, nongovernment debt instruments, and units of related stocks. He went on to explain that the precious metal contract would be the economic equivalent of precious metal ownership, that is to say, it would be a bullion value promissory note

(BVN). The BVN would be characterized as a security subject to SEC jurisdiction, while options on a metals future, or on the physical commodity itself would fall under CFTC regulation. Jurisdictional squabbles were to fleck the early stages of new product devlopment, as we shall see.

Similar disputes would also be sparked by the Amex plan to offer options on Treasury securities, on T-bills, notes and bonds, securities that the Special Committee believed would have broad appeal to retail firms and to professionals. Options on nongovernment debt instruments would be designed to complement Treasury options. They would include selected, broadly held corporate bonds, and a market basket of major bank certificates of deposit (CDs). Options on units of related stocks, on stock indices representing a particular industry or business group, represented an area requiring additional exploration. The program as a whole was a bold, far reaching one, and the Board unanimously approved rule amendments to authorize trading options on major domestic CDs and on BVNs. At the same time it authorized the administration to formulate specific proposals for trading the other options recommended by the Special Committee.

A cautionary note was in order, however, and Dr. Malkiel did not hesitate to sound it in a subsequent report to the Board. The Amex, he warned, "faced an uncertain market and regulatory climate" as well as strong competition from other exchanges. The American Stock Exchange could not be assured of becoming the principal market for each new option product proposed, and it was for this reason that the Special Committee had developed a multiproduct program. It was one "aimed at assuring Amex a fair participation consistent with member firm needs and Exchange capacity."

The concrete meaning of an "uncertain . . . regulatory climate" was to become clear all too soon. In July 1981 the Board had not only approved the Special Committee's proposal to trade precious metals options, but it had also authorized the administration to file proposals simultaneously with the Commodities Futures Trading Commission (CFTC) and the SEC. The former, however, had earlier proposed a pilot program permitting commodity option trading only by exchanges already trading futures contracts. In the Amex view, the CFTC plan imposed a restriction on competition that was arbitrary, unfair, and inconsistent with the Commodities Exchange Act. And so the Amex commenced a lawsuit to challenge the CFTC's program.

The CFTC countered with a two-pronged argument: not only did such a ruling fall within its authority, but the Amex suit was untimely. No decision to permit trading in options on futures prior to options on physicals had yet been made. The Court proceeded to grant the CFTC's motion to dismiss the suit.

Shortly thereafter, the SEC forwarded a preliminary negative reaction to the Amex proposal to trade options on bullion value notes (BVNs) under the Commission's jurisdiction. Essentially, the question was whether the SEC or the CFTC had jurisdiction. In view of the uncertainty, together with political and legislative efforts to more sharply distinguish the jurisdictional dividing line between the two agencies, the Amex decided it would not press the SEC for early formal action on the BVN proposal. As it turned out, the Amex never did trade options on BVNs. It developed instead a CFTC-regulated physical gold options contract, but because of difficulties we shall later discuss it did not begin trading these gold bullion options till the spring of 1985.

Jurisdictional uncertainties also held up the Amex plan to trade options on government securities. The Amex had filed a proposal to do so as early as 1977, only to withdraw it at the request of the SEC during the pendency of the moratorium. The particular interest of the Exchange at that time lay in trading options on Government National Mortgage Association (GNMA) paper. After the moratorium came to an end it was no longer certain it wanted to continue with that plan. Its longstanding interest in the area, however, qualified it to comment at length on a CBOE proposal to do so. The comment was negative: for numerous technical reasons the system proposed by the CBOE, in the judgment of Paul G. Stevens, senior vice-president in charge of the Amex's Options Division, would neither provide an efficient market mechanism nor adequately serve the needs of the mortgage industry.

The SEC nevertheless approved the CBOE proposal, but by that time the Amex had shifted its attention to options on Treasury bills (T-bills), "which have wider appeal," and also to Treasury bonds and notes. The SEC approval, however, provoked a storm of protest from the Chicago Board of Trade (CBT), which maintained in a suit against the Commission that it was lacking in jurisdiction. More specifically, the suit raised the issue of whether the SEC had authority to approve the trading of options on any financial instrument that was the subject of futures trading in a contract market designated by the CFTC. Not unnaturally, the CFTC authorized the filing of an *amicus* brief in support of the CBT. While the Amex anticipated the possibility that its ability to proceed with its own plans to trade options on government securities might be impaired by a CBT victory, it decided not to intervene.

The Amex changed its mind after the CBT won its suit against the SEC in the Seventh Circuit court of appeals. The Exchange "disagreed vigorously" with the Court's ruling. The overturning of the SEC's approval of the CBOE's GNMA options program sharpened the feeling at the Amex that its own plan to trade options on other government securities, specifically on Treasury bills and notes, had been placed in jeopardy. At the least, the program would have to be delayed pending the outcome of a motion filed by the SEC and CBOE for a re-hearing by the full court of appeals. The Amex decided to throw its weight on the SEC-CBOE side by entering an *amicus* brief in support of the motion.

The court denied the motion, but legal authority on the Amex had anticipated that result and pointed to the likelihood that the jurisdictional issue would be resolved legislatively rather than in the courts. It was. The chairmen of the CFTC and SEC, respectively, Philip Johnson and John Shad, reached an accord on jurisdictional boundary lines in the options area, and this accord was ratified by the Congress in the fall of 1982. Essentially, the trading of index futures on the commodity exchanges would be confined to broad-based index products, for example, an index future on the transportation industry as a whole. The securities exchanges subject to SEC regulation, however, were also permitted to trade such narrow-based ones as index options on the airlines. With the accord ratified, the SEC reapproved the Amex's rule proposals for trading options on Treasury instruments. (The CBT, however, continued to believe that the CFTC rather than the SEC had jurisdiction over these products.) Despite some apprehension on the Amex that the CBT would ask the Seventh Circuit Court of Appeals to stay the commencement of trading pending the outcome of a petition for review of the new SEC orders, trading began as scheduled on October 22, 1982. Volume in Treasury note and bill options amounted to a modest daily average of 700 to 800 contracts, but perhaps consoled by heavy volume in equities and stock options the administration pronounced itself "pleased with performance thus far."

The detailed studies of the possibility of trading options on Treasury Department securities had been done by Nathan Most's New Product

Development Committee, and it had taken nearly two years to bring those products on-line. With the resolution of jurisdictional disputes the process gathered speed. Within two months of the beginning of trading in T-bills and notes the SEC approved the Exchange's proposals to trade options on the Amex Market Value Index and on major bank certificates of deposit (CDs). In addition, the Exchange filed a proposal to trade options on eleven narrow-based indices in the following industry groups: Aerospace, Drugs, Electronics, Financial Services, Hospital Management/ Specialties/Supplies, Information Technology, Media/Entertainment, Merchandising, Metals, Oil and Gas, and Oil Services. Each of these industry categories consisted of stock groups, ranging from 11 to 42 in number, selected because of their market value, investor interest, and similar factors. The Amex planned to alter the stock groups periodically to maintain their quality and character and to do so in a manner that would preserve the continuity of the index values.

The mood of the Amex was upbeat. An "atmosphere of exuberance grips the Exchange these days," Levitt told the membership in 1982. The air was entrepreneurial, and once more the chairman reiterated a basic conviction. "Entrepreneurship," he reminded, "built this Nation's economy and built this Exchange." And the mid-range companies attracted to the Amex played "a special role in the creation of new jobs, new ideas, new products and new services."

TRANSITION?

Not that there were no problems to be confronted. One irritant stemmed from SEC approval in 1979 of a rule permitting the NASD to designate securities traded on the OTC as "national market system" (NMS) securities. To enable the securities of large OTC companies to be traded in a linked and competitive system, Congress in 1975 had included the concept of "qualified securities" in the national market provisions of the Securities Act. The SEC proceeded four years later to establish two tiers of securities. Those in the top tier automatically qualified, while those in the second tier, which were required to meet somewhat lower financial and trading criteria, were designated as qualified upon application by the company or by two or more market centers. The

Amex objected to the NMS securities concept on two grounds. In the first place, given the small and mid-range companies dominating the Amex list, the securities of most would be ineligible for the designation. In the second, the very term "national market system" securities was merely "a marketing tool [used] by the NASD to imply to companies and the public that this list of securities represents a trading system." The Amex saw no relationship between the NMS designation and the National Market System mandated by Congress. It objected in vain: on the eve of the 1990s the designation remained.

A threat rather than an irritant was the possibility that the National Conference of Uniform Law Commissioners would revise the Uniform State Securities Act in such a way as to remove the exemption of both "blue chip" and listed companies from state registration requirements ("Blue Sky laws"). Several states, moreover, were also considering removing the exemption in the late 1970s and early 1980s. Passage of such legislation would deny exemption to nearly half of all Amex-listed companies and prove a competitive boon to the NASD. The Exchange believed the anti-exemption movement to have been a product of "NASD lobbying efforts." The struggle against those efforts also continued into the late 1980s.

Finally, there was an experiment that failed. As early as the beginning of 1980 the Exchange had considered the possibility of trading gold coins. Indeed, the Board had approved an appropriation of $50,000 to permit SIAC to perform preliminary work on the necessary clearance and settlement system in February of that year. The program envisaged five-coin round lots trading in a specialist/dealer system, and by the end of the year the distinguished sociologist Dr. Kenneth Clark had been retained to assess public reaction to the contemplated inclusion of South African Kruggerands among the coins.

Six months later the Board authorized the formation of a wholly owned subsidiary to develop and operate a pilot program to trade gold bullion coins. Actual trading began in January 1982, with the Exchange offering access to its subsidiary, the American Gold Coin Exchange, by means of special trading permits. Volume for the first 16 days amounted to 1,482 coins, with only Canadian Maple Leafs available the first 14 days. Then, on February 10, the Austrian 100 Corona, Mexican 50 Peso, Mexican 1 oz. coin, and Kruggerand were added. Trading was slow. During the first four months a daily average of five trades took place on the Exchange, and while this doubled to ten a day over the next six months, aggregate losses totaled $178,000 in 1982.

While the gold coin program attracted the interest of some member firms and won a reputation for being a safe and reliable market in which to trade, it fell short of the Exchange's expectations. Member firm participation proved to be "extremely limited." With trading volume "far below the projected break-even level," and continued losses, the Exchange finally decided in the summer of 1985 to discontinue the program.

One swallow doesn't make a spring nor one failure much of a dent on the ongoing competitive success of the Exchange in 1983 and 1984. Both years joined the continuum of Amex prosperity. The year 1983 was extraordinary. On September 28 volume in warrants and equities surged past the previous record for a *full* year (1980). Ten weeks later, on December 14, the two-billion share level was reached for the first time— a gain of 56 percent over the total in 1982. (See Statistical Appendix.)

Institutional activity reflected in blocks of 10,000 or more shares represented one-fourth of the trading. (Five years before it had been less than 10 percent.) Options volume also continued to set new records, as it had every single year since the start of trading in 1975. Average daily volume reached a new high of 154,023 contracts.

Most heartening was the leap in new listings to 70 from 46 in 1982. Revenues, too, soared to an all-time high, with net income from all sources totaling $6,376,000—a remarkable increase of 41 percent over the previous year. Members' equity also set a record in 1983, ending the year at $45,554,000. Equity value had almost doubled since 1979. (In the last ten years it had risen two and a half times.) Finally, the banner year was reflected in the prices of stocks on the Amex, nearly one-third of which appreciated at least 50 percent in 1983. (Some 12 percent at least doubled in value during the year.) With understandable pride Chairman Levitt commented that the Exchange "does not simply *represent* growing companies—it is *itself* a growth company."

The Orwellian year 1984 saw a descent from 1983's dizzying heights in equity volume, but yet another landmark achieved in options. (See Statistical Appendix.) Average daily volume climbed more than 4,000 to 158,516 contracts. Revenue rose some $2.5 million, but an increase in expenses dropped net income from $6,376,000 to $4,653,000. Equity, though, continued to mount, going from $45,554,000 to $50,207,000. And, once more, new listings were up, from 70 to 91. Considering that 1984 was a period of great difficulty for the securities industry, it was another remarkable year on the Amex, with institutional activity accounting for nearly one-third of the trading. "Clearly," Levitt observed, "many fine stocks with a traditional retail following have now acquired strong institutional support as well."

INDEX OPTIONS

But options were where the action was, and both 1983 and 1984 witnessed the introduction of innovative products on the Amex. Some were stock options, but by far the most imaginative and productive of the new series were index options. (An index option differs from a stock option in this key respect: the index value serves as the underlying security. When the option is exercised, the holder receives an amount of cash that is determined by the difference between the closing index value and the exercise price.)

Interest in index products built steadily in the securities industry as a direct consequence of the commencement of trading in index futures on three commodity exchanges early in 1982. Concerned over the possibility that this type of activity on commodity exchanges might impinge detrimentally on trading in stocks and stock options, the securities industry responded by developing index products, which of course were subject to SEC jurisdiction. The first of these on the American Stock Exchange, as we have seen, were options on the Amex Market Value Index (XMI), approved by the SEC after the ratification of the Shad/Johnson accord.

The Exchange then followed with its proposal to trade options on 11 narrow-based stock indices. As of February 1983, the administration favored commencing its new program with an option on an original index representing a broad market average comprised of a number of major U.S. industrial corporations. (The index would be calculated on the basis of share prices to insure a balanced representation to the entire group of companies.) After that, in order of priority, would come options on the Amex's computer technology index, on the Amex's oil and gas industry index, and on the Amex Market Value Index (XAM). Finally, the administration planned to file a proposal with the CFTC to trade futures on its two broad indices.

The Exchange began to implement its program the following month by asking the SEC to approve its plan to trade options on the original index mentioned above. It would be comprised of the stocks of 20 major industrial corporations. Approval came swiftly for the Exchange's Major Market Index (XMI), and actual trading began, somewhat slowly, on April 29, with 8,600 contracts changing hands. To increase interest in the new product the Exchange mounted a major marketing effort. The campaign included advertising in important newspapers and business publications, industrywide dissemination of brochures and promotional material, and a 14-city tour to reach retail brokers and their clients directly. The administration voiced optimism about the future of the new product.

But was the Amex—and the other exchanges as well—moving too fast into this new and unexplored area? The Options and Derivative Products Committee of the Securities Industry Association (SIA) thought so. The products already on-line were burdening member firms with operational problems. And still more products were in the planning stage. The CBOE, for example, stated its intention to begin trading in options on the Standard and Poor (S&P) 500, and the NYSE planned to do the same with its NYSE Composite Index. In the meantime, the CBT was seeking a declaratory judgment in the Illinois courts entitling it to trade a futures contract on a 30-stock average identical to the Dow Jones Industrial Average. If the effort was successful, the Exchange planned a similar proposal to trade an Amex 30 index, identical to the Dow. The SIA Committee thought the pace too fast, and so in June 1983 it formally asked all the exchanges to defer the introduction of new options products till January 1984. The breathing spell would enable member firms to prepare more adequately to market existing broad-based indices through a better trained and regulated sales force.

The Amex was willing to go along, but in view of the reiteration by both the CBOE and NYSE of their intention to commence trading in the options we have just identified, the Exchange believed it had no alternative but to go forward with its own plans. Specifically, it would proceed, subject to regulatory approval, to introduce options on narrow-based indices, and options on the Amex Market Value Index. Actual trading in the latter began on July 8, with "favorable" volume levels. Trading in the former, when approved, would be conducted in direct competition with comparable indices on the CBOE and Pacific Stock Exchange. Competition in the new products, most especially in index options, was intense, so the Exchange made a move in the fall that it hoped would give it a competitive advantage. It granted the CBT an exclusive license to use the names "Major Market Index" and "Amex Market Value Index" for the trading of stock index futures. The Exchange believed that the agreement would fortify its competitive position in index options by providing specialists and market makers with a futures market in which to hedge risk. In the Amex view, cooperation with the CBT, the premier futures exchange, would provide additional competitive and strategic benefits over the long term as new products developed.

In the meantime, the SEC had approved a pilot program in narrow-based index options, and trading in the Computer Technology Index (XCI) commenced on August 26. Opening volume totaled 7,500 contracts. Then, on September 9, the Oil and Gas Index (XOI) was introduced, "with good initial trading interest." (XOI was a market-weighted measure of the performance of 30 active stocks representative of the oil and gas industry.) With the introduction of options on two broad-based (XMI and XAM) and two narrow-based indices (XCI and XOI) the Amex had positioned itself well for the competitive wars with the other exchanges. Nevertheless, the New Products Committee asked the staff "to explore other product areas that may offer attractive trading opportunities for investors and Amex members." And in view of the entry of the NYSE into the index option arena with a multimillion dollar advertising campaign, the Board authorized an additional $650,000 in advertising expenditures. That brought the Amex total to a million dollars.

It soon began to look like a good investment. In recent weeks, President Birnbaum reported to the Board in mid-October, the Major Market Index had averaged nearly 30,000 contracts a day, on some days representing nearly 20 percent of the Exchange's total options volume. However, the Amex advantage over the competition for trader interest, he warned, was a temporary one—whichever exchange offered a near-term expiration date for its contract was in the driver's seat. The Amex enjoyed this position in October, but in November the advantage would shift to the NYSE's composite index. Beginning on December 1 this shifting about would end. All exchanges would be permitted to list one-, two-, and three-month expiration series for broad-based indices, and this would eliminate the near-term expiration advantage. Thereafter, each product would have to attract order flow on its own merits.

The two new narrow-based industry indices were also doing well, Birnbaum reported. While the CBOE had initiated trading in two indices similar to the Amex's Computer Technology and Oil and Gas contracts, the Exchange's offerings enjoyed two advantages. One was a four-week head start, the other strong specialist performance. Together, they made it possible for the Amex to maintain a commanding share of the market. Meanwhile, the NYSE had launched its options program by introducing options on the NYSE composite index. First week volume of 9,000 daily contracts had tapered off to 5,000 a day. The self-confidence of the Amex was unshaken. Although the NYSE was "a formidable competitor, its performance to date has not had a demonstrable impact on the Amex's index option program." Having successfully met challenges thus far from the CBOE and the NYSE, the administration announced it would soon take up plans to develop an options contract on over-the-counter securities. It had filed a proposal to do so with the SEC in 1977, but then withdrew it during the moratorium.

The competition grew hotter and hotter. Not only the CBOE, but other exchanges as well, announced their intention to develop industry indices similar to those offered by the Amex on computers and on oil and gas. The Philadelphia Stock Exchange filed a proposal to trade indices on precious metals and gambling stocks, and the NYSE applied to trade 13 industry indices. But there were also positive developments for the Amex. The Illinois Supreme Court had upheld the right of Dow Jones and Company to prevent the use of its index as a subject for futures trading. That bode well for its closest surrogate, Amex's Major Market Index. And the Amex filed a proposal with the CFTC to trade options on physical gold.

The latter proposal was destined to suffer reexamination and delay, partly because of the CFTC's concern over the appropriateness of the specialist system for commodities trading. When it appeared the CFTC would not approve the plan, the Amex agreed to utilize a competing market maker system instead of the traditional specialist system. Other problems remained, however, not least of which was the administration's own recognition of the difficulty the Amex was likely to experience in competing with such other well-established similar contracts as the gold futures contract already trading on the Comex. And, that wasn't all.

The Exchange's strategy had been to design and market a gold options contract that would be compatible with stock options and index options, in the hope that it would appeal to securities salesmen and their customers. But this group was unfamiliar with the futures market, and needed proper training prior to licensing. The difficulty here was the

CFTC's requirement that securities salesmen complete the full commodities registration examinations before being permitted to trade the product. The Amex did obtain some relief from this requirement—in the form of an agreement to eliminate questions relating to agricultural commodities. In the Amex's view this provided significant inducement for major firms to continue in their efforts to license all salesmen for both securities and commodities products. Those controls, fundamental in securities markets, were "highly controversial" in the commodities markets and not present in them.

Despite the opposition on the part of the CBT and the Comex, the CFTC approved the Exchange's proposal to trade options on gold bullion through the facilities of an independent corporation established by the Exchange—the Amex Commodities Corporation. It had taken a long time. Trading did not commence till the spring of 1985, with New York City's Mayor Koch trading a symbolic first contract.[1]

Unsurprisingly, the Comex opposed the Amex plan. So too did the Chicago Board of Trade (CBT). The latter said it was against the board broker trading system agreed to by the Amex because that system possessed "the same anti-competitive weaknesses as the specialist system." To the Amex administration, however, it was "apparent" that the "real concerns" of the commodities exchanges had to do with the quality of regulatory control the Amex could provide, specifically, an audit trail and execution time stamping.

The Exchange thus adopted a host of innovative products in the options area in the opening years of the 1980s. To a considerable degree, its competitive alertness in the teeming arena was owing to one man in particular—Kenneth R. Leibler. Leibler's entry into the securities field was initially the direct result of a report he wrote at Syracuse University, where he majored in economics. (He graduated Magna Cum Laude and as a member of Phi Beta Kappa.) The subject of the report was stock options on listed securities. It led first to a job as an options trader at Marsh, Block & Company, and then to a managerial position at Lehman Brothers (which was to become Shearson Lehman Hutton Inc.). In November 1975, Leibler joined the American Stock Exchange as a director in the Options Division, where he helped guide the Exchange to its unbroken record of annual gains. His rise was rapid: to a vice-presidency in the division in 1977, to broader responsibility for the Exchange Administration and Finance in 1979, to a senior vice-presidency in July 1981.

It was from this elevated managerial position that Leibler addressed the Board in January 1984. He reminded the governors that when the Amex commenced its options program in 1975, the CBOE and two regional exchanges had formed the principal competition. The Amex had successfully captured and maintained about 30 percent of this market. Events in the new product arena in the past 12 months, however, foreshadowed far more intense competitive conditions.

Each of the options exchanges was attempting to position itself by filing extensive lists of index preferences with the SEC. The CBOE had proposed 17 indices; the NYSE, 14; and the Amex itself, 9. In addition, the Philadelphia Stock Exchange had recently begun trading two industry indices, and the Pacific Stock Exchange had announced start-up dates in two others. Finally, the NASD had entered a proposal to trade options on the most active NASDAQ securities—a form of side-by-side trading vigorously opposed by the Amex because of the overwhelming competitive advantage NASDAQ market makers would enjoy over any exchange market maker vying for order flow in the same option. The SEC, however, had developed an increasingly free market orientation in recent years and looked to competitive forces to contain abusive conduct among professionals.

Dual trading of the same product on two different markets was taking place too, and it was clear that the SEC had determined not to prohibit that either. And there were other causes for concern. The absence of minimum composition standards for index products might well foster more indices consisting of fewer stocks, more duplicative listings, and, ultimately, direct multiple trading among exchanges. Further complicating long-run planning on the Amex was the recent thrust by the commodities industry to list futures contracts on indices similar to those currently the subject of index options trading.

Summarizing on a cautionary note, Leibler reminded that of the three categories of new products introduced by the Amex and the other options exchanges over the past two years, namely, interest rate options, currency options, and index options, only the broad-based indices and the narrow-based Computer Technology index could be termed successes. "As expansion continues in the narrow-based indices," he concluded, "it is reasonable to assume that only a handful of attractive industry selections will ultimately survive."

STRATEGY ON THE AMEX

The Exchange was determined not to plunge thoughtlessly into the froth whipped up by the competitive frenzy. And there were other reasons for a stock exchange to take stock. As Chairman Levitt pointed out in the spring of 1984, competition with the NASD for equity security listings had become more acute in recent years, and the possible entry of the NYSE into the options arena might have a dramatic impact in that product area. (The fear was that NYSE's dominance in equities would give the Big Board a decisive advantage over other options exchanges.) The Amex needed to know whether it was properly positioned in the marketplace and making the most efficient use of its resources. Identification of the variables involved would enable it to reach basic strategic decisions. To obtain that information the Exchange decided to retain both a marketing consultant and a strategic planning consultant—Strategy Associates. Messrs. Birnbaum and Leibler would meet regularly with these consultants. The resultant study was one of major importance. Completed early in 1985, it analyzed in depth the competitive activities of the securities industry environment worldwide, and matched them against the strengths and weaknesses of the American Stock Exchange. The Amex, it concluded, possessed unique competitive advantages in four areas: the excellence of its specialist market making system, its strong market position in options, its reputation for integrity and surveillance, and its identification with growing companies.

The findings of the study, coupled with additional research on the part of the Exchange itself, formed the basis for a four-part strategic plan to guide management in the years ahead. The first component bespoke a determination to enhance equity marketing efforts; the second, to strengthen still more the Exchange's position in the options market; the third—judged critical to the strategic future of the Amex—to expand the part played by the Exchange in the internationalization of the securities industry. The fourth called on the Exchange to widen still more its leadership role in providing the industry with state-of-the-art technology.

This strategic plan was to light the way for pioneering steps taken by the Exchange on new product development, international markets, and technological innovation. Leibler was its chief architect, but he was more than that. A young man of great brilliance, he also led the Exchange's orchestrated efforts to achieve the goals of the plan. Needless to say, he won vigorous support from the executives placed in charge of the Exchange's divisions, from the technical staffs in those divisions, and, not least, from Chairman Levitt and the Board of Governors. When Robert Birnbaum resigned the presidency of the Amex to assume the presidency of the New York Stock Exchange in 1985, the Board, after conducting a careful search for his replacement, found him at home. In January 1986, at the age of 36, Kenneth Leibler was to become the youngest president of any exchange in the nation.

Leibler was given further opportunity to prepare himself for the responsibilities of that office, and in the process to strengthen the Amex's position in the options market, when the SEC decided in the spring of 1985 to allow the exhanges to trade options on OTC securities. The Amex was the first to take advantage of the opening. It did so by announcing its intention to list options on ten attractive OTC stocks. The CBOE followed by listing a dozen, seven of them in common with the Amex, thus assuring dual trading in those issues.

The administration was aware of the risks and burdens that would be placed on the staff, the floors, and the upstairs brokerage community. Nevertheless, given the SEC's mandate to compete, and the threats posed by the NASD, the NYSE, and the other options exchanges to the Exchange's position, the Amex, Leibler made clear, "can only view this competition as an opportunity to expand its product base and try to further solidify its premier position in these markets."

Trading of options on OTC securities began in the summer of 1985, with results that justified Leibler's confidence. The Amex dominated its two major competitors, the NYSE and the CBOE. At the end of eight trading sessions, it had captured two-thirds of the total business in the three options classes with which it was in competition with those exchanges. That outcome was not destined to prove a temporary fluke. By year's end the Exchange was capturing some 90 percent of total volume in options on OTC stocks, which by then were being competitively traded on four exchanges.

The Amex explanation of its success was almost self-deprecatory: history showed that once a consensus formed as to which exchange was primary in a particular option, most orders flowed there. What the explanation left out of account was the part played by alertness and careful preparation in achieving that primacy in the first place. Just before the start-up of trading in early June the administration intensified its marketing efforts by, among other things, making effective use of print media, and holding discussions with key options personnel at major firms. Mention of the use of automated trading systems on the Amex and a temporary suspension of transaction charges did little to harm those efforts. And certainly not to be discounted was the performance of the Amex's experienced specialists, a performance marked by a willingness to take large positions. By the spring of 1986 the Exchange's OTC options program had won "virtually 100 percent of the volume in nine out of ten stock options in which the Amex competed with the CBOE, and 95 percent of the trading volume in multiply-listed options (i.e., those traded competitively at other exchanges).

Maintaining that competitive edge in the options arena required reassessment of decisions already taken, and the projection of detailed plans into the longer-range future. Exchange executives did not consider themselves wedded to the past, and when a product failed to live up to expectations it was discarded. That was the fate, for example, of options on the Amex Market Value Index (XAM). Since participation in XAM had been "extremely limited" ever since the beginning of trading in 1983, the Exchange decided in January 1986 to delist it. Later that year XAM was replaced by another broad-based index option, XII.

XII was an Institutional Index Option that featured a European-style exercise system, that is, one in which the option can be exercised only on the date of expiration of the contract. The option was composed of 75 stocks most favored by institutional investors, as determined by the dollar value of shares held by such investors. The composition would be reviewed and updated quarterly on the basis of reports filed with the SEC by the largest domestic institutional investors. Interest in the new product was lively from the start, with an opening day volume of 30,000 contracts. Leibler emphasized the Exchange's plans "to continue its marketing and promotional efforts to make XII one of the most active index contracts in the country." By 1986 it was clear that index options were riding the wave of the future. Since their introduction on the Amex in 1983 volume in that product had "grown dramatically," with the volume increase in the Exchange's popular Major Market Index (XMI) also being accompanied by an increase in market share. In contrast, volume in stock options had declined over the same period. Despite the better performance of index options, however, the Exchange regarded itself in the spring of

1986 as "seriously committed to increasing the use of stock options." It had good reason to be: the Exchange was currently listing 130 options on underlying stocks, 19 of them OTC stocks, and the first quarter of 1986 had shown the Amex to be enjoying an all-time high market share in options on equities.

The Exchange was determined to increase still more the force of its presence in the entire options arena, and in May 1986 it adopted a strategic plan for enabling it to do so. Paul Stevens, executive vice-president of Operations, disclosed the details. In the first place, the Amex would continue to create and support additional proprietary products (of which XII would soon become an example). In the second, it would exploit technology and trading systems to maintain the Exchange's competitive advantage. Last, but not least, it would pursue international linkages between the Amex and foreign exchanges.

INTERNATIONAL LINKAGES

In the equities area it had already begun to do so. Kenneth Leibler had negotiated an agreement with the Toronto Stock Exchange in 1985 that created the first two-way electronic trading link between primary equity markets in different countries. The joint venture made it possible to offer investors "the most competitive prices in North America" in six of the most active interlisted Canadian securities.[2] With appropriate ceremonies the linkage took place on September 24. Having achieved a linkage for equities, the Exchange, once again under Leibler's leadership, began to explore international opportunities in Europe to increase its penetration of the options market.

Leibler's specific objective was to achieve a licensing agreement with the European Options Exchange (EOE) (a subsidiary of the Amsterdam Stock Exchange that was the largest listed options marketplace on the continent) to trade options on a European version of the Exchange's Major Market Index (XMI), a version that would be identical to and fungible with the XMI contract.

A joint venture with the EOE would bring greater international recognition to Amex markets—besides providing an additional four and a half hours of hedging opportunities for traders in both time zones. To make this possible, however, a host of difficulties, some technical, others legal, would have to be overcome.

In the first place, it would be necessary to devise a mechanism for enabling option orders to flow from Europe to the Exchange. Fortunately, a joint venture between the Amex and the Institutional Networks Corporation (Instinet) furnished such a mechanism. The agreement with Instinet, a firm that provided a computer facility enabling two institutional customers to meet, led to the development of joint software. This software made it possible for traders to effect through Instinet an automatic execution in the 20 stocks underlying the XMI option. The agreement also made possible an Exchange systems interface with Reuters Limited, to which firm Instinet had sold a controlling interest. Reuters was the largest distributor of financial information in Europe.

By February 1987 the Exchange had made significant progress in negotiating a number of agreements essential to the initiation of trading, and to the development of the electronic interfaces to coordinate that trading. Despite these agreements between the Amex, the EOE and the Options Clearing Corporation (OCC), however, other problems remained. For one thing, Dutch and American laws differed with respect to registration and disclosure requirements. For another, the EOE must comply with the SEC requirement that it develop an acceptable surveillance arrangement. To do so it would have to agree to share specific customer information in response to trading inquiries, and it would have to agree to attest to the accuracy of that information.

These and other issues required patient negotiations, but by the summer of 1987 they had been successfully resolved. (Leibler later reported that "the involvement of 22 political parties, a general election, and the signature of the Queen" were required in order "to complete just one section of our agreement" with the Dutch government!) From the point of view of the SEC, the most important accomplishment was an agreement between the Amex and the EOE to cooperate totally to insure the carrying out of compliance and surveillance inquiries. Following a number of promotional activities, including seminars held in New York and in Europe, the trading of XMI options on the EOE began in August, the OCC serving as common issuer and guarantor. The event marked the first trade agreement between a U.S. options market and a European exchange.[3]

To Exchange officials, the expansion of Amex interests into Canada and Europe represented steps taken in the direction of a strategic objective, that is, that of establishing the Amex as the leading internationally focused marketplace in the United States. The need for such a marketplace, and the opportunity to create it, were abundantly clear. Global economic interdependence had been growing ever since the end of World War II. Liberalization of self-protective laws and arrangements, together with technological innovation, had made it possible to allocate to cross-border investments ever larger proportions of pension funds, mutual funds, and other international assets. In country after country, the proportion of market capitalization held by foreigners was rising. And these foreign-held assets were in general the most likely to be traded. Any exchange facilitating transfers of such assets was bound to become an important player in the world's capital markets. The Amex administration realized this, and early in 1986 it created an International Division, and proceeded to draw up a detailed report to the Board of Governors that laid out some of the reasons for the Exchange's interest in Europe.

Europe represented approximately one-half of the equity market capitalization outside the United States. In addition, virtually every European securities market was undergoing significant change. This presented the Amex with an opportunity to penetrate an emerging market for both equity and options products. And since the Japanese were a growing presence in the European financial community, there might also be an opportunity for the Amex to break into the Far Eastern markets.

There were four specific goals in the Exchange's international plan. The first was to list quality, second-tier European companies that had not enjoyed a high level of international recognition. The second was that of "tapping options volume which originates in Europe and represents a primary means of European investment (especially by Europeans) in American markets." Thirdly, the Exchange should pursue opportunities to develop additional new products "with our European counterparts." Finally, developing relationships and expanding partnerships with key European players in the financial community would enhance the Exchange's strategic position.

Less than six months after officially opening its European office in Amsterdam on October 1, 1986, President Leibler could report significant progress toward the international objectives of the Exchange. For one thing, it seemed clear, after extensive research, and calls on nearly 200 companies throughout the U.K., Scandinavia, France, and Germany, that the U.K. held the greatest short-term potential for new listings.

The success of the Exchange's efforts would depend in large part, however, on SEC acceptance of modifications of foreign listing standards that the Amex had submitted to the Commission for approval. The Exchange was persuaded that listing requirements must take into account the laws and traditional business practices of foreign-based entities, particularly with respect to such matters as shareholder voting rights and independent directors; quorum requirements for shareholder meetings; and the issuance of quarterly earnings statements. The anticipated approval came shortly thereafter.

In the second place, Leibler continued, European institutional investors with significant U.S. holdings had found the Major Market Index an extremely attractive vehicle because of the absence of restrictions on the use of options in European portfolio management. The Exchange, he added, was planning on a joint marketing effort with major British and Dutch banks, and this was expected to increase still more the "incremental options volume" already being generated in both retail and institutional sectors.

Finally, preliminary discussions had been held with the London Stock Exchange (LSE) concerning the possibility of obtaining a nonexclusive license to permit fungible trading of the Financial Times Stock Exchange ("FTSE") 100 Index. The LSE's decision to continue to trade options on its trading floor, the president concluded, might enhance the Amex's ability to reach agreement on an options licensing linkage in the near future.

These activities by no means exhausted the efforts of the Exchange in the international arena. Because many foreign issuers chose not to comply with the registration or reporting requirements of the U.S. securities laws, institutional investors in the United States could acquire the securities of those firms only by complying in each instance with SEC rules governing private placements. The added expense, coupled with the virtual impossibility of effecting resales in the United States, was obviously stunting the growth of a potential market in this country. The securities of these foreign issuers were only traded in foreign markets.

To overcome the inhibiting conditions, the Amex began to evaluate the feasibility of creating a new, special purpose securities exchange eventually called SITUS (System for Institutional Trading of Unregistered

Securities)—through which U.S. institutions could readily purchase and resell the securities of foreign issuers. While a number of conceptual and practical problems remained to be addressed, the SEC appeared receptive to a plan that offered obvious benefits to both foreign firms and U.S. institutions, provided a means for preventing unregistered securities from getting into the hands of unsophisticated individual investors, and augmented the role of the United States and experienced U.S. investors in international markets. (The plan finally won SEC approval in the summer of 1988.)

INTERNAL AFFAIRS

Besides moving along the international sector of its strategic front, the Exchange, under Executive Vice-President Porter P. Morgan of the Marketing Division, also pursued another of its strategic goals. The major challenge facing the Division was that of increasing the Exchange's market share, as measured by the volume of shares traded. The difficulty was this: while Amex volume had more than quadrupled over the last ten years, rising from approximately 648 million in 1976 to 2,979,000,000 shares in 1986, it had not grown at the same rate as that of the NYSE and the NASD. In large measure this was due to a triad of circumstances. In the first place, increased participation of institutions in the securities markets appeared to be exerting a more positive effect on the NYSE than on the Amex. Secondly, one could not ignore the emergence of the NASDAQ market, which by mid-1986 was reporting 4,700 securities through its system. Finally, mergers and acquisitions, transfers to the NYSE, and delistings for cause also contributed to a relative decline in the Amex list.

To turn this situation around the Exchange adopted the following strategy for increasing the number of new listings. It expanded marketing coverage and took steps both to improve existing programs and services and to devise new ones. Among the latter were two significant innovations. The first was that of allowing a newly listed firm to select the specialist unit for its stock from a list of seven such units chosen by the Allocations Committee of the Exchange. The system worked with complete satisfaction to all concerned. The second was that of allowing more diversified upstairs firms to become affiliated with, that is to say, to own, a specialist unit—subject to an approved "Chinese Wall" separation essential to the maintenance of the integrity of the specialist system. (An additional advantage proved to be the bringing of more manpower, capital, and expertise to the trading floor.) The final steps taken by the Exchange to increase listings were the formation of an advisory investment banking committee in an effort to raise the visibility of the Amex in that community, and reaching out even more vigorously to Canada and the European business sector.

Over the past 18 months, Morgan reported in the spring of 1987, the Exchange had made significant progress toward its dual objectives of increasing market share and new listings. Volume on the Amex in 1985 rose at a faster pace than its competitors, reversing a ten-year trend. New listings were up, too. In 1984 a total of 63 companies had listed their common stock issues on the Exchange for the first time. In 1985 the number rose to 74. In the first six months of 1986, Morgan reported, the Amex listed 45 companies. (By the end of the year the number had surged to 103.) Stocks and warrants newly approved for listing showed the same trend, rising from 91 in 1984, to 108 in 1985, then zooming to an all-time high of 157 in 1986. Evidently, something was working—not least the men and women of the Amex.

So too were the Exchange's modern electronic devices. The Amex was determined to pursue vigorously its strategic objective of installing state-of-the-art technology that would make its marketplace second to none. Continually, it mounted pilot programs to increase the automaticity of Exchange operations, for example, AUTOAMOS in July 1985 and AUTO-EX in December of that year. (The latter significantly reduced delays in executing and reporting customer orders for selected Major Market Index (XMI) options contracts, and because of the system's clearance feature eliminated problems with uncompared trades.) In the three years from 1983 to 1986 the Exchange spent more than $40 million on innovative technology, a sum representing about 19 percent of its operating expenses. Among the most cost-effective electronic systems developed as a result of those expenditures were AUTOPER/AUTOAMOS, CMS, QUICKQUOTE, and AUTO-EX.[4] Together these systems gave the Amex a large competitive edge over both the NASD and the CBOE in handling orders up to 1,000 shares, or 10 contracts—an edge, that is to say, in information, order, execution, and trade processing.

In the fall of 1986, however, the CBOE committed $20 million to a three-year program to improve its capabilities in these areas. Mark Smith, vice-president of the Exchange's Planning Division, outlined the shape of the Amex response. The Exchange's strategy would focus on service improvements and on technology as well.

Key service programs, Smith emphasized, were interactive and must be developed together. Four of them—information services, member firm services, trading floor services, and trade processing services—covered the spectrum of market activity. During the next three years Exchange development programs would see to it that the support systems underlying these services were integrated. In addition, tools and techniques would be improved to raise productivity, and a new telecommunications pathway developed. The latter would enhance the ability of member firms to reach the Exchange through electronic means.

In his discussion of technology, Smith stressed how certain value systems might be used to extend the Amex marketplace and offer the benefits of its auction techniques to participants "off the trading floor and around the world." Technological development, he urged, must opt for a flexible architecture readily adaptable to a changing industry environment. At the same time, innovative systems and new approaches would also be necessary. The Exchange would continue as well to stress nontraditional linkages with foreign market centers, and the use of such electronic networks as Instinet, as well. Finally, of course, the Exchange would make sure that any restructuring of its technological resources would lead to increases in productivity. In sum, its "technology strategy" called for an aggressive three-year plan that would make the Amex a leader in automated services within the exchange community. In addition, the strategy provided a flexible support system enabling a rapid response to emerging competitive opportunities. The Amex planned to substantially restructure or replace the three major support systems for market data, order processing, and trade comparison during 1987.

That the Exchange's four-part strategy made an important contribution to the maintenance of its competitive edge can be seen not only by the increases in new listings in 1985 and 1986 that we have already noticed. All other measures point in the same direction. Among the trading records set in 1985—equity volume of 2.1 billion shares (an increase of 36 percent over 1984); options volume of 48.6 million contracts (up 21 percent over 1984); block trades of 29,094 (highest ever).

Amex revenues also reached a record height of $84.5 million, with net income of $5 million up from the previous year's $4.7 million, and the third highest in history. (See Statistical Appendix.)

Spectacular as were these results, they pale before those of 1986. In 1986, said Chairman Levitt, "the American Stock Exchange enjoyed the best year in its history." Nearly every statistical index registered an all-time record, whether in equities, options, revenues or net income. (See Statistical Appendix.) The latter nearly doubled, rising from $5 million to almost $9.5 million. The Amex share of the index options market went up to 13.20 percent (from 11.30 percent in 1985), and its share in equity options to 33.21 (from 30.45 the previous year). Competitively successful, all programs on go, and financially strong, the Amex entered the year of the "Great Plunge" full of confidence—both in itself, and in its vigorous and able young president, Kenneth Leibler.

N O T E S

1. Unhappily, by the time approval was secured, interest in gold had waned, and the new product was put on the back burner. In 1989 it was still dormant.

2. The six were Dome Petroleum, Ltd.; Golf Canada, Ltd.; Echo Bay Mines, Ltd.; Asamera, Inc.; Imperial Oil, Ltd.; and Husky Oil, Ltd. In the main, (except for Husky Oil, which left the list in 1987), all 54 recorded sharply increasing volumes between 1985 and 1989. In the four years between these dates shares in Dome Petroleum, Ltd., e.g., were traded in the following quantities (in millions): 56.3, 30.5, 70.9, and 125.8.

3. The very next month after the opening of trading the great Market Crash of September 1987 occurred. As of 1989 the trading of XMI on the EOE had not recovered.

4. The functions of these systems are briefly explained on pp. 143, below.

CHAPTER 6

THE GREAT PLUNGE
AND ITS AFTERMATH

It is altogether likely that the Great Plunge of October 1987 will take its place among the memorable panics and crashes of stock market history. In some respects it was unique. "What made this market break extraordinary," concluded the investigatory Task Force appointed by the President in the aftermath of the plunge ("The Brady Report") "was the speed with which prices fell, the unprecedented volume of trading, and the consequent threat to the financial system." Between Wednesday, October 14, and Tuesday, October 20, U.S. equity markets underwent "the most severe one-week decline in history." In that interim, the Dow fell from a little over 2,500 to just above 1,700, a decline of almost one-third. The loss in the value of all outstanding U.S. stocks amounted to approximately $1.0 trillion—a million dollars multiplied a million times.

The Brady Report explains how that happened. Two events triggered the sell-off. The first was the government's announcement that the merchandise trade deficit for August was $15.7 billion, about $1.5 billion higher than the figure expected by the financial markets. Heavy selling of dollars in the foreign exchange markets, then of Treasury bonds, ensued almost immediately—the former because traders believed that the dollar would have to fall further before the deficit could narrow, the latter, because traders feared that a weakening dollar "could both discourage international investment in U.S. securities and stimulate domestic inflation."

The second triggering event was an announcement that members of the House Ways and Means Committee "were filing legislation to eliminate tax benefits associated with the financing of corporate takeovers." Takeover shares had led the long bull market from 1982 to 1987, and as risk arbitrageurs unloaded those shares in the wake of the announcement, they led the market back down again.

The triggers "ignited mechanical, price-insensitive selling by a number of institutions following portfolio insurance strategies," with additional selling by a small number of mutual fund groups.

> The selling by these investors, and the prospect of further selling by them, encouraged a number of aggressive trading-oriented institutions to sell in anticipation of further declines. These aggressive trading-oriented institutions included, in addition to hedge funds, a small number of pension and endowment funds, money management firms and investment banking houses. This selling in turn stimulated further reactive selling by portfolio insurers and mutual funds. Selling pressure in the futures market was transmitted to the stock market by the mechanism of index arbitrage. Not surprisingly, trading volume and price volatility "increased dramatically" throughout the period.

The situation on the over-the-counter market appears to have been particularly difficult for investors. Unlike shares on the NYSE or the Amex, each NASDAQ stock is handled by a number of market makers, "none of which has either an express or implied commitment to maintain an orderly market." In consequence, some OTC market makers formally withdrew from making markets during the week of October 19. Others did the same thing "merely by not answering their telephones during this period." Still others, however, were willing to trade but were unreachable because they were overwhelmed by the volume of telephone calls and orders.

Perhaps the most damaging critique of performance on the NASD concerns the failure of "many" broker/dealers to utilize the automated equipment available to them. One system, SOES (Small Order Execution System), automatically executes all sell orders against the highest bid, and all buy orders against the lowest offer, in the system. SOES is available to all market makers, and prior to October 19, "46 of the top 50 market makers were active participants in at least some securities." But during the week of October 19 "many of them dropped out of SOES entirely." "Despite the high degree of automation in the over-the-counter market," the Report concludes, "the problems encountered in it during the market break appear to have been far more pronounced than the problems encountered on the exchange markets." In sharp contrast stands the technological performance of the Amex during the market break. Let us recall that the Exchange's Post Execution Reporting system ("PER") and Amex Options Switching ("AMOS") system provide member firms with the means to electroncially transmit equity and options orders directly to the post where the issue is traded for executing and reporting by a specialist. Both systems were subject to volume limits. The most recent increase in those limits before the Crash had taken place in 1983, when the Board approved raising PER and AMOS eligibility levels to 1,000 shares and 10 contracts, respectively. It is true that, in recognition of increases in average order sizes, the Board had approved raising these levels once again in February 1987 to 2,000 shares and 20 contracts, and that the SEC had approved the Amex's proposal to do so in July 1987, but the Exchange had not implemented these increased trading parameters before the Crash.

It *had*, however, instituted AUTOPER. Unlike PER, AUTOPER— as the acronym suggests—automatically executes trades when an order arrives at the post. A splendid refinement, AUTOPER enables specialists to enter execution data into PER by using touch screen terminals rather than executing by manual reporting on mark sense cards. And this was not the only enhancement put in place in time for the supreme test of the market break. Back in February 1987 the administration reported the successful installation of a new Market Data System (MDS) that reports quotes on screens above the trading floor. "Along with a new Electronic Gateway," the Report continued, "it is the first delivery of the new Amex technology program."

The strategic plan had its first payoff in October 1987. By an extraordinary coincidence, the Exchange, after months of testing, added another important refinement to its computerized trading floor systems on October 16, just three days before the Crash. "The enhancement," Chairman Levitt explained, "increased the fault tolerance of the Exchange's microcomputers." MDS processing of equity orders was separated from option orders, and this split of the traffic into separate paths allowed the system to update quotes and move greater masses of data far more rapidly. The plan was to throw the switch on Monday morning, October 19, to see how the new system performed under actual market conditions.

Systems analysts had no idea that on that day volume would triple on the Amex and subject the new technology to its most severe test in modern market history—with no chance for fine tuning. In the face of trading, which grew more hectic by the hour, the system, Levitt reported, "worked flawlessly." The SEC's independent investigation of the market break comes remarkably close to agreement with that evaluation. Despite the fact that PER averaged about 25,000 trades on October 19 and 20, in contrast with its normal delivery of orders and execution reports for 10,000 a day, the system "experienced relatively few problems."

On the front end, the SEC report continued, orders entered the PER system from the participating member firms "with no reported problems." Once in the system there was no queing of orders, with one exception. "On October 19, at 3:49 P.M., the PER system was shut down for the remainder of the trading day while the computer disk was changed."

Volume-related problems, however, "may have caused delays in turnaround time, i.e., the time from which the order is entered into PER to the time when the order is executed." The delays, the SEC investigation concluded, arose at the point of execution with AUTOPER, when some specialists temporarily eliminated the use of AUTOPER touch screens. They did so because the capacity of the screen is limited to the display of up to six orders entered through PER at a time.

When the screen is full because orders are entering the system faster than they can be executed, orders begin printing out on paper tickets in the order they are received by the PER system. After an order is executed on the screen, the next order not already printed in hard copy is displayed on the screen. Thus, the specialist must rely not only on the screen but on the paper tickets to ensure that orders are executed in proper priority and sequence.

The SEC conceded that the resort to the printing of orders "alleviated potential errors," and acknowledged that it did not know how many specialists had switched off AUTOPER during the week of October 19. The Amex knew, however; its records indicated that AUTOPER was not shut off on a broad basis at all. Indeed, "less than one percent of Amex listed securities were removed" during the period of the market break. Furthermore, in only one instance did an individual specialist remove a large number of securities from AUTOPER, and that occurred on October 21. As for delays, it was true that the speed of the PER system was affected by the volume surge. Yet over 80 percent of PER round-lot market orders entered after the opening during the Crash were reported back to the entering firm within three minutes, 99 percent within 15 minutes (the same as in September 1987).

In those cases in which AUTOPER was not used, it was the result of an operational decision by the specialist.

> Some specialists became concerned that proper sequencing could not be maintained when the display screen filled and additional incoming orders began printing automatically, a feature which avoids lengthy queueing. Similarly, during active market periods, more traffic arrives at the post through the crowd, and the number of limit orders previously entered on the specialist's book which become marketable increases dramatically. In such cases, some specialists shut off AUTOPER to ensure the same level of protection for PER orders as for other customer orders on the book and in the crowd.
>
> Efforts to address each of these conditions had commenced even before the market break. They included repositioning the terminals of some specialists to make them more visible, and redesigning the AUTOPER screen. Compared to the major changes planned by the NASD to upgrade the performance of its market makers, these improvements were cosmetic in nature. As the SEC acknowledged, the Amex "believes that PER generally worked well during the weeks of October 19 and 26."

Disagreement between the SEC and the Amex over the quality of specialist performance was more severe. The SEC report describes in the following terms the "extreme volume and volatility" to which the Amex market and its specialists were subjected during the October 16 to 23 period. On Friday, October 16, the Amex experienced a record-breaking day, with 18.4 million shares changing hands in 15,097 trades. The Amex Market Value Index declined by 12.25 points, or 3.7 percent, in comparison with a drop of 4.6 percent on the Dow. Volume on Monday, October 19, nearly doubled, to 35.4 million shares traded in 28,838 transactions, nearly triple the activity on an average day in September 1987. Tuesday, October 20, brought the third straight record-breaking day, with 43.4 million shares traded in 31,010 transactions. The remainder of the week of October 19 and Monday, October 26, saw continued high volume and heavy selling, pushing prices further downward.

Shaking his head, one Amex floor veteran said, "I never saw anything like it." Throughout the crisis, Chairman Levitt and President Leibler, the former reminisced, "spent long hours appraising the situation with floor governors, making quick decisions where needed and throwing the support of the institution behind the specialists and other trading members." With more and more of corporate America being offered for sale with each passing hour, and with few buyers at any price, the specialists intervened —increasing their participation in trades "some sixfold." By risking their own capital, and, in some cases "taking enormous losses, they kept the market open and accessible to the public, giving calmness an opportunity to reassert itself. The specialists," Levitt concluded, "proved to be the unsung heroes of the market break."

The SEC didn't see it that way. Its analysis of specialist performance on the Amex "indicated a general decline of performance on both October 19 and 20." While the majority of the specialists examined entered the market "long" on October 19, it alleged, they were not substantially so. The obligation of specialists to maintain continuity and depth in market activity, and fair and orderly prices, was met unevenly. While some increased their long positions on October 19, others did not. Indeed, in the afternooon of October 19, with prices tumbling, they were more likely to be sellers than buyers. And on October 20 specialist performance was even poorer, with price spreads between sales "considerably wider" than on the previous day. At best, the performance was a mixed one. "Although some specialists appeared to perform well under adverse conditions, others did not." Added to the SEC indictment was the charge that the Amex, like the NYSE, "experienced severe liquidity problems during the week of October 19 that resulted in numerous delayed openings, trading halts, and failures to open stocks."

Respectfully, but forcibly, the Amex pronounced its disagreement with this analysis. The devastating fact was that the SEC had based its evaluation on an examination of only 9 of the 843 common stocks and warrants listed on the Amex. The "limited sample," President Leibler pointed out, cast into question many of the SEC's conclusions and implications regarding specialist performance on the Amex during the market break. The Exchange, in contrast, did not limit its own investigation to any sampling at all. Instead, it examined trading in *every security* for the period of the market break." It's conclusion? There were indeed "individual situations where performance was substandard," and should have been better. The Exchange expected that either disciplinary action or reallocation would result in these cases. But the "aggregate data," Leibler said, "We believe . . . tells a positive story: the Amex market as a whole performed well."

The Exchange had begun its analysis of the October break by reviewing Automated Continuity and Depth Exception Reports, and Daily Transaction Journals for *all* issues to determine if performance had met the standards expected of specialists with respect to reasonable levels of continuity, depth, and participation. (However difficult it was to measure such standards during days of unprecedented market conditions.) The following schedule shows its finding regarding the specialist participation rate (expressed as a percentage of total volume):

DATE	PURCHASES	SALES
10/16	19.44	14.3
10/19	24.5	17.9
10/20	23.8	21.2
10/21	16.4	25.0
10/22	17.5	18.1
10/23	17.3	15.7
10/26	17.7	13.7

The figures clearly indicated that on October 19 and 20, the most volatile days, the average of all specialist purchases on the Exchange was 24.5 percent and 23.8 percent of total volume. When viewed in comparison to an average of only 12.7 percent for the entire preceding month, those figures demonstrated beyond cavil that, "from the perspective of the amount of specialist proprietary buying or selling, specialists fulfilled their affirmative obligations in the absence of public orders." Then, when the public interest reversed on October 21 and specialists were required to supply stock, they sold 25.0 percent of total volume, often at a substantial loss from inventoried positions.

As for the widening of point spreads, admittedly the average for all stocks during October—nearly 3/8 points—exceeded the 1/4-point average in September. But 91.2 percent of all transactions on the Amex occurred at variations of 1/4 point or less, further evidence of specialist effort to minimize trade-to-trade disparities.

Taking up next the SEC allegation of trading halts, delayed openings, and gap openings that occurred during the market break, Leibler promised a full review in accordance with existing surveillance procedures. Even before this was undertaken, however, it was worth reminding that trading halts and gap openings ought not necessarily to be construed as a weakness on the part of a specialist or his unit. Rather, they could be mechanisms permitting the "dissemination to the investing community of significant imbalances between supply and demand. The indication process which accompanies a halt or opening at a gap price allows investors an opportunity to re-evaluate their investment decisions, and permits the specialist to determine a 'fair price' based on orders in the marketplace prior to the resumption of trading."

The Amex review thus far, Leibler continued, indicated that some stocks remained closed simply because specialists had opened their most active issues first, to the benefit of the public. In some instances, corporate news developments added to the length of halts to allow for dissemination of the news. In others, delays or halts were not explainable in terms of market conditions or by the following of required procedures. Leibler promised that these instances would be followed up. For the majority of delayed openings and halts in trading, however, "the Exchange has identified no violations with respect to Amex rules or performance standards relating to specialist performance. For the most part, these stoppages were based on and supported by market conditions."

Turning to the trading in options, Leibler presented evidence comparable to that for equities to show that specialist participation "reached its highest level" in October, when options volume peaked. The following chart reveals that participation as a percentage of total trading volume (TTV):

MONTH	SPECIALIST PARTICIPATION (TVV)	TOTAL OPTION VOLUME (CONTRACTS, IN MILLIONS)
Jan. 88	25.4%	3.7
Dec. 87	23.9	3.6
Nov. 87	26.6	3.2
Oct. 87	26.5	7.6
Sept. 87	24.3	6.6
Aug. 87	24.1	7.2
July 87	24.2	6.2

Leibler acknowledged, however, that the Exchange's review of the performance of specialists and of Registered Options Trades (ROTs) in trading the Amex's Major Market Index (XMI) left a great deal to be desired. After conducting a trade-by-trade analysis of activity on October 20, and compiling and examining customer complaints, the Exchange's Performance Committee "had serious questions with respect to the specialist unit's fulfillment of its responsibility to maintain fair and orderly markets. The Committee unanimously determined that certain put transactions were unsatisfactorily priced." It proceeded to "severely admonish" the specialist unit involved for its "substandard performance," and to warn it that any recurrence would compel the Committee to consider reallocation. The unit was instructed to develop a plan to ensure adequate performance in the future.

In sum, as Chairman Levitt acknowleged, the Amex performance during the great market break of October 1987 was "not perfect." Additional examples include a major limitation—since corrected —of MDS, that is, the inability of both vendors and exchange systems to display three-digit options premium prices—premiums unimagined before October 19. After the Crash the Exchange also accepted the need for an increase in margin requirements for index options, and made them effective on November 2, 1987. Finally, on all markets, the Crash produced an abnormally high proportion of uncompared trades (known as DKs), transactions for which the buyer's and seller's reports of price, size, or other important information do not match. In relation to volume patterns, however, the exchanges performed much better than the OTC market in this respect. On the Amex, the DK rate never exceeded 5.5 percent; on NASDAQ, where the proportional volume surge was much less, the DK rate went as high as 10.5 percent.

Given the unprecedented pressures generated by the deluge, no market could have responded in ways that left no room for criticism and improvement. On the whole, however, and certainly in any relative sense, the Amex market had performed well, and its executives were justifiably proud not only of the way it had conducted itself but also of the strategic planning that had prepared it to do so.

Despite the great break in the stock markets, 1987 was the second best year in the history of the American Stock Exchange. Each of the following indices reached an all-time high: reported share volume, daily average share volume, total options and daily average contract volume, equity options contract volume, total shares and aggregate market volume of shares outstanding, and members equity. Revenues went to record levels, too, but so did expenses, so that net income declined by about $1 million from that of 1986. (See Statistical Appendix.)

Perhaps the most interesting facet of that fateful year was not that far more equity issues (stocks and warrants) were newly approved for listing than in the previous year (249 vs. 157), nor even that more companies listed a common stock issue on the Exchange for the first time in 1987 than in 1986 (152 vs. 103). More interesting still is the rise in new listings that came *after* the Plunge, and the main source of the rise. That source was the OTC, and companies transferred from that marketplace to the Amex because the performance of specialists on an auctions market, while not perfect during the long hours of the market break, was plainly superior to that of the broker/dealers functioning as multiple competing market makers on the OTC. However, it is fair to say that no system in place on any market could have withstood the avalanche of sell orders that fell with such fury on OTC and the exchanges in October.

THE MORNING AFTER

In the aftermath of the Great Plunge the Amex found itself— once again in the words of its irrepressible chairman—with some "formidable challenges" and "some solid reasons for optimism." From the perspective of early 1988, perhaps the principal challenge would be that of adjusting to whatever changes in the market environment might result from initiatives proposed by the various reports on the October Plunge, that is, those made by the Brady Commission, the SEC, GAO, and various congressional committees. Some critics recommended restrictions on portfolio insurance (a device designed to protect assets against market declines by selling stock-index futures as stocks fall—a technique blamed by the investment world for worsening the Crash); others blamed index arbitrage and program trading. Many supported the Brady study's recommendation that "circuit breakers" or "collars" be called into play in the event of very large drops in market values. Finally, there were a number of calls for regulation of the interlinked stock, futures, and options markets by a single regulatory body. Despite the ferment, the changes made in the late 1980s were limited and their efficacy not yet clear. There are certainly better communications between the markets, and joint clearing arrangements between options and futures markets. And both the NYSE and the Amex, in collaboration with the Chicago futures markets, have approved the imposition of trading halts in the event of extraordinary declines.

Finally, major firms on Wall Street have responded to investor perception that stock index arbitrage trading detracts from market stability by announcing that they have temporarily ceased that kind of trading.

Beyond these finger-in-the-dike gestures there remained great uncertainty at the end of 1988 on what, if anything, to do. In an address in November of that year, President Leibler pointed out some of the reasons that it was still not clear what *should* be done.

The October crash was a worldwide phenomenon. Yet some of these countries traded futures, others didn't. Some had computer trading, others didn't. Some closed their markets, others kept them open.

Bright people have honest differences when it comes to making sense of this complexity. Former Treasury Secretary Don Regan says Congress should ban stock index arbitrage. George Gould, the Undersecretary of the Treasury, says it shouldn't.

Nicholas Brady weighs the prospect of another crash and says we're looking down the barrel of a loaded gun. Yet Alan Greenspan says October has already gotten rid of most speculative excesses.

The President's new Working Group on Financial Markets goes before the Senate Banking Committee and the House Finance Committee and gets raked over the coals. Then it goes before the Agriculture Committee, which has oversight over futures trading, and gets praised.

The equity markets have their approach. The futures markets press their own agenda. Meanwhile, the various regulatory bodies and congressional oversight committees follow the laws of physics and present viewpoints that are equal but opposite.

For its part, the Amex proposed to continue along the entrepreneurial path that had served it so well in the past. It had established itself in the forefront of American exchanges offering programs, investment vehicles, and services to the international community. There was not only the Amsterdam connection, but a full-time office in London, and brokerage clubs in Britain, Switzerland, France, and the Far East. Before the end of 1988 it had opened a market for unregistered foreign securities, and filed with the SEC a proposal for an exciting new product, an international index (see below). The push for global markets had slowed somewhat since the Crash, but it had not been derailed. As President Leibler remarked at the end of 1988, the international strategy of the Exchange would continue to be what it had been from the beginning—one that was based "on a sustainable long-term commitment" involving "alliances with major institutions and other business sectors overseas."

The Amex had also won wide recognition of its technological leadership, and it had no intention of diminishing the enhancement of its systems. A long-planned expansion that added 6,500 square feet to its trading floor became fully operational in February 1988. The addition was equipped entirely with touch-screen terminals, a paperless system that had proved so successful in handling heavy volume that the Exchange proceeded to retrofit its other 20 trading posts with similar terminals.

Long an innovative force in making new products available to the investment community, the Exchange reaffirmed its commitment to that role in the year after the Crash. At the end of 1988 it was awaiting SEC approval of two major domestic and international products. One of the domestic vehicles was inspired by market studies made after the trading turmoil of October 1987. It was a new type of equity index product, based on a basket of heavily traded stocks. Investors purchasing Equity Index Participations (EIPs) would participate in the overall movement of all the stocks in the S&P 500. The second domestic vehicle, a different version of the first, would be based on the Amex's Major Market Index, which closely tracks the Dow Jones Industrial Average.

President Leibler explained that the new products would give an investor "the opportunity to buy or sell the market." Both offered "the benefits of owning stock, including the right to receive a proportionate share of dividends." Unlike options or futures, they could be held indefinitely, since there was no expiration date. Settlement was to be in cash, with no physical delivery of underlying securities. "Holders would be able, quarterly, to realize the market value of their holdings by exercising a 'cash out' privilege."

Of the two new international index products proposed, one (options) would be traded on the Amex, the other (futures contracts) on the Coffee, Sugar and Cocoa Exchange. The two institutions had developed the product jointly. Called the International Market Index, it measures the performance of 50 leading foreign stocks actively traded in the U.S. on either the Amex, the New York Stock Exchange, or the OTC market. The companies represented are from Europe, Australia, and the Far East, including Japan. They include such well-known names as Royal Dutch Petroleum, Jaguar, Toyota, and Sony. Leibler said that the new international products "will provide investors with opportunity and flexibility in global investment strategies." He expressed the view that the International Market Index "might become the investors' choice as the benchmark for international portfolios."

Not least, the Exchange continued at home its broad program of services to brokerage clubs, member firms and listed companies, and its sponsorship of seminars and conferences. While volume was down since the Crash, and the individual investor still hesitant at the end of 1988 to reenter the market, the Exchange pushed its marketing programs under Executive Vice-President Porter Morgan and Senior Vice-Presidents Robert Smith and Lee Cutrone.

It also adopted an imaginative new advertising program. "Extend Your Reach" was the brainchild of Ivers W. Riley, whom the Exchange had succeeded in enticing to the Amex in 1986 from a senior vice-presidency on the New York Stock Exchange. Trained in finance at UCLA and in Advanced Management at the Harvard Business School, Riley had gained extensive experience in the options and derivative securities field at the Chicago Board Options Exchange, before moving first to Paine, Webber, then to a founding partnership in an investment advisory and consulting firm specializing in options and futures, and from there to the NYSE. Not surprisingly in view of this rich background, he joined the Amex as senior executive vice-president and was given responsibility for the four key areas of marketing—new product development, strategic planning and corporate communications, as well as the management of the Exchange's international efforts. (It was Riley who developed the plan for the new international index.) Under his leadership and in response as well to the marketing initiatives of Messrs. Morgan, Smith, and Cutrone, new listings continued to mount after the Crash (reaching 111 before December 6, 1988, the second-highest number in modern history).

Perhaps it is even more accurate to say *because* of the Crash — because of the way the Exchange's advanced strategic planning had enabled it to handle the unprecedented demands of that extraordinary situation. Because, that is to say, of the impression made by the Amex on the financial community. Despite, therefore, the sobering impact of that experience on markets around the world; despite the clear recognition on the part of the Exchange leadership that a forceful rebounding of investment energy is dependent upon such complexly interrelated factors as the reinvigoration of American manufacturing competitiveness, the rewriting of tax legislation to correct the present bias favoring debt over equities, and sufficient reduction in the budget and trade deficits to enable the Federal Reserve to lower interest rates from the high levels necessary to attract the foreign investment that finances the federal debt, that leadership, tested in the flames of October 1987, remains calmly confident that the Amex is securely positioned for the demands and opportunities of the future. Chairman Levitt's remark that "there were indeed solid reasons for optimism" soon appeared to be justified. During 1988 the Amex Market Value Index gained 17.5 percent, finishing ahead of the NASDAQ Composite, NYSE Composite, Dow Jones Industrial Average, S&P 500, Wilshire 5000, and Value Line indices. And at the end of that year it counted 114 new listings, the second-highest number in 16 years, no fewer than 66 from the OTC market.

THE LEVITT LEGACY

Satisfying as were those results, the Exchange had more durable grounds for confidence in its future. During the Levitt years it had emerged not only as the leading spokesman for mid-range growth companies. It had also established itself as a public presence on the American landscape. As an exchange it was very much smaller than the NYSE or the OTC. But it was not merely an exchange. Unlike its rivals, the Amex actively sought a national role in public affairs. It did so by taking upon itself the task of addressing a host of issues vital to business and to the economy. In doing so it added so considerably to its stature that everyone thought it was bigger than it really was. In very important ways it was. And is.

This did not come about by accident but by design. From the beginning Levitt was determined to elevate the stature of the Exchange. To that end he joined Robert Mosbacher, (who was to become Secretary of Commerce in the Bush administration) in co-founding the American Business Conference (ABC) in July 1980. The ABC is a Washington-based coalition of 100 high growth companies that are listed in approximately equal numbers on the Amex, NYSE, and OTC and held in private hands. To qualify for membership, ABC companies must demonstrate an annual growth rate at least three times that of the economy, plus inflation. The focal emphasis on growth was bound to brighten the public image of the Amex, whose constituency is dominated by mid-range growth companies.

Levitt's reasoning in urging the formation of the ABC was straightforward. Large firms were organized in their trade associations, in the chamber of commerce, the National Association of Manufacturers, and other groups to lobby in defense of their interests. Despite their critical economic importance, mid-range companies lacked voice. They needed comparable organization to work for such objectives as reduced tax rates, which were higher for smaller and often more successful firms than for large ones, or for reduction or repeal of taxes on capital gains to spur investment. In a few short years the American Business Conference became one of the most influential business groups in Washington.

The Amex itself expanded its role in the nation's broader affairs under the guidance of Sarah Boehmler, and sponsored major two-and-a half day conferences in Washington, D.C., initially in the State Department's Loy Henderson Conference Room and later, after the conferees had become too numerous for that facility, in the Mayflower Hotel—to hear and discuss addresses by some of the country's political, academic, and business leaders. In 1988, for example, speakers included Senators Bill Bradley of New Jersey, Lawton Chiles of Florida, and Terry Sanford of North Carolina. The Reagan administration was represented by Secretary of Defense Frank C. Carlucci, by Lieutenant General Colin L. Powell, then the Assistant to the President for National Security Affairs, by Secretary of Commerce C. William Verity, by Deputy Secretary of State John W. Whitehead, by Chairman of the Council of Economic Advisers Beryl W. Sprinkel, and by Ken Duberstein, Chief of Staff to President Reagan.

Distinguished professors included historian Paul Kennedy of Yale, author of the widely discussed bestseller *The Rise and Fall of the Great Powers*, and two eminent professors of economics, Martin Feldstein of Harvard and Paul A. Volcker of Princeton— the latter two no less distinguished as former public servants (Feldstein as chairman of the Council of Economic Advisers and Volcker as chairman of the Board of Governors of the Federal Reserve System). Prominent editors, writers, and lecturers included Lou Cannon, Gerald Gardner, Michael Kinsley, Ann F. Lewis, Kevin P. Phillips, and Robert S. Strauss. Imported from the U.K. to serve as moderator was David Frost, a man whose résumé in TV, film, and publishing is so varied that he has been dubbed a "one-man conglomerate." (In previous years the ABC turned to local talent for the moderating task, to Barbara Walters, Jim Lehrer, or Leslie Stahl.)

No less impressive among the participants in the 1988 Conference were representatives of more than 300 international firms. They came from almost every country in Europe, from England, West Germany, Scotland, France, Switzerland, Italy, Norway, Sweden, Denmark, Belgium, Liechtenstein, the Netherlands, and Luxembourg; from Australia,

Japan, Hong Kong, and Singapore in the Far East; from Saudi Arabia, Kuwait, and Bahrain in the Middle East, and, closer to home, from the Bahamas, Bermuda, and Canada. In addition, participants from New York represented foreign firms all over the globe. The CEOs of Amex Listed Companies who participated were pleased by the presence of so many international investors in control of pension funds and other assets.

Among the speakers in 1988 was an Amex executive to whom Chairman Levitt had assigned the task of coordinating the conferences. Gordon Stewart had joined the staff of the Exchange in 1982 as the successor to John Sheehan. Given a vice-presidency and put in charge of Public Affairs, Stewart was to help implement the chairman's policy initiatives on a number of fronts. One concerned listings.

In order to attract listings, ceaseless pressure on newspaper editors not to drop the Amex stock tables was necessary. Success in courting listing prospects depended to a considerable degree on the CEO's ability to find his company's stock prices in his local paper. With space availability eroding at an alarming rate in the early 1980s, Bob Shabazian of Press Relations was given a full-time "war room" to develop and implement detailed plans to preserve the Amex tables in the nation's press. For two years Shabazian made personal calls on tough, hard-bitten newspaper editors all over the country to make sure that the Amex stock tables stayed in. In the main, they did.

No less successful were the efforts made by Stewart and others to bring TV to the Amex. The project was a favorite of Arthur Levitt. But the problems were formidable, and not least among them was opposition to the idea on the part of some floor members. From their point of view, TV would bring undesirable publicity to the traditionally private trading world. Another obstacle was physical—to make the kind of telecasts desired it would be necessary to "hard wire" the building at 86 Trinity Place, a fairly big budget item.

Lacking a fiber optic cable, the exchange put a satellite dish on the roof to take its place. But New York is a windy city, and that is especially true for the Amex, which is located near the water. Sometimes, the dish would blow over and it would be necessary for someone to run up to the roof in the middle of a shot to reposition it. And, if the weather were cold, someone would have to chip the ice off the dish with a hammer to make the picture clearer.

That "someone" was almost always Keith Silverman, who came to the Amex in 1985 to manage the Exchange's TV operation—as producer, cameraman, writer, and editor. Jerry-rigged though the early system necessarily was because of the lack of a video loop, the experiment converted the floor traders from doubting Thomases to hams as soon as the TV lights went on. Activity on the floor was no longer something discussed in a studio interview. It was brought directly to the viewer. And therein a major conceptual change was wrought—from an older idea that the floor was a private, closed arena to one in which its daily activity was seen to be of public interest.

Today, a main purpose of TV at the Amex is to put its own people on the air. It has been a means by which Chairman Levitt and President Leibler have communicated their views concerning important financial and other developments to the public, the former on "Good Morning America," for example, the latter on "Nightline." Both have appeared on many other national shows, including Dan Rather's nightly newscast. Among other prominent people who have been interviewed are two who do not require to be introduced to the reader, Malcolm Forbes and Walter Wriston. Louis Rukeyser broadcast the fifteenth anniversary program of "Wall Street Week" from the Amex trading floor.

The first "big break" for Amex TV was a decision by Ted Turner's Cable News Network (CNN) to plug into the Exchange's new video loop, and since 1984 CNN has been sending camera crews to the Exchange. FNN then entered into a similar arrangement with the Amex, and this was followed by one with the "Nightly Business Report," seen in New York on Channel 13. The Amex provided an office for the latter in an adjacent building at 74 Trinity Place and then split its video loop to run from that office to the trading floor. The arrangement, which brings the Exchange about $10,000 a year, enables the program to use the loop to broadcast, to get all the information from New York to Miami, where the nightly show is based.

The Amex has been able to expand its TV facility enormously through the use of a remote-controlled "robot camera" on the trading floor. There is no longer a need to tell a station to bring its own camera crew to the building for a telecast— just a reporter or guest. Two of the largest television networks in Japan, Tokyo Broadcasting and Fuji, send a reporter every day to the Amex floor for a five-minute telecast to Japan. The format for the hugely popular show calls for the reporter to provide an update on what's going on—to "give the numbers"—and then to interview someone from Wall Street, who is almost always Japanese or Chinese. The two networks broadcast at 5 P.M. (which is early in the morning in Japan) for about six months, then reverse the timing the rest of the year, reaching Japan at night.

The most exciting development in TV Amex in 1989 was the decision by Consumer News and Business Channel (NBC's cable outlet) to challenge Ted Turner's network by broadcasting twice an hour every hour from the floor of the Exchange. To facilitate the arrangement, sealed by a five-year contract, the Amex spent $100,000 to build a broadcast booth on the floor, "camera, lights, mikes, a set and everything else." CNBC planned to send over a reporter to interview people from the Wall Street area on the Amex floor.

As the Exchange prepared to enter the final decade of the century TV Amex was in good health.

So too was Radio Amex. "Doing more in radio" was another of Arthur Levitt's priority projects entrusted to Gordon Stewart for implementation. On Stewart's recommendation a second capable young man in his twenties was hired. Tom Mariam joined the Amex in June 1984.

Radio Amex Stock Reports to major urban markets were continued as necessary links to the past of John Sheehan, but Levitt and Stewart wanted to broaden the reach of this as well as all other Exchange facilities and services. In addition to the stock reports, Mariam developed a 20- to 30-second commentary for a New York station, and a three minute interview every Wednesday with a Los Angeles TV station. FNN radio began broadcasting live from the Amex trading floor in 1988. In January 1989 Larry Kofsky began to broadcast business news reports for FNN 16 times a day from a booth on top of the South Balcony. All 16 reports, each of them featuring Amex-related data provided every half hour by Amex's Corporate Communications department, are broadcast locally on WINS, the most listened to station in the city, particularly in the morning (which is when businessmen listen). Five minutes after the WINS broadcast, FNN does a broadcast for station KYW in Philadelphia and then ten minutes later one for KFWB in Los Angeles.

Undoubtedly, Radio Amex's finest innovation was the development of a weekly 15-minute radio show, "Amex Business Talk." Mariam first did a pilot talk show with Monty Gordon, the stock market analyst at Dreyfus Corporation, as his guest. Anxious to build the Amex presence in California, Mariam sent the pilot to a Los Angeles "super station," KJOI, which accepted it in May 1985.

After six months a second station, in Montgomery, Alabama, was added to the one in Los Angeles. Thereafter, additions came nearly once a month, and by the end of 1986 the program was being carried by about a dozen stations. From then on the popularity of the show "grew like Topsy," and by early 1989 "Amex Business Talk" was being aired over 100 stations. (Only one governing principle delimits the range of eligible subjects for discussion on "Amex Business Talk": it must have to do with money—a leeway that is considerable indeed.)

Following his early success in helping to stretch the reach of Amex TV and radio, Stewart accepted the chairman's mandate to develop the Exchange's positions in the areas of trade, defense, the federal budget, international finance, and problems of American competitiveness. A former speechwriter for President Jimmy Carter who wrote or co-authored most of Carter's major addresses during the latter half of the administration, Stewart was well equipped to do so. In addition, the Amex possessed a decided advantage over the NYSE enabling it to speak out on such subjects as ethics in government, reform of defense procurement procedures, fiscal policy, and international relations. The advantage derives from the relative homogeneity of the Amex's mid-range constituency of companies. Powerful conflicting interests represented in the NYSE list lessen the ability of that exchange to take any kind of public position on national issues, and it rarely does.

But more than this is required if the large public presence of the American Stock Exchange is to be explained. To a considerable degree, credit for the achievement is owing to one man in particular, namely, to Arthur Levitt. As we have seen, Levitt was determined from the beginning of his chairmanship in 1978 to enhance the image of the Exchange, and he had both the personality and interests necessary for that task. He participated with verve in numerous seminars, task forces, and other major meetings and rarely declined an invitation to appear on TV or speak on radio.

In his very first year as chairman, his growing reputation as a national spokesman for the interests of smaller businesses and for their entrepreneurial role in innovation and economic growth induced President Carter to name him chairman of the White House Conference on Small Business. The assignment was to take him to meetings with business leaders throughout the country and to lead to increased listings on the Exchange that had long been the historic home of such companies. It seemed quite natural that the Senate Select Committee on Small Business should have decided that same year to hold its hearings at the American Stock Exchange. Similarly, Levitt gladly accepted an invitation extended by National Security Advisor Frank Carlucci, a former Board member (who was to become Secretary of Defense late in the Reagan administration) to join a special task force of the Defense Science Board. The task force looked to Levitt to define the importance of growth companies in the industrial base of the nation, especially in relation to national defense. It was one instance among many in which the ability of the Amex to attract to its Board of Governors persons of national stature redounded to the interests of the Exchange and the wider causes for which it stood. Other prominent political leaders were no less supportive. Mayors Tom Bradley of Los Angeles and Ed Koch of New York gladly consented to accompany Amex representatives to testify before congressional committees.

Levitt's rising prominence also led to invitations to assume the leadership of causes that lay outside the bounds of the stock exchange—certainly beyond any strict definition of those bounds—but he accepted them not only because they appeared to him important in themselves but because his association with them would necessarily increase the visibility of the Exchange. His acceptance of the chairmanship of a Special State and City Commission on the development of the West Side of Manhattan identified the chief executive officer of the American Stock Exchange as the person in charge of supervising the transformation of the lower as well as upper West Side—and therefore of changes in the physical landscape of Wall Street. The task brought Levitt into daily contact with political leaders of both city and state, people with a large say about actions that would affect the destiny of the Amex and of every other financial institution in the area. The prestige of the chairman and of the institution he represented rose in tandem.

An invitation extended by another former governor of the Exchange, Jerry Sanford (he was later to become a U.S. Senator), perhaps took Levitt further afield from the stock exchange business than any other was to do. Sanford asked him to co-chair with Sonia Picado of Costa Rica the International Commission for Central American Recovery and Development. It was a task of awesome dimensions, yet one that, if successfully pursued, would once again enrich the prestige of the Amex chairman and the institution he headed.

In search of an integrated regional plan providing for the social and political as well as economic development of Central America, prominent representatives of the countries of the area met for almost two years. The most vital contributors to the resulting plan were the Central Americans themselves, but governments, central banks, and international organizations everywhere have paramount interests in promoting peace, democracy, and development, in formulating an integrated approach to ending war, and in moving toward civil rights, civil justice, and economic growth with equity. The Commission's report was warmly endorsed by all five Central American presidents, by the secretary general of the United Nations, by Chancellor Kohl, and by the United States. President Oscar Arias of Costa Rica, who in receiving the Nobel Prize had called for an international response to the problems of Central America, told President Bush in the spring of 1989 that the report was the response for which he had hoped.

In these and in other ways Levitt has worked—and of course been assisted by other Amex executives (for example, it was Gordon Stewart who drew up the work plan of the Commission, outlined the way in which it should discharge its functions, shape its report, and avoid involvement in the American presidential election of 1988)—to raise the prestige of the Exchange, to enhance its political influence with the Congress and with other governmental agencies, national, state, and local, and to diminish the perceptual gap that exists between the view of the New York Stock Exchange as the older, more tradition-laden and prestigious exchange and that of the Amex as an upstart lacking the ivied patina of tradition. He regarded this gap as a principal impediment to the ability of the Exchange to attract new companies and to retain their loyalty.

Increases in new listings in recent years testify to the success of his strategy. It is no longer true that the New York Stock Exchange alone speaks for the business community and its interests. For this Arthur Levitt is deserving of much of the credit.

The Amex lives! And that also means that the Amex continues to retain the loyalty of men and women long associated with it. Two of its employees are still on the job after 60 years. One "Bernie" Maas, became an executive in the Amex administration; the other, "Mike" Pascuma, loved the life of the trading floor too much to ever think of leaving it. In 1989 the former was in his upper seventies, the latter already in his ninth decade.

Their lives at the Amex help to explain and give human dimension to the long, vibrant history of this uniquely American institution. Both men owed their initial opportunities at the Amex to intercessions in their behalf. Bernie Mass wanted to go to West Point but couldn't pass the eye test. Fortunately, a friend of his mother worked for an accounting firm that had the Exchange as a client, and Bernie was offered a job in the Securities Division. The pay was $17 for a five an a half day week. Officially, he was a "dividend clerk" whose chief duty was to establish the ex-dividend dates of stocks. "In reality," he says, "I did everything."

He seems also to have seen and remembered everything. Bernie began work in 1929 about six months before Black Tuesday, the first October Crash. "People were just too busy to panic," he says of that historic day. "Brokers scrambled around from 10 A.M. to the closing bell at 3 P.M. It did give the impression of pandemonium. But the real problems took place off the floor." Bernie not only recalls "quite a lot" about the Crash. He also has vivid memories of the Bank Holiday of 1933, the beginnings of the Securities and Exchange Commission, "and other watermarks of the industry."

After a series of promotions, Bernie Maas became a vice-president in charge of the Securities Division. While he officially "retired" in 1976, he never left the Exchange and continued to work full time as a consultant. The Amex is the richer for it. There are only a handful of men on Wall Street with the perspective and wealth of knowledge of Bernie Maas. Exchange officials constantly rely on his expertise in the areas of listing and delisting, international liasons, and market development.

Mike Pascuma records early experiences similar to Bernie's. As a lad of about 17 he had approached a friend on Thames Street who had a bar and restaurant and asked for help in landing a job on the stock market. Brokers were in the habit of stopping off after work to chat, relax, and down a few, so that it was without difficulty that "Mike's" friend fixed him up with a job on the old Curb.

Mike remembers those early days well. He started with Jesse Hyman and Company as a runner, then became a "quote boy." "Nowadays," he points out, "all you have to do is punch a button on a machine to get the price of a stock, but back then you used the phone to get quotes from the floor." Mike's next step up the ladder took him to the order room to take some of the orders coming into the firm by phone. He owed his opportunity to move to the trading floor to the fact that the employer (the broker) and his clerk were Jewish. The occasion was a Jewish holiday and the boss decided to entrust the responsibilities of the floor to his young Catholic employee. Afterward, Mike says he worried all night long for fear errors would appear the next day!

Trading had been hectic, and in those days before the technological revolution that we have sketched in these pages, it was entirely dependent on hand signaling. Fortunately, the young man acquitted himself well, and stuck with the Exchange all during the depressed 1930s and World War II—except for a period with the armed services. "We didn't make any money till the late 1950s and 1960s," he says. In 1989, at the age of 80, he is senior member of the Pascuma Group, which for 10 years has also included his son Michael, Jr. Joshingly, the older Mike says that other brokers tell him they are glad his son is not like him. "We couldn't take two of you." Mike earned a reputation for being "tough": he refused to buy or sell at the first quarter point change in the price of a stock but held out for better prices. "My customers were my employers and I wanted to do the best I could for them."

Like "Bernie" Maas, Mike Pascuma vividly recalls the Great Crash of 1929. When pressed to contrast the earlier crash with that of 1987, he stresses the larger human costs of 1929. "Brokers were able to buy stocks on a margin of 10 percent, and when prices plunged they found themselves dangerously extended. No one could get up any money and your positions were sold out." Losses were grievous and the most important of these were those of broker friends who committed suicide by jumping out of windows. The higher margins required at the time of the later crash had a moderating effect on loss—although some specialists "took quite a beating" because of their efforts to make markets in collapsing stocks. At any rate suicides do not appear to have taken place. Talk on the Street at the time was that computers jumped out the window in 1987.

The Pascumas are by no means the only father and son team operating on the Exchange in the late 1980s. Joseph Streicher and his son Judd make up a specialist unit; Louis ("Lou") Herman and his sons Richard and James ("Dick" and "Jimmy") work on the trading floor and so does James ("Jimmy") Gilligan—another specialist —and his son Patrick ("Pat"). In the "old days," Bernie Maas remembers, units were more apt to be composed of brothers than of fathers and sons. He recalls one broker who brought charges against his own brother. "He called me an s.o.b.(!)," the bringer of the charges complained!

Change in the constitution of family units is by no means the only difference observable in the people at work on the floor. The advent and increasing importance of women, as brokers as well as clerks, also strikes the eye. ("The clerks do a good job," says Pascuma. They yell like boy clerks to their brokers.") Pascuma does his yelling over the phone. In the old days, he says, you could see all across the floor and communicate with your clerks by using hand signals. "Now, the clerks buzz me, I go to the phone and buzz them back." "Thank God I got no trouble with my feet," he adds.

Banks of monitors have transformed his working day into a series of bobs and weaves, starts and stops. "You move quick. You cover a lot of ground here," he adds. Those remarks must surely qualify as the understatements of the week. In the mid-1960s he clocked himself at 11 1/2 miles a day, and 20 years later estimated he was still covering 8 to 10 daily miles of Amex floor. That worked out to a good 50 miles a week, 2,500 a year, and more than 100,000 in his half-century (in 1985) as a trader! By 1985, he estimates, he had circled the globe three or four times by foot—all without leaving the trading floor of the American Stock Exchange at 86 Trinity Place. Four years later he was still going strong. So was Bernie Maas, at his desk at the Amex every working day—at the age of 78. And so too was the American Stock Exchange—at approximately the age of 100.

STATISTICAL
APPENDIX

SOURCE:
American Stock Exchange 1991 Fact Book,
Equities and Options

PRESIDENTS OF THE AMERICAN STOCK EXCHANGE	EFFECTIVE DATE	CHAIRMEN OF THE AMEX BOARD OF GOVERNORS	EFFECTIVE DATE
John L. McCormack	March 1911	Clarence A. Bettman	February 1939
Edward R. McCormick	June 1914	Fred C. Moffatt	February 1941
John W. Curtis	February 1923	Edwin Posner	February 1945
David U. Page	February 1925	Edward C. Werle	February 1947
William S. Muller	February 1928	Mortimer Landsberg	February 1950
Howard C. Sykes	February 1932	John J. Mann	February 1951
E. Burd Grubb	February 1934	James R. Dyer	February 1956
Fred C. Moffatt	February 1935	Joseph E. Reilly	February 1960
George P. Rea	April 1939	Edwin Posner	February 1962
Fred C. Moffatt (pro tem)	July 1942	David S. Jackson	February 1965
Edwin Posner (pro tem)	February 1945	Macrae Sykes	February 1968
Edward C. Werle (pro tem)	February 1947	Frank C. Graham, Jr.	February 1969
Francis Adams Truslow	March 1947	Paul Kolton	January 1973
Edward T. McCormick	April 1951	Arthur Levitt, Jr.	January 1978
Joseph F. Reilly (pro tem)	December 1961	James R. Jones	November 1989
Edwin Posner (pro tem)	January 1962		
Edwin D. Etherington	September 1962		
Ralph S. Saul	November 1966		
Paul Kolton	June 1971		
Richard M. Burdge	January 1973		
Robert J. Birnbaum	May 1977		
Kenneth R. Leibler	January 1986		

Source: Robert Sobel, *Amex, A History of the American Stock Exchange, 1921–1971* (N.Y.: Weybright & Talley, 1972), p. 363; Amex internal records (1972–1989).

Note: Prior to 1939, there was no Board chairman. The president was elected from among the Board of Governors. The Exchange's first paid president was George P. Rea; its first full-time chairman was Paul Kolton.

ALL-TIME TRADING RECORDS: EQUITIES (AS OF 12/31/90)

SHARE VOLUME

DAILY		WEEKLY	
43,432,760	October 20, 1987	158,680,590	October 19, 1987
35,409,165	October 19, 1987	103,240,445	October 26, 1987
34,593,620	October 21, 1987	93,796,575	August 20, 1990
30,489,710	October 16, 1989	92,235,479	March 10, 1986
26,654,405	August 3, 1990	85,849,975	January 12, 1987
26,558,745	October 22, 1987	85,838,325	February 26, 1990
24,848,015	August 23, 1990	85,832,640	February 24, 1986
23,834,490	January 7, 1986	85,757,990	August 6, 1990
23,286,680	May 24, 1990	85,011,500	October 16, 1989
23,272,490	August 6, 1990	84,557,225	March 3, 1986

MONTHLY		YEARLY	
399,813,250	October 1987	3,505,954,875	1987
365,517,005	August 1990	3,328,918,325	1990
344,926,185	March 1987	3,125,107,840	1989
332,941,270	March 1990	2,978,611,984	1986
330,857,810	August 1989	2,515,025,340	1988
323,276,050	January 1990	2,100,815,250	1985
318,010,549	March 1986	2,080,922,014	1983
309,858,695	January 1987	1,626,072,625	1980
308,099,980	May 1990	1,545,140,660	1984
304,759,900	October 1989	1,435,765,734	1968

TRADING IN FOREIGN ISSUES

Foreign issuers are an important constituency of the Exchange, trading in their shares and ADRs accounting for 15.2 percent of equity volume. Canada continues to be the country with the most foreign issues on the Amex.

FOREIGN ISSUES (INCLUDING CANADIAN)

YEAR	NO. OF ISSUES	SHARE VOLUME	PERCENT OF TOTAL SHARE VOLUME
1960	148	51,265,386	17.9
1965	99	80,539,250	15.1
1970	67	76,822,710	9.1
1975	71	49,507,160	9.2
1980	56	443,531,740	27.3
1981	54	273,803,190	20.4
1982	51	254,516,900	19.0
1983	52	244,139,280	11.7
1984	53	197,757,930	12.8
1985	51	353,299,270	16.8
1986	55	383,847,660	12.9
1987	60	351,435,290	10.0
1988	56	202,974,260	8.1
1989	65	428,864,060	13.7
1990	77	504,393,240	15.2

CANADIAN ISSUES ONLY

YEAR	NO. OF ISSUES	SHARE VOLUME	PERCENT OF TOTAL SHARE VOLUME
1960	107	38,691,325	13.5
1965	63	59,401,880	11.1
1970	48	61,075,110	7.2
1975	52	28,001,560	5.2
1980	39	338,568,420	20.8
1981	38	240,092,240	17.9
1982	34	219,567,450	16.4
1983	36	144,686,180	7.0
1984	38	128,361,280	8.3
1985	36	182,583,520	8.7
1986	40	236,254,960	7.9
1987	44	243,318,190	6.9
1988	41	137,826,160	5.5
1989	45	217,654,060	7.0
1990	50	212,123,540	6.4

FOREIGN AND CANADIAN ISSUES

Of the 26 non-Canadian foreign equity issues listed at the end of 1990, seven were traded in the form of American Depository Receipts (ADRs), or American Shares. These certificates, which are not shares themselves, represent the shares of foreign corporations. The non-Canadian foreign issues listed on the Exchange are organized under the laws of Africa, Bermuda, the Cayman Islands, Denmark, France, Great Britain, Greece, Ireland, Israel, Liberia, Mexico, the Netherlands Antilles, Norway, and the Philippines.

ALL FOREIGN ISSUES (INCLUDING CANADIAN)*

YEAR-END	NO. OF ISSUES	PERCENT OF LIST	MARKET VALUE**	PERCENT OF TOTAL MKT. VAL.
1960	148	15.7	$ 6,208,835,797	25.7
1965	99	9.6	9,651,758,658	31.1
1970	67	5.5	8,108,509,648	20.5
1975	71	5.6	10,692,908,872	36.4
1980	56	5.8	28,329,131,655	34.2
1981	54	5.6	24,591,378,683	38.0
1982	51	5.4	16,298,291,193	26.4
1983	52	5.5	22,507,744,670	27.9
1984	53	5.7	17,456,422,350	25.0
1985	51	5.4	22,644,434,548	26.0
1986	55	5.8	23,184,629,720	24.2
1987	60	5.6	22,975,899,435	23.2
1988	56	5.1	27,240,037,039	24.5
1989	65	6.1	30,139,423,562	23.0
1990	77	7.2	27,434,593,295	26.8

CANADIAN ISSUES ONLY*

YEAR-END	NO. OF ISSUES	PERCENT OF LIST	MARKET VALUE**	PERCENT OF TOTAL MKT. VAL.
1960	107	11.4	$ 5,950,436,566	24.6
1965	63	6.1	8,393,350,817	27.1
1970	48	3.9	7,345,741,718	18.6
1975	52	4.1	9,854,235,860	33.6
1980	39	4.0	25,676,563,300	31.0
1981	38	4.0	24,126,228,263	37.2
1982	34	3.6	15,931,075,061	25.8
1983	36	3.8	22,149,724,200	27.4
1984	38	4.1	17,109,058,726	24.5
1985	36	3.8	21,764,794,111	25.0
1986	40	4.2	22,488,099,283	23.5
1987	44	4.1	22,352,247,060	22.5
1988	41	3.7	26,374,397,125	23.8
1989	45	4.3	28,681,885,875	21.9
1990	50	4.7	24,504,669,233	24.0

*Includes securities with unlisted trading privileges.

**For companies that trade ADRs, only the value of ADRs outstanding (not shares outstanding) is included in this total.

NEW EQUITY LISTINGS IN 1990

There were 21 stock splits of 3-for-2 or greater and three reverse splits of 1-for-2 or less on the Amex in 1990.* Thirty-seven of these securities were listed in conjunction with an initial public offering.

TICKER SYMBOL	LISTING DATE	COMPANY NAME	STATE/ COUNTRY	BUSINESS DESCRIPTION
ELN	1/3	Elan Corporation, plc (ADR)	Ireland	Research/development drug formulation technology
RCG	1/11	Resurgens Communications Group, Inc.	GA	Long distance telephone operator services
HIL	1/12	*The Hillhaven Corporation	WA	Operates nursing homes
DXA.WS	1/12	*Kingdom of Denmark	Denmark	Put warrants on the Nikkei Stock Average
SXA.WS	1/17	*Salomon Inc	NY	Put warrants on the Nikkei Stock Average
IMF	1/18	*The Inefficient-Market Fund, Inc.	NY	Closed-end investment capital appreciation fund
GBI	1/22	*Granada Biosciences, Inc.	TX	Food animal biotech production/services
GNF	1/22	*Granada Foods Corporation	TX	Produces poultry, red meat products
BTB.WS	2/1	*Bankers Trust New York Corporation	NY	Put warrants on the Nikkei Stock Average
SUG	2/7	*Southern Union Company	TX	Natural gas distribtuion; oil and gas
SXO.WS	2/15	*Salomon Inc	NY	Put warrants on the Nikkei Stock Average
PLX	2/16	Plains Resources Inc.	TX	Oil and gas exploration, development, production
NVX	3/1	*North American Vaccine, Inc.	Canada	Develops immunobiological products
SFT.WS	3/7	*Salomon Inc	NY	Put warrants on the Financial Times Index
CYE	3/20	Cheyenne Software, Inc.	NY	Computer software and equipment
EPT	3/28	Epitope, Inc.	OR	Research and development of diagnostic reagents
SXZ.WS	4/4	*Salomon Inc	NY	Call warrants on the Nikkei Stock Average

TICKER SYMBOL	LISTING DATE	COMPANY NAME	STATE/COUNTRY	BUSINESS DESCRIPTION
SMO	4/4	Santa Monica Bank	CA	Commercial Banking
NFC	4/6	NFC, PLC (ADR)	England	Transport services
FIL	4/12	*Sanifill	TX	Non-hazardous waste landfills
AMI	4/16	American Medical Holdings, Inc.	CA	Services U.S. and international hospitals
VX	4/17	Veronex Resources Ltd.	Canada	Exploration and development of oil and gas
DEL	4/18	Del Electronics	NY	Manufactures high voltage power systems
PXA.WS	4/18	*Paine Webber Group Inc.	NY	Call warrants on the Nikkei Stock Average
PXB.WS	4/18	*Paine Webber Group Inc.	NY	Put warrants on the Nikkei Stock Average
PEF	4/19	*Pacific-European Growth Fund Inc.	MN	Closed-end investment fund
EXW.WS	4/26	*A/S Eksportfinans	Norway	Put warrants on the Nikkei Stock Average
UG	4/30	United-Guardian, Inc.	NY	Reserach and development of fine chemicals; pharmaceuticals
FTP.WS	5/1	*Salomon Inc.	NY	Put warrants on the Financial Times Index
ISB	5/2	Interchange Financial Services Corp.	NJ	Commercial banking
SHC	5/17	Schult Homes Corporation	IN	Designs and builds manufactured homes
CHC	5/24	*Chiles Offshore Corporation	TX	Offshore oil and gas drilling
TGU	5/24	*Templeton Global Utilities Inc.	FL	Closed-end investment company
CLU	5/25	Celutel, Inc.	PA	Operates cellular telephone system
CNB	5/31	Community National Bancorp, Inc.	NY	Commercial banking

Continued on next page

*Initial public offering.

TICKER SYMBOL	LISTING DATE	COMPANY NAME	STATE/COUNTRY	BUSINESS DESCRIPTION
GBL	6/8	Gamma Biologicals, Inc.	TX	Blood transfusion products
SU	6/13	Summa Medical Corporation	NM	Developer of cancer drugs
XYX	6/14	Xytronyx, Inc.	CA	Develops biotech/health products
HTL	6/20	*Heartland Partners, L.P.	IL	Real estate development
IDT	6/20	Information Display Technology, Inc.	PA	Manufactures and markets visual displays
BEI	6/27	*Benchmark Electronics, Inc.	TX	Manufactures circuit boards
RCV	7/9	*Rhône-Poulenc S.A. (CVR)	France	Manufactures chemicals for medicine, agric, and consumer
FH	7/12	*Foundation Health Corp.	CA	Administers health care services
ZAP	7/13	Helionetics, Inc.	CA	Manufactures electronic power products
ESX	7/17	*Essex Financial Partners, L.P.	VA	Savings bank
TGN	7/19	Tecogen Inc.	MA	Manufactures cogeneration systems
UVL	7/19	Universal Voltronics Corporation	NY	Electrical components
SZH	7/27	*Sierra Capital Realty Trust VIII	CA	Real estate investment trust
BLM	7/31	Belmac Corporation	FL	Developer of pharmaceutical products
BPC	8/8	*Bradmar Petroleum Corporation	OK	Oil and gas exploration, development, production
CII	8/16	CII Financial, Inc.	CA	Insurance holding for workers' compensation
SPO	8/27	*Salomon Phibro Oil Trust	NY	Oil investment vehicle
HWK	9/5	H.W. Kaufman Financial Group, Inc.	MI	Insurance brokerage and agency
HEN	9/7	Henley International Inc.	TX	Manufactures medical and therapy products

TICKER SYMBOL	LISTING DATE	COMPANY NAME	STATE/COUNTRY	BUSINESS DESCRIPTION
RT	9/17	*Resorts International, Inc.	NJ	Operates casinos and hotels
MAB	9/18	Mid-America Bancorp	KY	Commercial banking
PAM	9/18	*Pamida Holdings Corp.	NE	Operates chain of discount department stores
FPU	9/19	Florida Public Utilities Co.	FL	Natural gas, electric and water services
VCR	9/26	Go-Video, Inc.	AZ	Designed first dual-deck V.C.R.
PSA	10/1	*Storage Properties, Inc.	CA	Real estate investment trust
ARI	10/23	American Reliance Group, Inc.	NJ	Property and casualty insurance
ECG	10/24	Eco Corporation	Canada	Ecological services
MAJ	10/25	Michael Anthony Jewelers, Inc.	NY	Manufactures handcrafted gold jewelry
HRY	11/2	*Hallwood Realty Partners, L.P.	TX	Acquires and manages real estate
SGG.WS	11/5	*Société Générale Warrants Limited N.V.	France	Put warrants on the CAC-40 index
CFX	11/13	Cheshire Financial Corporation	NH	New Hampshire savings bank
ETC	11/13	Environmental Tectronics Corporation	PA	Manufactures environmental measuring instruments
CBM	11/15	Cambrex Corporation	NJ	Producer of specialty chemicals
ELN.U	11/15	*Drug Research Corporation, plc (ADR)	Ireland	Drug development technology
PWP.WS	11/20	*Paine Webber Group Inc.	NY	Put warrants on the CAC-40 Index
GFY	11/20	*PLM Equipment Growth Fund II	CA	Owns/leases used transportation equipment
DHC	12/6	*Danielson Holding Corporation	CT	Financial services

*Initial public offering.

Continued on next page

TICKER SYMBOL	LISTING DATE	COMPANY NAME	STATE/ COUNTRY	BUSINESS DESCRIPTION
USI	12/10	U.S. Intec, Inc.	TX	Roof materials manufacturer
MXX	12/12	International Murex Technologies Corp.	Canada	Develops and manufactures in vitro diagnostic test systems
TSX	12/17	Texscan Corp.	TX	Cable television equipment company
XCL	12/21	The Exploration Co. of Louisiana, Inc.	LA	Oil and gas exploration and production
MMS	12/24	Mid Maine Savings Bank	ME	Savings bank
TBK	12/27	Tolland Bank	CT	Savings bank

*Initial public offering.

STOCK SPLITS

There were 21 stock splits of 3-for-2 or greater and three reverse splits of 1-for-2 or less on the Amex in 1990*

STOCK SPLITS

NAME OF COMPANY	SPLIT RATIO	SHARES OUTSTANDING	
		BEFORE	AFTER
**Americus Trust for American Home Products Shares	2-1	1,859,541	3,719,082
**Americus Trust for Coca-Cola Shares	2-1	3,377,414	6,754,828
**Americus Trust for DuPont Shares	3-1	2,760,686	8,282,058
**Americus Trust for GTE Shares	2-1	4,636,543	9,273,086
Chambers Development Company, Inc. (Cl. A Com.)	2-1	24,381,131	48,762,262
Chambers Development Company, Inc. (Com.)	2-1	8,344,740	16,689,480
Clear Channel Communications, Inc. (Com.)	3-2	3,825,233	5,737,850
Continuum Company, Inc. (The) (Com.)	2-1	4,467,452	8,871,510
Crown Crafts, Inc. (Com.)	2-1	3,425,383	6,764,839
Frederick's of Hollywood, Inc. (Com.)	3-2	3,760,478	5,640,717
Imperial Holly Corporation (Com.)	3-2	6,741,809	10,112,713
Johnson Products Co., Inc. (Com.)	3-1	405,326	1,215,978
Keane, Inc. (Com.)	3-2	2,501,197	3,757,359
Lillian Vernon Corporation (Com.)	3-2	6,192,184	9,288,276
Metro Mobile CTS, Inc. (Cl. B Com.)	3-1	46,080,483	57,638,027
OEA, Inc. (Com.)	2-1	3,669,950	7,339,900
Selas Corporation of America (Com.)	2-1	1,230,538	2,461,076
SIFCO Industries, Inc. (Com.)	3-2	3,288,374	4,932,561
Thermo Cardiosystems, Inc. (Com.)	3-2	4,600,000	6,899,994
Turner Broadcasting System, Inc. (Cl. A Com.)	3-1	23,698,699	69,249,447
Turner Broadcasting System, Inc. (Cl. B Com.)	3-1	27,870,797	81,765,741

*Limited to companies on the Amex as of December 31, 1990.
**Consists of Units, PRIMEs and SCOREs.

BLOCK TRANSACTIONS
(AT LEAST 10,000 SHARES, SELLING AT $1 PER SHARE OR MORE)

DOLLAR VALUE		SHARE VOLUME	
Wang Laboratories, Inc. (Cl. B)	1/7/86	Wang Laboratories,Inc. (Cl. B)	1/7/86
$191.2 million		10,000,000 shares	
10,000,000 shares		$191.2 million	
Imperial Oil (Cl. A)	5/31/90	B.A.T Industries p.l.c	2/6/85
$69.5 million		6,000,000 shares	
1,405,000 shares		$25.5 million	
B.A.T Industries p.l.c.	5/24/90	B.A.T Industries p.l.c.	5/24/90
$62.4 million		5,200,000 shares	
5,200,000 shares		$62.4 million	
Affiliated Publications Inc.	4/15/86	B.A.T Industries p.l.c.	4/12/85
$55.8 million		5,000,000 shares	
1,156,800 shares		$21.8 million	
Brascan Ltd. (Cl. A)	4/30/79	Dome Petroleum Ltd.	3/3/88
$54.6 million		4,399,000 shares	
2,400,000 shares		$4.3 million	

ALL-TIME TRADING RECORDS: EQUITIES (CONTINUED)

AMEX MARKET VALUE INDEX— DAILY INCREASES/DECREASES

INCREASES		DECREASES	
+23.81	October 21, 1987	-41.05	October 19, 1987
+18.06	October 30, 1987	-24.54	October 26, 1987
+8.29	October 29, 1987	-24.34	October 20, 1987
+7.01	August 3, 1984	-16.56	October 13, 1989
+6.60	March 28, 1980	-12.95	Octboer 22, 1987
+6.46	January 28, 1982	-12.25	October 16, 1987
+6.39	January 4, 1988	-10.01	September 11, 1986
+5.84	February 4, 1987	-9.55	January 8, 1988
+5.67	April 22, 1980	-8.58	November 30, 1989
+5.64	January 6, 1983	-8.54	August 23, 1990

WEEKLY INCREASES/DECREASES

INCREASES		DECREASES	
+16.30	January 5, 1987	-59.34	October 19, 1987
+16.26	February 2, 1987	-23.26	October 12, 1987
+15.46	September 28, 1981	-19.07	November 30, 1987
+14.27	July 30, 1984	-17.66	September 8, 1986
+13.38	December 14, 1987	-17.48	October 9, 1989
+10.93	January 3, 1983	-17.32	August 20, 1990
+10.82	December 7, 1987	-15.36	September 14, 1981
+10.58	July 27, 1987	-15.21	January 22, 1990
+10.38	May 31, 1988	-12.99	March 3, 1980
+9.95	August 23, 1982	-12.56	October 27, 1989

Continued on next page

YEARLY	HIGH		LOW	
1976	54.92	(December 31)	42.16	(January 2)
1977	63.95	(December 30)	54.81	(January 12)
1978	88.44	(September 13)	59.87	(January 11)
1979	123.54	(December 31)	76.02	(January 2)
1980	185.38	(November 28)	107.85	(March 27)
1981	190.18	(August 13)	138.38	(September 25)
1982	170.93	(November 11)	118.65	(August 12)
1983	249.03	(July 26)	169.61	(January 3)
1984	227.73	(January 6)	187.16	(July 25)
1985	246.13	(December 31)	202.06	(January 8)
1986	285.19	(June 25)	240.30	(February 4)
1987	365.01	(August 13)	231.90	(December 4)
1988	309.59	(July 5)	262.76	(January 12)
1989	397.03	(October 10)	305.24	(January 3)
1990	382.45	(January 5)	287.79	(October 31)

EQUITIES VOLUME

Investor interest in Amex issues reached its second-highest level ever in 1990 with more than 3.3 billion shares changing hands. Block trading, a prime indicator of institutional activity, hit two all-time highs: 37.7 percent of dollar volume and 43.3 percent of share volume. Average trade size grew to more than three times its 1980 level, 1800 versus 573.

ANNUAL VOLUME

YEAR	SHARE VOLUME*	TURNOVER RATIO (%)	AVERAGE DAILY VOLUME	DOLLAR VOLUME	TRADES	AVERAGE TRADE SIZE
1960	286,039,982	18.0	1,112,996	$ 4,235,685,712	NA	NA
1965	534,221,999	30.9	2,119,929	8,874,874,754	NA	NA
1970	843,116,260	29.5	3,319,355	14,266,040,599	NA	NA
1975	540,934,210	17.0	2,138,079	5,678,028,284	1,269,681	426
1980	1,626,072,625	38.9	6,427,165	35,788,327,624	2,839,544	573
1981	1,343,400,220	30.3	5,309,882	24,520,205,419	2,124,071	632
1982	1,337,725,430	29.1	5,287,452	21,056,649,904	1,835,108	729
1983	2,080,922,014	38.8	8,224,988	31,237,023,941	2,664,345	781
1984	1,545,140,660	28.0	6,107,275	21,376,098,408	1,607,460	961
1985	2,100,815,250	33.1	8,336,568	27,838,566,791	1,715,169	1,225
1986	2,978,611,984	40.0	11,773,170	45,356,898,691	2,222,526	1,340
1987	3,505,954,875	42.5	13,857,529	50,469,993,686	2,548,350	1,376
1988	2,515,025,340	28.8	9,940,812	30,921,806,605	1,588,421	1,583
1989	3,125,107,840	35.5	12,401,222	44,401,174,619	2,031,015	1,539
1990	3,328,918,325	34.1	13,157,780	37,714,827,819	1,849,847	1,800

Continued on next page

BLOCK TRADING**

YEAR	NO. OF BLOCKS	BLOCK SHARE VOLUME	PERCENT OF TOTAL SHARE VOLUME	BLOCK DOLLAR VOLUME	PERCENT OF TOTAL DOLLAR VOLUME
1970	2,260	57,648,900	6.8	$ 989,280,487	6.9
1975	1,803	39,882,700	7.4	428,650,212	7.6
1980	9,895	206,856,066	12.7	3,991,188,469	11.5
1981	10,463	233,299,045	17.4	4,275,261,742	16.2
1982	12,330	297,636,074	22.3	3,517,187,576	17.9
1983	20,629	506,002,950	24.0	6,754,744,054	21.4
1984	18,820	484,989,760	31.0	6,237,579,567	29.2
1985	29,094	837,737,820	39.0	8,947,865,182	34.0
1986	44,421	1,215,937,020	40.8	15,381,476,846	35.4
1987	53,814	1,328,435,400	37.9	18,944,517,560	36.0
1988	39,865	1,060,931,100	42.2	11,429,198,877	36.7
1989	51,907	1,197,298,000	38.3	14,838,169,595	33.4
1990	60,830	1,442,626,150	43.3	14,209,010,827	37.7

*In round lots and includes warrants.
**A block is a trade of 10,000 shares of more.
NA=Not Available.

LISTINGS

The number of outstanding shares of common and other stock issues listed on the Exchange rose for the tenth consecutive year. Year-end aggregate market value was down 21.8 percent due to the drop in the market.

EQUITY ISSUES (COMMON, AMERICUS TRUSTS, PREFERRED, WARRANTS)*

YEAR-END	NO. OF ISSUES	NO. OF SHARES OUTSTANDING	AGGREGATE MARKET VALUE**	AVG. PRICE PER SHARE LISTED
1960	942	1,584,889,172	$24,170,932,525	$15.25
1965	1,028	1,726,201,246	30,986,708,582	17.95
1970	1,222	2,857,275,369	39,535,679,374	13.84
1975	1,267	3,180,800,830	29,365,930,815	9.23
1980	973	4,179,545,476	82,916,682,074	19.84
1981	959	4,436,952,696	64,791,101,004	14.60
1982	945	4,603,612,000	61,711,676,500	13.41
1983	948	5,357,298,000	80,808,449,812	15.08
1984	930	5,517,346,900	69,847,014,194	12.66
1985	940	6,339,768,349	87,013,822,402	13.73
1986	954	7,451,062,478	95,849,287,530	12.86
1987	1,073	8,253,485,077	99,171,058,732	12.02
1988	1,100	8,730,464,213	110,985,891,729	12.71
1989	1,058	8,816,726,863	130,795,337,552	14.83
1990	1,063	9,767,749,621	102,301,457,254	10.47

*Includes securities with unlisted trading privileges.

**For companies that trade ADRs, only the value of ADRs outstanding (not shares outstanding) is included in this total. For Americus Trusts, the value is based on units tendered and the closing price of a unit.

LISTINGS (CONTINUED)

EQUITY ISSUERS

New listings rose as more companies went public, transfer activity picked up, and a diverse group of issuers (banks, securities firms, a corporation and a national government) made their Amex debut by listing an equity derivative.
New Equity Issuers Stocks and ADRs Derivative Products

			NEW EQUITY ISSUERS				
			Stocks and ADRs		Derivative Products		
YEAR	TOTAL ISSUERS	TOTAL	OTC TRANSFERS*	IPOs*	AMERICUS TRUSTS	WARRANTS & CVRs	COMMODITIES TRUSTS
1975	1,215	27	27	0	0	0	0
1976	1,161	29	29	0	0	0	0
1977	1,098	35	35	0	0	0	0
1978	1,004	36	36	0	0	0	0
1979	931	40	40	0	0	0	0
1980	892	51	51	0	0	0	0
1981	867	82	79	3	0	0	0
1982	822	36	33	3	0	0	0
1983	822	49	39	10	0	0	0
1984	791	63	45	18	0	0	0
1985	782	74	40	33	1	0	0
1986	796	103	51	50	1	1	0
1987	866	152	64	56	24	8	0
1988	896	114	68	45	0	1	0
1989	860	50	32	17	0	1	0
1990	859	73	34	31	0	7	1

*May contain spin-offs, consolidations and mergers.

AMEX COMPANIES

The typical Amex company may be described in terms of averages or medians (half are above the median and half are below). The skewed size distribution of listed companies accounts for the fact that the averages shown below are all much greater than the medians: a relatively small number of exceptionally large companies pull up the averages for the group as a whole.

	AVERAGE	MEDIAN
Total Assets (mils.)	$347.9	$68.5
Shareholders' Equity (mils.)	$90.6	$23.7
Sales (mils.)	$247.1	$60.3
Net Income (mils.)	$5.5	$1.2
Market Value (mils.)	$140.3	$21.
Employees	2,260	458
Long-Term Debt (mils.)	$ 92.0	$13.0
Shares Outstanding (mils.)	14.9	5.2
Pre-Tax Income (mils.)	$ 12.2	$ 1.7

GEOGRAPHIC DISTRIBUTION OF AMEX LIST

Amex companies are represented by 47 states. Sixteen states serve as headquarters for at least ten Amex-listed corporations apiece. New York, California and Texas together are home to 44.1 percent of the list.

STATE	COMPANIES WITH STOCK LISTED	PERCENT OF TOTAL
New York	181*	19.7
California	136	14.8
Texas	88	9.6
New Jersey	53	5.8
Florida	51	5.5
Pennsylvania	39	4.2
Connecticut	37	4.0
Massachusetts	35	3.8
Illinois	29	3.2
Ohio	22	2.4
Michigan	20	2.2
North Carolina	16	1.7
Colorado	13	1.4
Virginia	12	1.3
Missouri	10	1.1
Oklahoma	10	1.1
	752	81.8

* Includes twenty-five Americus Trusts.

TOP 10 AMEX LEADERS BY:

AMEX SHARE VOLUME*

ISSUE	1990 AMEX SHARE VOLUME (MIL.)
1. Amdahl Corporation (AMH)	132.8
2. Wang Laboratories, Inc. (Cl. B) (WAN.B)	132.8
3. Continental Airlines Holdings, Inc. (CTA)	116.5
4. Magma Copper Company (Cl. B) (MCU)	94.6
5. Echo Bay Mines Ltd. (ECO)	79.0
6. Diasonics, Inc. (DIA)	58.4
7. Metro Mobile CTS, Inc. (CL A) (MMZ.A)	50.1
8. The New York Times Co. (Cl. A) (NYT.A)	45.1
9. B.AT Industries p.l.c. (ADRs) (BTI)	37.0
10. Western Digital Corporation (WDC)	34.1

PRICE GAIN*

ISSUE	1990 PERCENT PRICE GAIN
1. Universal Voltronics Corp. (UVL)	200.0
2. Damson Energy Co., L.P. (Cl. B) (DEP.B)	166.4
3. OEA, Incorporated (OEA)	162.8
4. Damson Energy Co., L.P. (Cl. A) (DEP.A)	162.8
5. Schult Homes Corporation (SHC)	105.9
6. Thermo Cardiosystems, Inc. (TCA)	91.0
7. New Line Cinema Corporation (NLN)	87.5
8. arr Laboratories, Inc. (BRL)	82.1
9. Tech/Ops Sevcon, Inc. (TOC)	72.5
10. General Employment Enterprises (JOB)	68.4

*Limited to issues with a closing price of at least $2.00 on December 31, 1990.

Continued on next page

MARKET VALUE*

ISSUE	MARKET VALUE, YEAR-END 1990 ($ MIL)
1. B.A.T Industries p.l.c. (ADRs) (BTI)	16,741.2
2. Imperial Oil Ltd. (Cl. A) (IMO.A)	9,610.4
3. Viacom Inc. (VIA)	2,735.0
4. Courtaulds plc. (ADRs) (COU)	2,371.2
5. Brown-Forman Inc. (Cl. B) (BF.B)	1,836.1
6. Carnival Cruise Lines, Inc. (Cl. A) (CCL)	1,734.2
7. Turner Broadcasting Sys., Inc. (Cl.A)(TBS.A)	1,678.1
8. Giant Food Inc. (Cl. A) (GFS.A)	1,628.7
9. ALZA Corporation (Cl. A) (AZA)	1,536.5
10. The New York Times Co. (Cl. A) (NYT.A)	1,514.3

SHARES OUTSTANDING*

ISSUE	SHARES OUTSTANDING, YEAR-END 1990 (MIL.)
1. B.A.T Industries pl.lc. (ADRs) (BTI)	1,521.9
2. NFC Public Limited Co. (ADRs) (NFC)	524.4
3. Courtaulds plc. (ADRs) (COU)	395.2
4. Imperial Oil Ltd. (Cl. A) (IMO.A)	191.3
5. Corona Corporation (Cl. A) (ICR.A)	166.4
6. Wang Laboratories, Inc. (Cl. B) (WAN.B)	165.4
7. Gulf Canada Resources Ltd. (GOU)	155.9
8. Turner Broadcasting (Cl. A) (TBS.A)	149.2
9. Carnival Cruise Lines, Inc. (Cl. A) (CCL)	134.7
10. Amdahl Corporation (AMH)	109.9

*For companies that trade ADRs, these tables are based on shares outstanding, not ADRs outstanding.

Continued on next page

NET INCOME

SALES

COMPANY	SALES ($ MIL)	COMPANY	NET INCOME ($ MIL)
1. B.A.T Industries p.l.c. (ADRs) (BTI)	15,281.2	1. B.A.T Industries p.l.c. (ADRs) (BTI)	2,090.8
2. Ford Motor Co. of Canada, Ltd. (FC)	13,223.2	2. HC Communications, Inc. (Cl. A) (BHC)	819.8
3. Imperial Oil Ltd. (Cl. A (IMO.A)	8,642.0	3. Imperial Oil Ltd. (Cl. A) (IMO.A)	393.8
4. Continental Airlines Holdings, Inc. (CTA)	6,684.9	4. Ford Motor Co. of Canada, Ltd. (FC)	271.2
5. Bergen Brunswig Corp. (Cl. A) (BBC)	4,442.3	5. The New York Times Co. (Cl. A) (NYT.A)	266.6
6. Courtaulds plc. (ADRs) (COU)	4,328.6	6. Brascan Ltd. (Cl. A) (BRS.A)	242.5
7. The Turner Corp. (TUR)	3,576.0	7. Carnival Cruise Lines, Inc. (Cl. A) (CCL)	193.6
8. Giant Food Inc. (Cl. A) (GFS.A)	3,248.9	8. Cominco Ltd. (CLT)	185.3
9. American Petrofina, Inc. (Cl. A) (APLA)	3,036.4	9. Amdahl Corporation (AMH)	153.0
10. The Penn Traffic Company (PNF)	2,725.5	10. Courtaulds plc. (ADRs) (COU)	145.4

Continued on next page

TOTAL ASSETS

COMPANY	TOTAL ASSETS ($MIL.)
1. B.A.T Industries p.l.c. (ADRs) (BTI)	18,655.5
2. Imperial Oil Ltd. (Cl. A) (IMO.A)	13,409.7
3. First Empire State Corp. (FES)	7,922.2
4. Citadel Holding Corp. (CDL)	5,632.2
5. I.C.H. Corporation (ICH)	5,545.6
6. Brascan Ltd. (Cl. A) (BRS.A)	5,195.8
7. American Capital Corp. (ACC)	4,963.9
8. Continental Airlines Holdings, Inc. (CTA)	4,772.6
9. Viacom Inc. (VIA)	4,015.0
10. American Medical Holdings, Inc. (AMI)	3,916.8

SHAREHOLDERS' EQUITY

COMPANY	SHAREHOLDERS EQUITY ($ MIL.)
1. B.A.T Industries p.l.c. (ADRs) (BTI)	7,560.7
2. Imperial Oil Ltd. (Cl. A) (IMO.A)	6,202.4
3. Brascan Ltd. (Cl. A) (BRS.A)	2,130.8
4. Gulf Canada Resources Ltd. (GOU)	1,998.4
5. Ford Motor Co. of Canada, Ltd. (FC)	1,369.9
6. Amdahl Corporation (AMH)	1,176.0
7. BHC Communications, Inc. (Cl. A) (BHC)	1,149.
8. Cominco Ltd. (CLT)	1,125.6
9. The New York Times Co. (Cl. A) (NYT.A)	1,067.
10. American Petrofina, Inc. (Cl. A) (APLA)	1,060.7

Note: Limited to stocks listed on the Amex at year-end 1990. Financials are for most recent fiscal year reported as of December 31, 1990.

MEMBERSHIP

SPECIALIST SYSTEM

Specialists are members of the Exchange whose obligation is to maintain a fair and orderly market in the securities in which they are registered. Towards that end, they perform three functions. First, specialists act as brokers' brokers, holding away-from-the-market orders entrusted to them by brokers on behalf of customers. These limit orders constitute the "book" and specialists are responsible for seeing to it that they are executed when the market reaches the specified limit price. Second, specialists work as facilitators, employing their extensive knowledge of the market in a stock to bring together potential buyers and sellers. This skill is particularly important when large blocks of stock are brought to the floor. Third, specialists serve as dealers when there is insufficient public interest to accommodate willing sellers or buyers at prices reasonably close to the last trade. In these instances, specialists buy for or sell from their own account to improve price continuity and/or depth. Specialists participate as dealers on all odd-lot orders.

Amex specialists participating as principal accounted for 11.1 percent of equities trading volume on the Exchange in 1990. Their stabilization rate on trades in which they participated was 88.6 percent. Thanks in part to their participation, 57.7 percent of all transactions occurred at the same price as the previous sale and 92.5 percent occurred within 1/8 point of the last sale. Average trade-to-trade price variation, an inverse measure of market quality, fell to its lowest level in recent history, 6.5 cents.

TRADING STATISTICS

	SPECIALIST TRADING		TRADE-TO-TRADE PRICE VARIATIONS FREQUENCY		
YEAR	PARTICIPATION RATE*	STABILIZATION RATE**	1/4 PT. OR LESS	1/8 PT. OR LESS	AVERAGE
1970	15.7%	95.4%	98$	81%	9.9
1980	14.6	6.1	99	86	8.9
1981	13.5	6.3	98	85	8.9
1982	12.0	5.9	99	89	8.0
1983	11.6	6.3	99	88	8.0
1984	11.2	6.3	99	90	7.4
1985	10.1	4.6	99	91	7.1
1986	10.6	4.3	98	90	7.5
1987	12.3	3.9	98	89	7.8
1988	10.6	2.0	99	92	7.0
1989	11.1	91.5	99	92	6.7
1990	11.1	88.6	99	93	6.5

*Specialist purchases plus sales as a percentage of total purchases plus sales.
**Specialist purchases below the last different price plus sales above the last different price, as a percentage of all specialist purchases plus sales.

MEMBERSHIP (CONTINUED)

SPECIALIST UNITS

YEAR	NUMBER OF UNITS*	NUMBER OF SPECIALISTS*	AVERAGE NO. SPECIALISTS PER UNIT	AVERAGE NO. STOCKS PER UNIT
1970	34	174	5.1	33.9
1980	29	200	6.9	30.0
1981	29	202	7.0	29.7
1982	30	219	7.3	28.0
1983	28	233	8.3	30.0
1984	29	220	7.6	28.2
1985	26	211	8.1	31.7
1986	25	198	7.9	33.3
1987	23	209	9.1	41.9
1988	24	213	8.9	41.1
1989	25	217	8.7	38.2
1990	25	215	8.6	38.4

MEMBERSHIP SALES

Membership on the American Stock Exchange, Inc. is of four types—regular, options principal, associate and allied. Regular and options principal memberships, commonly called "seats," provide direct access to the trading floor.

- Regular members may transact business in equities and options. There are presently 661 regular members.
- Options principal members may execute principal transactions in options only. There are 203 options principal members.
- Associate membership provides wire access to the trading floor where orders are executed by regular members.
- Allied membership is held by general partners and principal executive officers of member organizations.

In addition, the Exchange has 36 limited trading permit holders who may execute principal transactions in XMI and XII index options only.

The record high price of $420,000 for a seat was reached on October 9, 1987 and again on October 16, 1987. The all-time low price of $650 was set in 1942.

MEMBERSHIP (CONTINUED)

REGULAR MEMBERSHIP SALES

YEAR	HIGH	LOW	LAST
1960	$ 60,000	$ 51,000	$ 52,000
1965	80,000	55,000	80,000
1970	185,000	70,000	115,000
1975	72,000	34,000	44,000
1980	252,000	95,000	250,000
1981	275,000	200,000	250,000
1982	285,000	180,000	285,000
1983	325,000	261,000	261,000
1984	255,000	160,000	165,000
1985	160,000	115,000	135,000
1986	285,000	145,000	285,000
1987	420,000	265,000	275,000
1988	280,000	180,000	180,000
1989	215,000	155,000	155,000
1990	170,000	83,500	83,500

OPTIONS PRINCIPAL MEMBERSHIP SALES

YEAR	HIGH	LOW	LAST
1980	$160,000	$ 73,000	$160,000
1981	185,000	152,000	180,000
1982	225,000	155,000	225,000
1983	270,000	220,000	225,000
1984	180,000	150,000	150,000
1985	120,000	100,000	115,000
1986	225,000	165,000	225,000
1987	345,000	170,000	225,000
1988	225,000	175,000	175,000
1989	175,000	125,000	130,000
1990	130,000	52,000	60,000

Note: Tables based on date of sale consummation.

MEMBERS' TRADING

Specialist activity, excluding transactions in odd-lots, amounted to 58.2 percent of all member proprietary trading in 1990.

PURCHASES PLUS SALES (SHARES)*

YEAR	SPECIALISTS	ALL MEMBERS	ALL MEMBERS AS PERCENT OF TOTAL
1960	60,088,110	98,321,760	17.2
1965	127,361,775	216,198,700	20.2
1970	276,162,555	409,148,921	24.3
1975	139,993,775	212,732,019	19.7
1980	486,838,935	678,423,995	20.9
1981	364,726,468	595,371,336	22.2
1982	326,460,322	548,216,269	20.5
1983	481,040,515	822,393,910	19.8
1984	340,154,452	630,917,779	20.4
1985	419,715,890	838,616,699	20.0
1986	626,156,956	1,210,442,202	20.3
1987	866,616,642	1,413,743,434	20.2
1988	527,651,555	924,638,289	18.4
1989	695,759,965	1,135,329,866	18.2
1990	733,336,485	1,260,428,739	18.9

*Excluding odd lots.

The standard unit of trading on the American Stock Exchange is the round lot (generally 100 shares). Odd-lot transactions (those involving fewer shares than a round lot) are executed by specialists on the trading floor and are not normally entered onto the ticker tape or counted as part of reported volume.

ODD-LOT TRADING

YEAR	ODD LOT VOLUME	ODD LOT VOLUME AS A PERCENT OF TOTAL	YEAR	ODD-LOT VOLUME	ODD LOT VOLUME AS A PERCENT OF TOTAL
1960	21,829,966	3.68	1984	12,827,369	0.41
1965	37,812,125	3.42	1985	16,270,600	0.39
1970	44,284,040	2.56	1986	17,519,119	0.29
1975	11,336,376	1.04	1987	17,694,830	0.25
1980	19,848,965	0.61	1988	11,376,512	0.23
1981	16,417,763	0.61	1989	14,180,568	0.45
1982	14,144,599	0.53	1990	8,713,647	0.26
1983	19,863,625	0.48			

GOVERNMENT AND CORPORATE BONDS

On January 31, 1975, the American Stock Exchange introduced trading of U.S. Government securities in odd-lot denominations (units of $1,000 to $99,000) in certain Treasury Notes (2 to 10 years maturity) and Treasury Bonds (20 years or more maturity).

By year-end 1976, there were approximately 270 issues listed, including most Federal Agency securities and one-year U.S. Treasury Bills. On April 4, 1977, all outstanding three- and six-month U.S. Treasury Bills were added to the program.

Agency issues include Federal Home Loan Banks, Federal National Mortgage Association, Federal Farm Credit Banks and Federal Land Banks.

As of December 31, 1990, there were 260 Corporate and 689 Government issues listed.

GOVERNMENT BOND TRADING

Government bond volume averaged $10,749,842 a day in principal amount during 1990, a decrease of 23.0 percent from 1989.

GOVERNMENT BONDS YEAR	PRINCIPAL AMOUNT ($000)	GOVERNMENT BONDS YEAR	PRINCIPAL AMOUNT ($000)
1975	$ 44,805	1985	$2,117,007
1980	761,228	1986	2,421,255
1981	964,955	1987	3,016,038
1982	1,392,736	1988	3,691,901
1983	1,808,921	1989	3,518,454
1984	2,086,817	1990	2,719,710

CORPORATE BOND TRADING

Corporate bond volume averaged $3,032,087 a day in principal amount during 1990, an increase of 7.8 percent from 1989.

CORPORATE BONDS YEAR	PRINCIPAL AMOUNT ($000)	CORPORATE BONDS YEAR	PRINCIPAL AMOUNT ($000)
1975	$259,395	1985	$644,882
1980	355,723	1986	810,151
1981	301,226	1987	686,922
1982	325,145	1988	603,882
1983	395,089	1989	708,836
1984	371,857	1990	767,118

CORPORATE BOND LISTINGS*

YEAR-END	NO. OF ISSUES	PRINCIPAL AMOUNT OUTSTANDING	TOTAL MARKET VALUE	AVERAGE PRICE
1960	63	$1,064,502,930	$ 954,792,454	$89.69
1965	98	1,422,110,590	1,319,703,311	92.80
1970	169	3,178,354,510	2,044,735,556	64.34
1975	197	4,421,821,224	2,998,605,993	67.82
1980	225	6,195,258,443	4,853,002,615	78.34
1981	237	6,863,444,443	4,894,243,593	71.31
1982	244	7,419,099,691	6,213,798,988	83.75
1983	262	8,764,565,391	7,443,389,349	84.93
1984	290	12,670,599,101	9,646,216,836	76.13
1985	347	22,853,452,911	17,655,245,818	77.25
1986	341	24,118,069,806	19,845,653,627	82.28
1987	324	25,461,827,026	19,069,341,030	74.89
1988	309	25,557,448,968	20,993,531,457	82.14
1989	279	27,279,065,889	21,443,266,531	78.61
1990	260	27,195,333,970	29,458,671,424	108.32

*Includes securities with unlisted trading privileges.

MARKET INDICES

MARKET VALUE INDEX

The American Stock Exchange introduced the Market Value Index and 16 subindices on September 4, 1973, with base levels of 100.00 as of the close of trading on August 31, 1973. The Market Value Index replaced the Price Change Index, which had been used since April 1966.

On July 5, 1983, the Market Value Index was adjusted to one half of its previous level. As a result, the Index and subindices are now measured against a base level of 50.00.

Changes in these indices from one day to the next reflect changes in the aggregate market value of common stocks, ADRs and warrants that are listed on both days. Equivalently, index changes are a weighted average of price changes in component issues, with each issue being weighted by its initial shares outstanding. The Market Value Index and its subindices are not altered by stock splits, stock dividends or trading halts, nor are they affected by new listings, additional issuances, delistings, suspensions or cash dividends.

The fact that the indices are not affected by cash dividends means that they reflect the total return of the underlying issues, not just their price performance.

AMEX MARKET VALUE INDEX, 1981-1990
(SEPT. 4, 1973 = 50)

MARKET VALUE INDEX (CLOSING LEVELS)

MONTH	1970	1975	1976	1977	1978	1979	1980	1981	1982
January	57.86	37.10	48.15	55.58	60.70	79.62	137.71	172.52	147.83
February	58.84	38.64	51.69	55.13	61.43	80.37	151.74	169.47	133.07
March	56.88	39.97	52.12	55.59	64.47	89.85	116.52	180.30	130.06
April	46.26	42.12	51.29	56.08	68.18	92.09	126.69	178.13	135.23
May	41.31	44.34	51.58	56.09	72.44	93.47	135.84	188.50	135.62
June	38.82	46.73	52.66	60.16	72.78	100.38	146.81	187.32	125.40

MONTH		1983	1984	1985	1986	1987	1988	1989	1990
July	41.28	44.98	51.84	60.08	77.37	99.35	157.25	180.99	124.50
August	43.52	43.32	50.99	58.99	84.21	108.81	162.39	174.97	140.01
Sept.	49.17	41.57	50.98	59.44	84.41	112.59	165.78	146.43	141.59
October	46.36	41.40	49.44	56.51	68.38	101.82	168.00	156.01	159.91
Nov.	47.05	42.91	49.47	61.44	74.20	113.89	185.38	166.43	168.09
Dec.	49.21	41.74	54.92	63.95	75.28	123.54	174.50	160.32	170.30
Jan.		181.20	216.91	224.07	243.07	300.47	269.10	323.02	350.07
Feb.		186.60	210.22	227.43	257.35	321.76	288.46	322.47	352.90
March		194.54	211.34	229.59	270.03	332.66	296.43	328.31	361.75
April		213.19	210.42	227.44	268.97	325.19	303.14	345.08	343.10
May		230.36	198.63	231.69	282.60	326.39	294.19	356.66	363.06
June		242.32	200.08	230.89	284.20	338.13	309.25	358.97	361.21
July		238.38	188.67	233.92	261.56	358.03	306.18	376.56	353.60
Aug.		230.14	215.41	235.25	273.85	361.36	294.80	382.19	323.39
Sept.		230.28	215.45	222.31	260.69	356.45	301.63	388.76	307.72
Oct.		211.77	208.18	228.61	265.59	260.36	300.95	370.58	287.79
Nov.		225.56	204.27	242.26	264.81	242.39	294.36	373.84	301.79
Dec.		223.01	204.26	246.13	263.27	260.35	306.01	378.00	308.11

GEOGRAPHIC SUBINDICES OF THE MARKET VALUE INDEX (CLOSING LEVELS)

	1983	1984	1985	1986	1987	1988	1989	1990
New England	481.00	387.61	424.45	436.03	401.36	425.33	485.20	418.19
Middle Atlantic	282.48	281.28	370.75	408.19	373.80	411.66	486.81	430.29
North Central	289.25	280.82	361.57	410.68	380.21	429.67	576.71	398.95
South Atlantic	418.32	431.79	563.01	638.94	720.51	904.94	1,120.12	881.59
South Central	272.76	238.86	270.30	247.33	199.37	266.25	366.08	301.79
Mountain	121.52	108.45	121.26	95.22	101.77	104.97	115.84	108.31
Pacific	270.57	242.30	327.02	358.39	344.38	399.58	464.40	356.12
Foreign	130.38	117.65	134.75	145.80	178.79	209.43	265.29	213.05

INDUSTRIAL SUBINDICES OF THE MARKET VALUE INDEX (CLOSING LEVELS)

	1983	1984	1985	1986	1987	1988	1989	1990
High Technology	525.00	374.87	383.81	349.26	364.91	368.83	376.69	332.10
Capital Goods	201.90	202.84	260.29	273.28	264.87	321.55	401.37	335.31
Consumer Goods	213.48	195.49	274.30	335.83	304.83	393.07	504.76	396.80
Service	359.20	403.65	537.77	662.25	626.67	710.63	930.78	732.38
Retail	410.36	465.89	746.10	769.80	655.04	949.31	1,193.34	1,000.70
Financial	290.32	351.54	455.40	478.49	355.34	378.49	407.45	351.31
Natural Resources	157.50	135.60	146.30	137.94	176.97	202.21	258.52	215.22
Housing, Construction & Land Development	312.55	305.48	373.50	390.10	335.02	429.99	446.11	230.58

EQUITY DERIVATIVE PRODUCTS

INTRODUCTION

As a leading international marketplace for the trading of equities and options, the American Stock Exchange continues to expand the range of financial instruments available for public auction market trading. The extent and diversity of Amex equity derivatives are testimony to the important role played by the American Stock Exchange in meeting the needs of issuers and investors alike.

INDEX WARRANTS: The first warrants on foreign stock indices to trade in the U.S. were listed on the Amex in 1990. Amex warrants in Japanese, French and British indices offer significant flexibility to investors seeking to hedge existing positions or benefit from changes in securities markets around the world.

CURRENCY WARRANTS: Foreign currency warrants provide Amex investors with a mechanism to hedge against currency risk or speculate on it, as they choose.

CONTINGENT VALUE RIGHTS: Similar to limited put warrants, these securities have been used to provide downside protection to stockholders of newly merged companies.

COMMODITY TRUST UNITS: Commodity-based securities enable sophisticated investors to hedge or speculate over a longer time frame than is possible in the futures markets, and without other limitations normally inherent in such investment.

AMERICUS TRUSTS: These instruments enable investors to separate the price appreciation aspect of common stocks from their income aspect, so that some investors can enjoy greater current income while others can invest for capital gains each group using separate parts, or components, of the same stock.

TRADING VOLUME

	YEAR WHEN FIRST ISSUE WAS LISTED	NO. OF ISSUES	1990 VOLUME	PERCENT OF TOTAL VOLUME
WARRANTS ON FOREIGN STOCK INDICES				
Nikkei Index Warrants	1990	8	391,108,500	11.75
CAC 40 Index Warrants	1990	2	2,619,700	0.08
Financial Times Index Warrants	1990	2	42,274,600	1.27
Total		12	436,002,800	13.10
COMMODITY TRUST UNITS				
Oil Trust Units	1990	1	13,929,700	0.42
Contingent Value Rights	1986	3	59,038,700	1.77
FOREIGN CURRENCY WARRANTS				
Yen	1987	11	21,294,600	0.64
Deutsche Mark	1987	5	2,609,700	0.08
Total		16	23,904,300	0.72
AMERICUS TRUSTS	1985	75	196,086,100	5.89
Total		107	728,961,600	21.90

MARKET VALUE (YEAR-END)

	NO. OF ISSUES	SHARES OUTSTANDING	MARKET VALUE	PERCENT OF TOTAL MARKET VALUE
WARRANTS ON FOREIGN STOCK INDICES				
Nikkei Index Warrants	8	63,337,000	$ 698,503,625	0.68
CAC 40 Index Warrants	2	4,888,000	16,173,500	0.02
Financial Times Index Warrants	2	11,000,000	48,812,500	0.05
Total	12	79,225,000	763,489,625	0.75
COMMODITY TRUST UNITS				
Oil Trust Units	1	16,000,000	54,000,000	0.05
CONTINGENT VALUE RIGHTS	3	125,841,000	661,552,750	0.65
FOREIGN CURRENCY WARRANTS				
Yen	11	26,100,000	82,844,750	0.08
Deutsche Mark	5	10,800,000	5,996,875	0.01
Total	16	36,900,000	88,841,625	0.09
AMERICUS TRUSTS	75	130,990,000	7,082,092,500	6.92
Total	107	388,956,000	$8,649,976,500	8.46

AMEX OPTIONS PROGRAM

INTRODUCTION

The Amex stock options program began on January 13, 1975 with the listing of call options on six NYSE-listed securities. The program was expanded in 1983 with the listing of options on broad-market and industry-based stock indices. In 1985, the Amex launched trading of options on over-the-counter (OTC) securities, marking the first time since the mid-1970s that competitive trading in stock options was permitted. In 1990, the Exchange began freely listing and multiply trading options on exchange-listed securities under a new SEC rule that effectively abolished the Options Allocation Plan restricting options trading on listed stocks to a single options market.

At year-end 1990, the Amex was trading 218 individual stock options (including 50 options on OTC securities); long-term options with expirations up to two years on 10 actively traded common stocks; five broad-based index options, including the Major Market Index (XMI), the Amex's flagship index option; and two industry-based index options.

HISTORICAL AMEX OPTIONS TRADING

NUMBER OF CONTRACTS TRADED (000)				AVERAGE DAILY CONTRACTS			
YEAR	CALLS	PUTS	TOTAL	YEAR	CALLS	PUTS	TOTAL
1975	3,531	—	3,531	1975	14,352	—	14,352
1976	9,036	—	9,036	1976	35,714	—	35,714
1977	9,655	423	10,078	1977	38,312	2,898*	39,990
1978	13,540	841	14,381	1978	53,732	3,336	57,068
1979	16,506	961	17,467	1979	65,240	3,800	69,040
1980	24,955	4,093	29,048	1980	98,636	16,179	114,815
1981	26,430	8,430	34,860	1981	104,465	33,320	137,785
1982	27,680	11,111	38,791	1982	109,407	43,917	153,324
1983	28,069	10,899	38,968	1983	110,945	43,078	154,023
1984	28,731	11,373	40,104	1984	113,563	44,953	158,516
1985	35,186	13,414	48,600	1985	139,627	53,230	192,857
1986	48,875	16,568	65,443	1986	193,182	65,485	258,668
1987	52,952	17,997	70,949	1987	209,296	71,136	280,433
1988	34,225	10,776	45,001	1988	135,278	42,591	177,869
1989	37,448	12,408	49,856	1989	148,605	49,237	197,842
1990	26,958	13,930	40,888	1990	109,331	58,122	167,453

*Based on 146 trading days.

HISTORICAL AMEX OPTIONS TRADING

CONTRACTS EXERCISED (000)				OPEN INTEREST (000)			
YEAR	CALLS	PUTS	TOTAL	YEAR	CALLS	PUTS	TOTAL
1975	75	—	75	1975	458	—	458
1976	252	—	252	1976	963	—	963
1977	328	16	344	1977	1,078	56	1,134
1978	429	55	484	1978	1,127	57	1,184
1979	611	28	639	1979	1,322	98	1,420
1980	1,352	113	1,465	1980	1,649	405	2,054
1981	1,719	1,093	2,823	1981	2,090	577	2,667
1982	1,928	933	2,861	1982	2,223	891	3,114
1983	3,533	958	4,491	1983	2,785	963	3,748
1984	2,566	1,285	3,851	1984	1,763	581	2,344
1985	3,255	743	3,998	1985	2,432	735	3,167
1986	5,170	921	6,091	1986	2,229	660	2,889
1987	5,509	1,454	6,963	1987	1,945	476	2,421
1988	3,433	1,064	4,497	1988	1,650	503	2,153
1989	4,615	1,001	5,616	1989	1,857	628	2,485
1990	2,800	1,829	4,629	1990	1,372	701	2,073

AVERAGE PREMIUM PER CONTRACT ($)		SETTLEMENT VALUE ($ MILLIONS)	
YEAR	AMOUNT	YEAR	AMOUNT
1975	409	1975	1,443
1976	279	1976	2,524
1977	192	1977	1,935
1978	242	1978	3,482
1979	342	1979	5,967
1980	431	1980	12,534
1981	410	1981	14,289
1982	371	1982	14,380
1983	408	1983	15,918
1984	262	1984	10,492
1985	238	1985	11,578
1986	291	1986	19,048
1987	363	1987	25,803
1988	275	1988	12,398
1989	303	1989	17,160
1990	313	1990	12,841

1990 TOTAL OPTIONS VOLUME BY PRODUCT

(AVERAGE DAILY OPTIONS VOLUME)

	EQUITY OPTIONS	INDEX OPTIONS	INTEREST RATE OPTIONS*	TOTAL AMEX OPTIONS	YEAR-TO-DATE 1990
Jan.	3,754,550	714,557	101	4,469,208	4,469,208
(22)	(170,661)	(32,480)	(5)	(203,146)	(203,146)
Feb.	2,797,898	479,727	20	3,277,645	7,746,853
(19)	(147,258)	(25,249)	(1)	(172,508)	(188,948)
Mar.	3,143,983	450,131	110	3,594,224	11,341,077
(22)	(142,908)	(20,461)	(5)	(163,374)	(180,017)
Apr.	2,656,046	557,550	1	3,213,597	14,554,674
(20)	(132,802)	(27,878)	(0)	(160,680)	(175,358)
May	3,050,386	618,952	25	3,669,363	18,224,037
(22)	(138,654)	(28,134)	(1)	(166,789)	(173,562)
June	2,544,134	580,303	1	3,124,438	21,348,475
(21)	(121,149)	(27,633)	(0)	(148,783)	(169,432)
July	3,117,410	516,604	0	3,634,014	24,982,489
(21)	(148,448)	(24,600)	(0)	(173,048)	(169,949)
Aug.	3,081,032	636,379	0	3,717,411	28,699,900
(23)	(133,958)	(27,669)	(0)	(161,627)	(168,823)
Sep.	2,299,641	461,221	15	2,760,877	31,460,777
(19)	(121,034)	(27,563)	(1)	(148,598)	(170,096)
Oct.	3,303,195	643,944	0	3,947,139	35,407,916
(23)	(143,617)	(27,998)	(0)	(171,615)	(169,160)
Nov.	2,401,908	533,556	0	2,935,464	38,343,380
(21)	(114,377)	(28,276)	(0)	(142,653)	(169,782)
Dec.	2,047,636	496,819	—	2,544,455	40,887,835
(20)	(102,382)	(24,841)	—	(127,223)	(167,453)
Total	34,197,819	6,689,743	273	40,887,835	
(253)	(135,169)	(32,282)	(1)	(167,453)	

*Ceased trading November 19, 1990.

AMEX PROFITS (OR LOSSES =/−) 1970–1990

YEAR		YEAR	
1970	$ 20	1980	$ 3,793
1971	181	1981	5,192
1972	164	1982	4,508
1973	−626	1983	6,376
1974	−1,089	1984	4,653
1975	−316	1985	5,043
1976	1,032	1986	9,439
1977	764	1987	8,307
1978	1,528	1988	2,606
1979	1,295	1989	4,284
		1990	325

Source: Amex Annual Reports